# THE DRAMATIC DECADE

Other books by the author

*Beyond Survival: Emerging Dimensions of Indian Economy* (1984)
*Off the Track* (1987)
*Saga of Struggle and Sacrifice* (1992)
*Challenges Before the Nation* (1992)

# THE DRAMATIC DECADE
## The Indira Gandhi Years

—◦◦◦—

# PRANAB MUKHERJEE

RUPA

First published by
Rupa Publications India Pvt. Ltd 2015
7/16, Ansari Road, Daryaganj
New Delhi 110002

*Sales Centres:*

Allahabad Bengaluru Chennai
Hyderabad Jaipur Kathmandu
Kolkata Mumbai

ISBN: 978-81-291-3574-2

First impression 2015

10 9 8 7 6 5 4 3 2 1

The moral right of the author has been asserted.

Printed at Repro Knowledgecast Limited, India

*I dedicate this book to the millions of political
activists who have protected and nurtured
democracy in India*

CONTENTS

*Preface*                                                            *ix*

Prologue                                                              1

1. Muktijuddho: The Making of Bangladesh                             13

2. The Midnight Drama: Declaration of the Emergency                  44

3. Jayaprakash Narayan's Offensive                                   71

4. Putting the House in Order: Actioning Reforms                     84

5. The Stunning Defeat and Its Aftermath                             106

6. Battle Lines Drawn in the Congress                                123

7. Towards the Second Split                                          146

8. The Birth of Congress (I)                                         160

9. Crisis in the Janata Party                                        177

10. Back in the Saddle: Indira Gandhi's Return to Power              201

11. New Challenges Face Congress (I)                                 212

12. The 1980 Lok Sabha Elections and After                          223

Epilogue                                                             249

*Appendices*                                                         251
*Acknowledgements*                                                   311
*Index*                                                              313

# PREFACE

As I step into my eightieth year, it is time for introspection—
a time to look back at the vast, almost unimaginable changes I
have witnessed in our country. For five of these eight decades,
given my career in public life, I have had the rare privilege of
being a participant in many of the defining moments of our
country's democratic history. Our nation and its people have, and
continue to, offer me an abundance of love, faith and affection
in a measure that I find deeply humbling and inspiring. It is
their welfare which has been the foundation and raison d'être
of my public life.

*The Dramatic Decade* straddles many worlds. At one level it
is the story of a boy who moves from a flickering lamp in a
remote village in West Bengal to the glittering chandeliers of
India's national capital—a long journey, marked by some successes,
as also some disappointments, and fascinating encounters. Yet,
this book is more than just a collection of fond remembrances.
As I have been fortunate enough to have personally witnessed
extraordinary events in this nation's past, it is a retelling of India's
political history as I have experienced it.

*The Dramatic Decade* is the first of a trilogy; this book covers
the period between 1969 and 1980. It begins with my entry

into public life as a member of the Rajya Sabha and covers three epochal events—the war that led to the liberation of East Pakistan; the events leading up to, and following, the declaration of the Emergency in 1975; and the emergence of coalition politics in India with the formation and coming to power of the Janata Party in 1977. Each of these events significantly shaped the political landscape and discourse of our country. I intend to deal with the period between 1980 and 1998 in Volume II, and the period between 1998 and 2012, which marked the end of my active political career, in Volume III.

In covering the decade between 1970 and 1980, there is a lot I have retrieved from my personal diaries. While I had, tragically, lost substantial segments of this material when my house was flooded, I was also fortunately able to recollect and rewrite large segments of the diary. After the waterlogging episode, I made it a point to create the first draft in my own hand, then get two or three copies typed and printed for safekeeping.

The process of writing this book has been revelatory—revisiting the past often is. I offer *The Dramatic Decade* to you, the reader, and trust you will enjoy reading it as much as I have enjoyed putting it together.

Pranab Mukherjee
New Delhi, November 2014

# PROLOGUE

Winter gripped the capital, wrapping it in a sheet of mist. 11 December 1935, the day I came into the world.

Over the years I have noticed that while the daily routine of my work life carries on unabated, on this day, my thoughts take me far away. My immediate surroundings—the capital's massive functioning apparatus, South Block, North Block and the distances beyond—become indistinct in my mind. Instead, I see clusters of trees, kutcha (unpaved) roads and mud houses. I remember the sting of my schoolmaster's cane, the aroma of payesh (kheer) made by my mother. My mind sprints towards Mirati, the village I grew up in.

Mirati lies two miles north of the town of Kirnahar in the district of Birbhum in West Bengal. My family originally hailed from Bilwagram in the Nadia district. In 1880, my grandfather bought some property and settled in Mirati. It wasn't a prosperous village—there was just one pucca dwelling (that of the zamindar) while all other families, including mine, lived in mud houses. We owned a fair amount of cultivable land in the village, but much of it was given out to sharecroppers. Even before the Tebhaga movement of 1946-47 (which demanded that two-thirds of the produce from the land should go to the sharecropper cultivating the land, and only one-third to the landowner), my father had introduced his own rules for dividing the harvest, more generous than what other landowners practised: the harvest was divided into five parts, two parts each to the sharecropper and the landlord while the remaining one-fifth was used to cover farming expenses.

Ours was a relatively content village, in that there were no major disputes. There might have been some heated arguments over the distribution of the harvest, or some drunken brawls, but that was generally the extent of it. And whenever a dispute of any consequence arose, my father would be the chosen arbitrator. He would discuss the issue with the village elders, and then resolve it according to village tradition. If my father was not around, my mother's help was sought. For a period, then, our home became an informal court.

■

I was a restless child, forever up to mischief and with a penchant for avoiding studies as much as I could. I would rather play away my day with the neighbourhood boys than go to school. This is not to say that I did not get thrashed for this indiscipline, both by my mother and the schoolmaster, but at that time I thought it well worth to endure the thrashing to pursue my deep interest in having a good time!

It could be said that between 1940 and 1945 I did *not* go to school, preferring instead a life of playing games, climbing trees or running along with the grazing herds of cows. In 1946, however, I was enrolled at the Kirnahar Shib Chandra High English School[1] in Class V. A well-known school in the area, it was about two-and-a-half kilometres away from home, which meant travelling five kilometres every day on foot—and that too

---

[1]This is the name of the school as it was known at that time.

barefoot, as was commonplace in those days. Much of the journey entailed walking over a raised path with ditches on either side. During the rains, when the entire area was several feet deep in water, I would take off my shirt and shorts and wade through the water wearing a gamchha (towel), changing back into my presentable, school-worthy attire once I reached higher ground. In 1973, when I was a minister, I got that road paved.

It was in high school that I first began taking some interest in studies, routinely ranking first or second in class. Around twenty-two or twenty-three of us from my school took the matriculation examination[2]—the final school exam—at the end of Class X. We were the first batch from my school to take this particular school-leaving exam. In 1952, after the school final exam, I enrolled at Vidyasagar College in Suri and stayed in the hostel all through my college years from 1952 to 1956. Our college enjoyed a great reputation, known to be generally ahead of a number of other colleges under Calcutta University at the time. After graduating from college in 1956, I went on to Calcutta and did my postgraduation—both in modern history and political science—from the university. Having enrolled as a 'private' student, my education took me longer than it does most regular students (private students had to put in an extra year). In 1960, after I had got my first postgraduate degree, I enrolled in law college and, three years later, obtained a law degree, too.

■

My father, Kamada Kinkar Mukherjee, was a staunch nationalist and a dedicated Congress worker. After the Lahore session in

---

[2]In 1952, the Central Board of Secondary Education took on the responsibility of secondary education from the university, and the school-leaving exam, till then referred to as matriculation, came to be known as the school final examination.

1929, when the Congress pledged to observe 26 January as Independence Day, we would raise the Congress flag at home every year on this day. If my father was home, he would unfurl the flag and read the Independence pledge; if he was away, my mother took his place, though she sometimes allowed my older brother the privilege (and if he, too, was away, I was given the responsibility). Having joined the Congress in 1920, my father remained an active member till 1966.

Father had a great talent for organizing people. Our home stood thirty miles south of the Ajay River, and twenty-five miles north of the Mayurakshi River. The large area between these two rivers was assigned to my father by the party. He was out all day, travelling on foot or by bullock cart, explaining to people the various facets of the national agitation for Independence. He travelled from village to village, sharing meals with the locals and preaching the Congress ideology. Rabindranath Tagore once jokingly remarked to my father that he (Father) was compensating for the behaviour of our forefathers who disdained the poor, calling them low caste and keeping them at a distance.

Father participated in virtually all agitations launched by the Congress before Independence and courted arrest innumerable times. I recall an amusing incident from those times, one that my mother recounted for many years after. A police party turned up one day to confiscate all our possessions. We had been warned in advance, so we had shifted all our cattle and grain to the houses of various people in the village. Father's papers also had been similarly removed and given to neighbours for safekeeping. Not finding much to confiscate, a sub-inspector in the police party asked me, 'You used to have cows at home, I've seen them. Where have they gone now?' Straight-faced, I replied, 'Cows? We ate them.' The sub-inspector was astounded. 'What are you saying? You are Hindus and you ate your cows?' I, all of eight years old then, said, 'Actually, Father has been in jail for a long time. So we sold the cows for some money to feed ourselves.'

Even when a large number of Congress workers and leaders in West Bengal were swept away by Netaji Subhas Chandra Bose's fervour and became his followers, my father was among the handful of people who remained steadfast in their loyalty to Mahatma Gandhi. He, along with a few others, was charged with the responsibility of running the Birbhum District Congress. While he held party posts at the district level and was also a member of the West Bengal legislative council, he had little enthusiasm for working in the government and preferred to work at the grass-roots level or at the level of the party organization.

Father taught us the value of self-respect, maintaining that it was enormously important. Many years later, in 1978, when the Congress split under Indira Gandhi, he told me: 'I hope you will not do anything that will make me ashamed of you. It is when you stand by a person in his or her hour of crisis that you reveal your own humanity. Don't do anything which will dishonour your forefathers' memory.' His meaning was clear, and I didn't, then or later, waver from my loyalty to Indira Gandhi.

■

I was a late entrant into student politics, getting involved only when I was studying law. In 1962, during the India-China border skirmishes, I worked with other student leaders to organize blood donation and fundraising camps. Slowly thereafter, I became involved with the law college students' union, becoming the Chairman of the University Law College Students' Association in 1962–63.

My active political career started in the mid-1960s, when I joined Ajoy Mukherjee's Bangla Congress. Originally a

Congressman, Ajoy babu, in keeping with the Kamaraj Plan (which had many Congress ministers across the country quitting office in the early 1960s to devote themselves to party work), resigned his ministerial berth and took over as President of the West Bengal Congress. But it became difficult for him to get any work done because the real power within the West Bengal Congress rested with Atulya Ghosh.

Though the Congress had successfully held West Bengal in the first three general elections after Independence, there had been significant internal problems within the West Bengal Congress right from the outset, with Atulya Ghosh and Prafulla Chandra Sen on one side and Arun Chandra Guha, Surendra Mohan Ghosh and Prafulla Chandra Ghosh on the other. Things came to a head in the state Congress in 1950 when a group of West Bengal Congressmen led by Prafulla Ghosh left the party while Atulya Ghosh's control and influence over the West Bengal unit was slowly established. (My father worked with Atulya Ghosh and was a member of the West Bengal Pradesh Congress Working Committee from 1948.) Ultimately, in 1966, there was a split in the West Bengal Congress, with the group headed by Ajoy Mukherjee striking out on its own.

The Bangla Congress was formally launched on 1 May 1966. While in the process of setting up this party, Ajoy babu had called a meeting of Congress workers at Shyam Square, Calcutta (5-6 February). I attended that meeting, though I was not a Congress regular then. I told Ajoy babu: 'Look, I've studied politics. If there is any writing-related work you would like me to do for the party, I will.' Ajoy babu replied: 'Okay, come to the office.'

It was on 8 June 1966, when on a tour of the state with Ajoy babu, that I first mooted the idea of a 'United Front' to him: 'Ajoy da, if we want to defeat the Congress, we have to unite all parties… If we fight the elections on a common platform, we could defeat the Congress.' Ajoy babu then began efforts in that direction.

The first United Front government, led by Ajoy Mukherjee and Jyoti Basu, was formed in West Bengal in 1967. Two factors led to the formation of this front—the split in the Bengal unit of the Congress and the intense anti-Congress sentiment that had grown in the state by that time. Though efforts were made to bring all non-Congress parties on one platform to oppose the Congress in the 1967 elections, the efforts did not succeed. The state went to elections in a three-cornered contest between the People's United Left Front (PULF), the United Left Front (ULF), and the Congress.

The major non-Congress parties were divided into two blocks. One group, consisting of the Communist Party of India (Marxist) (CPI[M]), the Revolutionary Socialist Party, the Revolutionary Communist Party and the Socialist Unity Centre, among others, formed the ULF and was led by Jyoti Basu. The second group, the PULF, consisted of the Bangla Congress, the Forward Bloc, the Communist Party of India (CPI), among others, and was led by Ajoy babu. In this three-cornered contest, the PULF secured 63 seats while the ULF got 68 seats. After the elections, these two groups came together on the basis of the 18-point programme[3] and formed the government with the support of some others.

While the United Front government was formed amidst state-wide rejoicing, the economic situation in the state and the country was deteriorating. The situation did not improve even after this election, as a result of which the first non-Congress government formed in the state did not last long.

---

[3]According to this programme, 'high on the United Front's list of priorities were particular attention to the plight of the peasants and to land reform generally, educational reforms and a liberation of the forces of freedom and progress.' See Geoffrey Moorhouse, *Calcutta* (London, 1971).

Given the economic situation, particularly Food Minister Prafulla Ghosh's handling of the food policy, representatives of the CPI(M) in the United Front's coordination council began creating trouble, to Ajoy babu's great annoyance. Seeing that Ajoy babu was becoming increasingly frustrated by the internal discord and dissatisfaction, some Congressmen started wooing him back into the party. The idea was that if the 34 MLAs of the Bangla Congress joined hands with the 127 Congress MLAs, the group would form a majority in the assembly (then constituting 280 members) and could form the government. Here, I'm only repeating the little that Ajoy babu told us.

It was decided that on 2 October, Mahatma Gandhi's birthday, Ajoy babu would resign as Chief Minister, and the All India Congress Committee (AICC) would simultaneously withdraw his expulsion from the party. The larger plan was that the expulsion of all 34 Bangla Congress members would be withdrawn and a Congress ministry would be formed in West Bengal, with Ajoy babu again becoming Chief Minister.

Before this could happen, however, Barun Sengupta, a correspondent with *Anandabazar Patrika,* got wind of this plan and reported it in the newspaper. He had even got hold of the resignation speech Ajoy babu had intended to broadcast. The story created a sensation, and there was complete pandemonium. A meeting was called at the residence of Kanai Bhattacharya to discuss the matter.

All United Front leaders arrived at Kanai babu's house. Ajoy babu spoke on the matter in detail, after which it was decided that the CPI(M) would temper its agitational stance and would no longer embarrass or humiliate Ajoy babu.

As a consequence of this meeting and the decisions taken, Ajoy babu decided to remain in the Bangla Congress and agreed not to resign as Chief Minister. However, the meeting also sealed the division in the ranks of the Bangla Congress. Led by Prafulla Ghosh, 17 of the 34 MLAs of the Bangla Congress decided to quit the party and go back to the Congress. The Governor wasted no time in receiving their letters, and asked Ajoy babu to immediately convene a session of the assembly to prove his majority. In response, Ajoy babu told the Governor that as he had already called for the assembly session to be reconvened, he would not move the date forward, and that it was the ministry's prerogative to decide when assembly sessions should be held. The Governor was not convinced, and told Ajoy babu, 'After listening to them [the Bangla Congress MLAs who had quit the party], I feel you no longer have a majority in the assembly. Hence you have to first prove to me that you have the requisite numbers.'

It must be borne in mind that at this time the country at large, too, was in the throes of major political change. It was not only in West Bengal that the Congress had been defeated in the 1967 elections, but also in many other states like Bihar, Orissa, Tamil Nadu and Kerala.

During 1966 there was upheaval in some provincial Congress committees, and a number of prominent Congress leaders from these states decided not to go along with the clique in the party. As a result, some of them were driven out of the party, and they went on to form regional outfits and contested against the Congress in the 1967 elections. Mahamaya Prasad Sinha of Bihar formed the Kranti Congress, Dr Harekrushna Mahatab and Pabitra Mohan Pradhan of Orissa formed the Jana Congress and Ajoy Mukherjee of West Bengal set up the Bangla Congress. These parties formed the governments in their respective states after the elections, and their leaders became chief ministers: Mahamaya Prasad Sinha in Bihar and Ajoy Mukherjee in West Bengal. In Orissa, the non-Congress parties formed the government with

Rajendra Narayan Singh Deo of the Swatantra Party as Chief Minister and Pabitra Mohan Pradhan of the Jana Congress as Deputy Chief Minister.

After the general elections, the Congress governments in Uttar Pradesh and Madhya Pradesh collapsed because of the defection of some Congress MLAs under the leadership of Charan Singh in Uttar Pradesh and Govind Narayan Singh in Madhya Pradesh. With the support of some non-Congress parties, they then formed the government in their respective states, thus increasing the number of non-Congress ruled states after these elections.

It is then that an idea of an all-India party was floated. A steering committee was formed, and West Bengal was represented by Ajoy Mukherjee, Professor Humayun Kabir and Sushil Kumar Dhara. In November 1967, the steering committee convened a conference in Indore to announce the new party. The key people who attended this conference were Charan Singh, Mahamaya Prasad Sinha, Ajoy Mukherjee, Govind Narayan Singh, Pabitra Mohan Pradhan, Professor Humayun Kabir, Dr Harekrushna Mahatab and Shyamlal Yadav. It was at the conclusion of this three-day conference that the Bharatiya Kranti Dal (BKD) was announced. Henceforth, participating state parties became the state units of the BKD.

On 21 November, Ajoy babu received a missive from the Governor, telling him that his government had been dismissed. The reason given was that he had refused to convene the assembly session to prove his majority. Thereafter, amid great secrecy and in the dead of night, a new ministry was sworn in with Prafulla Ghosh as Chief Minister. The 127-member Congress legislature party pledged its support to this ministry.

The very next day, the United Front called a public meeting to protest against the manner in which an elected government had been dismissed. However, the police did not allow the meeting to continue till the end, breaking it up with a lathi charge. This incident, naturally, added fuel to the existing fire, and indignation grew further. The protests continued in spite of Section 144—which prohibits public assemblies—being clamped down in Calcutta. Many, including myself, were arrested.

Meanwhile, the assembly convened to prove Prafulla Ghosh's majority. At the very start of the session, the Speaker, Bijoy Banerjee, following a precedent, ruled, 'The people seated on the treasury benches when I concluded the last Vidhan Sabha session are not the ones I see there today. There are some strangers on the treasury benches. The old ministers are not there. The ministry has changed while the assembly was not in session. This is completely undemocratic, since the ministry is responsible to the assembly. The ministry cannot be changed outside the Vidhan Sabha.' Thus, he suspended the proceedings of the assembly indefinitely. There was absolute pandemonium thereafter. Prafulla Ghosh had a paperweight flung at him. Some other MLAs, however, surrounded him and ensured that he did not get hurt.

Political instability continued and, ultimately, the assembly was dissolved and President's Rule was imposed in the state. This state of affairs continued till March 1969, when the United Front coalition came to power for the second time with a thumping majority.

Though elections to the state assembly were announced for September-October 1968, they couldn't be held due to the devastating floods in Jalpaiguri and Cooch Behar. They were finally held in February-March 1969.

The Bangla Congress (now a constituent of the BKD) faced a peculiar problem during this election. As a result of a BKD directive that no constituent parties could align with the Marxists, we were faced with the possibility of fighting the Congress on our own—a near impossible task in West Bengal at that time. It is then that we decided to exit from the BKD and restore the Bangla Congress. Professor Humayun Kabir and his supporters joined the BKD; they contested the elections of 1969, but were routed. Meanwhile, the BKD was renamed the Lok Dal, which then focused its activities in Uttar Pradesh, Bihar and Madhya Pradesh.

Incidentally, I was elected to the Rajya Sabha as one of the six members from West Bengal that year.

# CHAPTER ONE

# MUKTIJUDDHO:
# THE MAKING OF BANGLADESH

O n the midnight of 14-15 August 1947, India was partitioned into two dominions—India and Pakistan—and the two subcontinental neighbours embarked on markedly distinct political trajectories. In India, after the assassination of Mahatma Gandhi on 30 January 1948, the mantle of leading the nation fell on Pandit Jawaharlal Nehru, the architect of modern India. From 15 August 1947 to 27 May 1964, he was the gentle colossus who guided India, laying the foundations of the country's modern democratic administration by enacting the magnificent Constitution of India. Within five years of Independence, the right to choose their rulers was transferred to the people of India, and they exercised this power in the general elections of 1952, conducted impartially by an independent Election Commission on the basis of universal adult franchise.

After establishing modern democratic practices and institutions in India, Nehru also set in motion the process of modern economic development and laid the cornerstone of India's foreign policy with the Non-Aligned Movement. This soon became a movement against colonialism and a cry for liberation for a large number of Asian, African and Latin American countries, thus placing India in the position of the leader of the third world.

With Nehru's death in 1964 came a political vacuum, as is bound to happen with the exit of a charismatic leader. The Indian National Congress suffered electorally in the general elections of 1967: while it just managed a slender majority in the Lok Sabha, it failed to get even that in a large number of states. A number of political parties emerged as powerful regional players, thus weakening the hegemony of the Congress. Organizational contradictions, which came to the fore with Nehru's death, finally led to the split of the Indian National Congress in 1969.

And then came the bold leadership of Indira Gandhi. Under her command the Congress, with the support of a range of political parties such as the Dravida Munnetra Kazhagam (DMK) and the Communist Party of India (CPI), emerged victorious in the mid-term general elections of 1971, getting a two-thirds majority in the Lok Sabha and later, in 1972, recovering many of the state assemblies it had lost earlier.

■

As these events were unfolding in India, eastern Pakistan was in the throes of momentous change. In the first ever free general elections in Pakistan, the Awami League of East Pakistan, led by Sheikh Mujibur Rahman, won a clear majority in the Pakistan National Assembly (PNA). With this, the history of the subcontinent reached a turning point in 1971.

The year began positively for Pakistan, with democracy on the ascent and elections looming. However, it ended with the country being partitioned: a Pakistan consisting of two geographically distant parts—East and West Pakistan separated by 1,600 kilometres of Indian territory—became two nations: Pakistan and Bangladesh.

The inherent contradictions of the entity that was Pakistan as demarcated by the Radcliffe Line were evident even when the country was born, but increasingly so in the subsequent politics of the newly emergent nation. With a minority of the population share of the country, West Pakistan had a significantly larger share of revenue allocation which facilitated industrial and infrastructural development and agricultural reforms. Not only that, West Pakistan elites—Punjabis and Afghans—dominated the country's politics, to the near exclusion of the Bengalis of East Pakistan. However, economic neglect and political exclusion were not the only issues burning East Pakistan's psyche. There was also the issue of ethnic and linguistic discrimination. Was the split, then, not inevitable?

■

The politics of Bengal, particularly the role played by Muslim politicians and legislators, is of significance in this context. And, to understand this better, it is necessary to go back in time.

As mandated by the Government of India Act 1935, provincial assembly elections were held in 1937 throughout British India for control of the autonomous provincial assemblies. Congress got a majority in five provinces—the United Provinces of Agra and Oudh (UP), Central Provinces and Berar (now Madhya Pradesh), Bihar, Orissa and the Madras Presidency (where, with 74 per cent of all seats, it eclipsed the Justice Party). In the North-West Frontier Province (NWFP), the Congress, with minor party support, was able to form a ministry. Similarly, in Bombay, where it fell just short of gaining half the seats, it was able to draw on the support of small pro-Congress groups to form a majority.

Bengal, Assam and Punjab saw an indecisive verdict, though the Congress and Muslim League got a big chunk of seats.[4] In Sindh, the Sindh United Party got a clear majority.

In Bengal, the Congress got about 52 seats, the Muslim League got 39, while A.K. Fazlul Huq's Krishak Praja Party (KPP) got 36, seats.[5] The fractured verdict resulted in Fazlul Huq first trying to build a coalition government with the Congress—he preferred to join hands with the Congress and other nationalists rather than the Muslim League. Though Sarat Chandra Bose (Subhas Chandra Bose's elder brother), a prominent Congress leader in Bengal and the leader of the Congress Party in the assembly, agreed to join hands with Fazlul Huq, no consensus could be reached on the joint programme. An angry Fazlul Huq decided to seek the support of the Muslim League instead.

> Thus a Krishak Praja Party-Muslim League coalition government, with support from scheduled caste and some independent upper-caste Hindu MLAs came to power... The Muslim League took full advantage of its governmental authority in Bengal to extend its support base over the Muslim masses. It also befriended Huq and persuaded him to join the League within a short time with many of his followers. In fact, in his anxiety to accommodate every interest that could support his government, Huq became a minority within the ministry. This, as also his abandonment of the election pledges, caused rumblings in [the] KPP. As early as March 1938 a majority of the KPP assembly party sat with the opposition to register their protest... Huq realised

---

[4] See 'Imperial India and the Growth of National Identity', *Schwartzberg Atlas*, Volume 5, p. 222.
[5] Syed Umar Hayat, 'Muslim Political Ascendancy in Bengal', *Pakistan Journal of History and Culture*, Volume XXVIII, No. 2 (2007), p. 119.

that he could save his ministry only with Jinnah's support and joined the League at its annual session at Lucknow in December 1937. Between 1937 and 1940, Huq was drawn into the vortex of Muslim League politics although he never felt comfortable in the landlord-dominated party.[6]

Fazlul Huq had a chequered political career as he was aligned to, or part of, various political parties between 1941 and 1946. He became the first Premier of Bengal in 1937 (joining the Muslim League shortly thereafter), but this government did not last for its full term, and collapsed in December 1941. Though he moved the famous Lahore Resolution in the Muslim League Council in 1940 (later interpreted as a demand for a single state of Pakistan), he did not support the proposal for a separate dominion of Pakistan in 1946, as a result of which his party lost miserably in the face of an ascendant Muslim League.

As Premier of Bengal, Fazlul Huq's unique contribution was in safeguarding the interests of Bengal's peasantry. Rescuing them from the clutches of moneylenders, he provided the debt-burdened peasants relief through the Debt Recovery Settlement Board. Significantly, Fazlul Huq was responsible for creating a powerful middle class which became the foundation of Bengal's politics in subsequent years.

The verdict of 1946 clearly demonstrated the able leadership of Huseyn Shaheed Suhrawardy and the organizational ability of Abul Hashim, General Secretary of the Muslim League. Ahead of this election, Suhrawardy had offered Fazlul Huq a deal—forty Muslim constituencies to Fazlul Huq's nominees if they filed their nominations as Muslim League candidates. Fazlul Huq rejected the proposal outright and contested elections on

---

[6]Nitish K. Sengupta, *History of the Bengali-Speaking People* (New Delhi, 2001), pp. 426-27.

a separate manifesto. The result was clear. The Muslim League won 115 of the 121 Muslim seats while nationalist Muslims and Fazlul Huq's party were completely washed out, as was the Congress (though the Congress fared well in general seats, winning 87 out of 90).[7] This was also the first time that the Communist Party contested elections, winning three seats: Jyoti Basu, Ratanlal Brahmin and Rupnarayan Roy were elected.

In spite of the mandate, Suhrawardy did not form the government immediately. With the view that a large part of the population would have no representation in such a government, he endeavoured to co-opt the Congress into a coalition. Senior leaders of both parties tried to work things out, but their efforts were unsuccessful. Consequently, on 23 April 1946, Suhrawardy formed his cabinet with seven other members of the Muslim League and Jogendra Nath Mandal, leader of the Scheduled Castes Federation, the lone Hindu minister in the cabinet. The family of the Nawab of Dacca was not represented in this cabinet, though the Nawab of Bogra, Muhammad Ali, held a cabinet post. Most of the ministers were from the upper middle class.

This government's darkest hour came only a few months later. The Muslim League had announced 16 August 1946 to be observed as Direct Action Day to press for their demand for Pakistan. While it was expected that the agitation would be against the British, in Calcutta it turned into a communal confrontation between Hindus and Muslims instead. Hindus and Sikhs were targeted on the assumption that they were opposed to the creation of Pakistan. While there are many published accounts of this period, two experiential accounts stand out. Sheikh Mujibur Rahman, founder of Bangladesh and the then

---

[7]Nitish K. Sengupta, *Land of Two Rivers: A History of Bengal from the Mahabharata to Mujib* (India, 2011), p. 454.

leader of the student wing of the Muslim League, provides a glimpse into this time of irrationally raised passions in his book, *The Unfinished Memoirs*,[8] as does Tapan Roychowdhury in his *Bangal Nama*.[9]

It didn't stop at Calcutta, though. Riots spread to Noakhali in Bengal, and then Bihar and Punjab. Hindu–Muslim amity was thrown to the winds and sanity was lost for the time being. This was in sharp contrast to the glorious Hindu–Muslim unity demonstrated against British rule in November 1945, when Hindus and Muslims jointly demonstrated on the streets of Calcutta against the British policy of divide and rule. Perceptions of safety radically changed in Calcutta from what they were before 16 August: while Calcutta streets were perceived to be safe for Hindus and Muslims before this day, they became unsafe thereafter.

■

The period after the Second World War was one of momentous political change in India. In its wake, Congress-led ministries resigned from the United Provinces of Agra and Oudh, the Central Provinces, Bihar, Orissa, NWFP, Bombay and Madras in protest against the unilateral decision of the British government to make India declare war against the Germany-led Axis forces and become a part of the Allied forces led by Britain, without assessing public opinion in India.

To resolve the crisis and effect a political resolution, a powerful ministerial mission headed by Sir Stafford Cripps was sent to India to hold discussions with ten Indian leaders to ensure their

---

[8]Sheikh Mujibur Rahman, *The Unfinished Memoirs* (New Delhi, 2012).
[9]Tapan Roychowdhury, *Bangal Nama* (Kolkata, 2007).

cooperation with the war efforts of the British government. However, the mission failed as Congress leaders did not agree with the stance taken by the British government. On 8 August 1942, the Congress launched the Quit India Movement under Mahatma Gandhi.

As a result, Congress leaders were arrested and the party was banned. However, Mahatma Gandhi's message reached every corner of the country, spurring people to rise against the British government in massive numbers. Subhas Chandra Bose left the country and, via Germany, reached Japan to take over the leadership of the Indian National Army (INA). By 1944, Netaji had liberated the Andaman and Nicobar Islands with Japanese support.[10] With the surrender of Germany, Italy and Japan, the Second World War ended in 1945, catalysing heightened political activity. The ban on the Congress was lifted, its leaders were released from jail and a dialogue between them and the British government began.

On 2 September 1946, an interim government took office in India with Governor General Lord Archibald Wavell as the President of the Executive Council and Jawaharlal Nehru as Vice President. The other members were Sir Claude Auchinleck, Sardar Vallabhbhai Patel, Dr Rajendra Prasad, Asaf Ali, C. Rajagopalachari, Sarat Chandra Bose, Dr John Mathai, Sardar Baldev Singh, Sir Shafaat Ahmad Khan, Jagjivan Ram, Syed Ali Zaheer and C.H. Bhabha. Five seats were offered to members of the Muslim League, which they initially refused; however, on 15 October 1946, they accepted the offer and Liaquat Ali Khan, Ibrahim Ismail Chundrigar (both later served Pakistan as prime ministers), Abdur Rab Nishtar,

---

[10]R.V.R. Murthy, *Andaman and Nicobar Islands: Development and Decentralization* (New Delhi, 2005), p. 29.

Raja Ghazanfar Ali and Jogendra Nath Mandal joined the government. (Jinnah's choice of Mandal as a Muslim League nominee was an effort to counter the Muslim card of the Congress.) Significantly, none of the other Muslim League members were from Bengal.

According to the plan declared by the British government on 3 June 1947, shadow ministries were to be set up in the to-be-partitioned provinces of Punjab and Bengal so as to look after all interests. The shadow cabinet of East Punjab was headed by Dr Gopi Chand Bhargava while that of West Punjab was headed by the Nawab of Mamdot, Iftikar Hussain; the West Bengal ministry was led by Dr P.C. Ghosh, a member of the Congress Working Committee (CWC). This done, members of the legislative assembly from Muslim majority districts and non-Muslim districts were to meet separately and decide which dominion—India or Pakistan—they would like to join.

In the meantime, boundary commissions were set up for Punjab and Bengal and both were headed by Sir Cyril Radcliffe.

When on 17 August, 1947 the Radcliffe report consisting of 16 pages was released of which 9 pages were devoted to Bengal, there were many surprises. Khulna and Chittagong Hill districts, which had hoisted [the] Indian national flag two days ago, became parts of Pakistan. Murshidabad and Malda districts which had hoisted [the] Pakistani flag were made parts of India. The districts of Jalpaiguri, Malda and Nadia remained in India while losing substantial territory from the districts to Pakistan. On the other hand, although Jessore and Dinajpur were allotted to Pakistan, a subdivision each from both the districts (Bongaon subdivision in Jessore and Balurghat subdivision in Dinajpur), were allotted to India. The state of West Bengal as it emerged from Radcliffe's scissors was also moth-eaten. The districts of Darjeeling and Jalpaiguri were physically separated from West Bengal mainland. The Muslims were sad to see that Calcutta had gone to West Bengal, as also the Muslim majority district of Murshidabad. What weighed with Radcliffe in giving Murshidabad to India while, as a compensatory measure, giving Khulna to Pakistan was that the entire length of the Hooghly river from the point where it branches off from the Ganges should be with India in order to maintain the navigability of the Calcutta port. The Hindus were sorry that the predominantly Buddhist district of Chittagong Hill tracts had been given to Pakistan. All its normal communication routes to the outside world lay through the Chittagong district and apparently that had influenced Radcliffe's judgement, although he failed to notice in his haste that the hill tracts of Chittagong had a long border with Lushai Hills district of the Indian province of Assam. As all the parties had given a guarantee that they would accept [the] Radcliffe award without any question, they had to keep quiet and accept whatever had been decreed by Radcliffe in what was by far the strangest, most illogical and arbitrarily drawn boundary line in history between two countries.[11]

Realizing that neither country could rightly claim all of Punjab, Bengal and Assam, the central leadership of the Muslim League, particularly Jinnah, and the Congress were eager to get whatever areas they could out of the scheme of Partition. However, some leaders in Bengal floated the idea of an undivided Bengal— Maulana Akram Khan and H.S. Suhrawardy were totally opposed to the partition of the province—and Congress and Muslim League leaders met on several occasions to work out a formula

---

[11]Nitish K. Sengupta, *History of the Bengali-Speaking People* (New Delhi, 2001), p. 524.

to avoid it. In his book, *The Unfinished Memoirs*, Mujibur Rahman wrote of a conspiracy against Suhrawardy while the partition plan was being finalized. His claim that the Muslim League leadership in Bengal was kept in the dark about the partition of Bengal is hardly surprising given Suhrawardy's unambiguous position and his support for an undivided Bengal. The cross-party discussions in Bengal yielded a formula, an important ingredient of which was that a constituent assembly would be elected by the people of Bengal and the elected members of this assembly would then decide whether to join India or Pakistan or remain independent. This formula was endorsed by the provincial Muslim League Council. When Sarat Chandra Bose (who had joined hands with Suhrawardy after being pushed out of the interim government), Kiran Shanker Roy, Suhrawardy and other Muslim League leaders laid out this formula, the Congress's central leadership rejected it. According to Sarat Chandra Bose's statement, Mahatma Gandhi and Jawaharlal Nehru advised Bose to talk to Sardar Vallabhbhai Patel who, in turn, told him bluntly: 'Don't behave in a funny manner. We must have Calcutta in India.' Thus disappointed, they returned home.

The ground reality, too, made the task of the proponents of an undivided Bengal difficult. After the riots of Calcutta and Noakhali, Hindus were wary and hesitant of living in a province dominated by a Muslim majority, as would be the case in an undivided Bengal. Dr Syama Prasad Mookerjee, President of the All India Hindu Mahasabha and a prominent leader of Bengal, was a strong supporter of a partitioned Bengal and was able to influence the public mood substantially in its favour. At that moment, he emerged as the undisputed leader of Bengali Hindus. In this scenario, therefore, the Governor General refused to consider any new scheme unless it was agreed to by both the Congress and the Muslim League.

In the meantime, Suhrawardy's popularity rapidly declined because of the almost continuous communal rioting in Bengal as also due to his support and strong advocacy for a united Bengal. On the pretext that he had been elected to the Bengal assembly from a constituency which fell in West Bengal, he lost his position as the leader of the Muslim League in the East Bengal assembly to Sir Khawaja Nazimuddin, Nawab of Dacca, who declared that Dacca would be the capital of East Bengal. In his autobiography, Mujibur Rahman claims that by doing this, Khawaja Nazimuddin completely blocked the chance of staking a claim to Calcutta as the capital of Pakistan. According to him, if Calcutta had become a part of East Bengal, it would certainly have been the capital of Pakistan. He also claimed that Suhrawardy's overall popularity among the Muslim masses of Bengal would have propelled him to the office of Prime Minister of Pakistan.

■

The genesis of Bangladesh remained in this discord within the Muslim League and marginalization of several prominent leaders like H.S. Suhrawardy, Fazlul Huq and Abul Hashim. After Partition, the Muslim League in Bengal was largely dominated by zamindars and landed aristocrats. In his book, Mujibur Rahman stated that Suhrawardy's drive to abolish the zamindari system was one of the reasons for his defeat in the leadership election of the Muslim League in East Bengal, as a large number of legislators were zamindars. Even when Mujibur Rahman tried to influence the newly-elected Sylhet legislator to support Suhrawardy, he failed. It is said that when they came to participate in the leadership election, they demanded three ministerial berths from Suhrawardy and a commitment that the zamindari system would not be abolished. Suhrawardy refused to make any commitment and they voted against him.

Significant changes in national politics, too, further accentuated the marginalization of East Bengal politicians. Jinnah died in 1949, and Khawaja Nazimuddin first became Governor General of Pakistan, and then Prime Minister after the assassination of Liaquat Ali Khan in 1951. With Nazimuddin becoming Prime Minister (though he was replaced a couple of years later by Muhammad Ali of Bogra), Ghulam Mohammad, a civil servant, took over as Governor General of Pakistan. Ghulam Mohammad's appointment marked the ascendancy of bureaucrats in Pakistan's politics. In fact, the real rulers of Pakistan were the civil servants, the military and the landed aristocrats who, along with certain industrial groups, held overwhelming control. The central Muslim League leadership kept a few East Pakistan leaders—like Nazimuddin and Muhammad Ali of Bogra—in the forefront to showcase that East Bengal leaders were also participants in the overall Pakistani establishment. But they were used as puppets to serve the interests of the real rulers.

After the formation of the government in East Bengal, a significant number of Congress leaders from East Bengal migrated to West Bengal; similarly, important Muslim League leaders from West Bengal went to East Bengal. As in the formation of government so also in the leadership of the Muslim League, the middle-class intelligentsia, which emerged in the 1930s, was marginalized, for which the Muslim League paid a heavy price in the 1954 election to the East Bengal legislative assembly.

■

In the meantime, the rashtrabhasha (national language) agitation gained momentum. Muslim League leaders, including Jinnah, were adamant that Urdu be the national language of Pakistan. The Pakistan constituent assembly discussed the issue in February 1948, and almost all Muslim League members backed this demand. Babu Dhirendranath Datta, a Congress member of the assembly, voiced the demand that Bengali be added as the other national language, given that it was the mother tongue of the majority of the population of the country. This demand was bitterly criticized by Muslim League members, and Prime Minister Liaquat Ali Khan accused Datta of being an Indian agent focused on destroying Pakistan. This criticism notwithstanding, the reaction in Bengal was unambiguous. The East Bengal Muslim Students League and Tamaddun Majlish (a cultural organization) protested against Urdu being imposed as the only state language, and reiterated Datta's demand. With the support of senior Muslim League leaders such as Kamruddin Ahmed and Shamsul Haq as well as Mujibur Rahman, they set up the Rashtrabhasha Bangla Sangram Parishad (Bengali State Language Agitation Council), and decided to observe 11 March 1948 as Bangla Bhasha Day.

The large-scale student support and turnout came up against a police and administrative crackdown, and the protesting student activists were mercilessly beaten and many arrested. In the East Bengal assembly, then in session, many members including Fazlul Huq, Muhammad Ali of Bogra, Tofazzal Ali, Khairat Hossain and Anwara Khatun strongly condemned the Muslim League and the government. The government repression had the effect of bringing people together in wider support for the cause, as a result of which the government agreed to initiate a dialogue with the leaders of the agitation. However, shortly thereafter, on 16 March, the movement was called off so as to welcome Jinnah, the Governor General of Pakistan, who was scheduled to visit Dacca.

On 24 March, Jinnah addressed a public rally at Race Course

Maidan and reiterated that Urdu would be the only state language of Pakistan.[12] He repeated this resolve later at the convocation at Dacca University. At both events, students voiced their opposition loudly and clearly, shouting out: 'No, we don't accept.'

Jinnah's Dacca declaration only strengthened the agitation and, in February 1952, it took a serious turn in the form of riots, with a large number of students being beaten or jailed, even killed. The impact of the language movement and its inept handling by the central Muslim League leadership unleashed an active Bengali sub-nationalism.

■

While the language movement was gradually gathering momentum, there were beginnings of turmoil within the Muslim League. Nazimuddin had not included any of Suhrawardy's people in his cabinet in 1947, and this had the effect of uniting Suhrawardy's supporters as well as people like Muhammad Ali of Bogra, Dr Abdul Malek, Tofazzal Ali and a big chunk of Muslim League legislators, who then formed a pressure group. And, while such discontent was brewing, Maulana Akram Khan expelled some old Muslim League council members from the party. Those who had been thus removed made a complaint against this arbitrary expulsion to the all-India President of the Muslim League. Chaudhry Khaliquzzaman, the then Party President, told them bluntly that they would have to work under Khawaja Nazimuddin and that Akram Khan would decide who could and should be a member of the League.

All this led to the formation of the All Pakistan Awami Muslim League. In 1949, the dissidents, mainly the followers of

---

[12]'Language Movement Hero Passes Away', *The News Today*, 6 November 2014.

Suhrawardy, were instrumental in establishing this party. Abdul Hamid Khan Bhashani, a prominent Muslim League leader of East Pakistan, became the Founder-President and continued in this capacity till 1957, when he left to form the National Awami Party. Mujibur Rahman was associated with this party from the very beginning and worked hard to establish it and spread its influence across East Bengal. The exodus of prominent and popular Bengali Muslim leaders out of the Muslim League had a far reaching effect. The Awami League grew stronger over the years and Mujibur Rahman emerged as the uncrowned leader of this organization over the course of time.

■

Elections to the East Bengal legislative assembly were declared in 1954. At the initiative of three prominent Muslim leaders of Bengal—Suhrawardy, Fazlul Huq and Maulana Bhashani— a United Front was established. It consisted of the Awami League, Fazlul Huq's Krishak Praja Party (KPP), Nizam-e-Islam and a few others. The United Front achieved massive success in these elections: out of 309 seats, the ruling Muslim League Party got only 9,[13] and all prominent leaders of the Muslim League, including Nurul Amin, who was the Premier of East Pakistan, were defeated. This was in stark contrast to the League's performance in 1946 when it had virtually made a clean sweep. It was decided that Fazlul Huq would form the government, which he did first with four members; he then expanded the ministry to include leaders of the Awami League and some other parties. Of the Awami League leaders, Ataur Rahman Khan, Abul

---

[13]'The Election of the United Front', *Bangladeshi Awami League*, albd.org/index. php/en/party/history/80-the-election-of-the-united-front.

Mansur Ahmed, Abdus Salam Khan, Hashimuddin Ahmed and Mujibur Rahman joined the ministry.

In his autobiography, Mujibur Rahman states that rather than introspect and take corrective measures, East Pakistan Muslim League leaders instead left their respective areas and began operating out of West Pakistan, focusing on toppling the United Front government.

■

Developmental work in West Pakistan was being carried on in full swing. Industrial enterprise and agricultural development were given a significant fillip with the massive aid received from the United States and other countries. In contrast, hardly any economic development took place in East Pakistan. It was turned into a supplier of raw materials for West Pakistan and a market for its finished products. Archer K. Blood, an American diplomat, in his book, *The Cruel Birth of Bangladesh,* says:

> Since independence real political control of Pakistan had been in the hands of the Pakistani military, the upper ranks of the civil servants and a small number of wealthy industrialists, with all three groups from West Pakistan. East Pakistan's numerical superiority was nullified by the failure of parliamentary democracy to take effective root in Pakistan, as it had in India. The highly centralized, often authoritarian structure of Pakistan government in the West Wing resulted in West Pakistan getting the lion's share of foreign assistance and internal development funds.[14]

■

---

[14]Archer K. Blood, *The Cruel Birth of Bangladesh* (Bangladesh, 2013).

Lack of development, undemocratic practices, and the arbitrary manipulation of parliamentary democratic systems led to the final revolt of the people of East Pakistan against the ruling West Pakistan. Mujibur Rahman emerged as the leader of this revolution. If one studies his eventful life during these years, one can understand how he gradually prepared himself and his people for the creation of the sovereign nation of Bangladesh.

On 5 June 1955, he was elected as a member of the Pakistan constituent assembly. A few days later, on 17 June, a 21-point charter of demands for an autonomous East Pakistan was adopted at a public meeting at Paltan Maidan in Dacca. On 23 June, the Executive Council of the Awami League resolved that if the demand for autonomy was not considered, all Awami League members would resign from the legislature. On 25 August, in his address to the constituent assembly, Mujibur Rahman observed:

> Sir, you will see that they want to place the word 'East Pakistan' instead of 'East Bengal'. We have demanded so many times that you should use the word Bengal instead of Pakistan. The word 'Bengal' has a history, has a tradition of its own. You can change it only after the people have been consulted. If you want to change it then we have to go back to Bengal and ask them whether they accept it. So far as the question of one unit is concerned, it can come in the Constitution. Why do you want it to be taken up just now? What about the state language, Bengali? What about joint electorate? What about autonomy? The people of East Bengal will be prepared to consider one unit with all these things. So I appeal to my friends on that side to allow the people to give their verdict in any way, in the form of [a] referendum or in the form of [a] plebiscite.

This was the crux of the demands of the people of Bengal

from the days of the rashtrabhasha agitation till the declaration of the Liberation War by Mujibur Rahman on 26 March 1971.

■

On 7 October 1958, the central government of Pakistan under Prime Minister Malik Sir Feroz Khan Noon was dismissed by the Governor General, Iskander Mirza. Martial law was declared, and General Ayub Khan, Commander-in-Chief of the Pakistani Army, was appointed Chief Martial Law Administrator. Shortly afterwards, General Ayub Khan forced Iskander Mirza to step down and go into exile, and assumed absolute authority of governing the whole of Pakistan on 27 October 1958. Under him, military rule continued till 1962 when, in June, he introduced a civilian government through his idea of 'basic democracy'. A large number of established political leaders, including Mujibur Rahman, were debarred from contesting elections ostensibly because of charges of corruption against them. (On 11 October 1958, within four days of the declaration of martial law by Feroz Khan Noon, Mujibur Rahman was arrested, and was released and re-arrested a number of times till 18 June 1962.) On the basis of the principles of 'basic democracy', General Ayub Khan was elected President of Pakistan, defeating Fatima Jinnah (Muhammad Ali Jinnah's sister) by a huge margin.

On 24 January 1964,[15] the Awami League was revived (it had been banned during the period of martial law), and immediately put forth the demand for a parliamentary form of government based on adult franchise. Maulana Abdur Rashid Tarkabagish and Mujibur Rahman were elected the President and General

---

[15]*Political Parties in South Asia*, edited by Subrata Mitra, Mike Enskat and Clemens Spiess (USA, 2004), p. 218.

## Party Position 1970 Elections

### Seats and percentage of total vote polled

| Party | Punjab | Sind | NWFP | Baluchistan | West | East | Total |
|---|---|---|---|---|---|---|---|
| Awami League | 0 (0.07%) | 0 (0.07%) | 0 (0.2%) | 0 (1.0%) | 0 | 160 (74.9%) | 160 (38.3%) |
| Pakistan Peoples Party | 62 (41.6%) | 18 (44.9%) | 1 (14.2%) | 0 (2.3%) | 81 | 0 | 81 (19.5%) |
| PML (Q) | 1 (5.4%) | 1 (10.7%) | 7 (22.6%) | 0 (10.9%) | 9 | 0 (1.0%) | 9 (4.5%) |
| PML Convention | 7 (5.1%) | 0 (1.7%) | 0 | 0 | 7 | 0 (2.8%) | 7 (3.3%) |
| Jamiat e Ulema Islam | 0 (5.2%) | 0 (4.3%) | 6 (25.4%) | 1 (20.0%) | 7 | 0 (0.9%) | 7 (4.0%) |
| Markazi Jamiat Ulema Pakistan | 4 (9.8%) | 3 (7.4%) | 0 (0%) | 0 | 7 | 0 | 7 (4.0%) |
| National Awami Party (Wali) | 0 | 0 (0.3%) | 3 (18.4%) | 3 (45.1%) | 6 | 0 (1.8%) | 6 (2.3%) |
| Jamaat e Islami | 1 (4.7%) | 2 (10.3%) | 1 (7.2%) | 0 (1.1%) | 4 | 0 (6.0%) | 4 (6.0%) |
| PML (Council) | 2 (12.6%) | 0 (6.8%) | 0 (4.0%) | 0 (10.9%) | 2 | 0 (1.6%) | 2 (6.0%) |
| PDP | 0 (2.2%) | 0 (0.04%) | 0 (0.3%) | 0 (0.3%) | 0 | 1 (2.2%) | 1 (2.9%) |
| Independents | 5 (11.8%) | 3 (10.7%) | 7 (6.0%) | 0 (6.8%) | 15 | 1 (3.4%) | 16 (7.1%) |
| **Total seats** | **82** | **27** | **25** | **4** | **138** | **162** | **300** |

*Source:* http://www.elections.com.pk/contents.php?i=7#Party. Accessed on 1 November 2014.

## Provincial Party Position 1970 Elections

| Party | Punjab | Sind | NWFP | Baluchistan | West Pakistan | East Pakistan |
|---|---|---|---|---|---|---|
| Awami League | 0 | 0 | 0 | 0 | 0 | 288 |
| Pakistan Peoples Party | 113 | 28 | 3 | 0 | 144 | 0 |
| PML (Qayyum) | 6 | 5 | 10 | 3 | 24 | 0 |
| PML (Convention) | 15 | 4 | 1 | 0 | 21 | 1 |
| JUI | 2 | 0 | 4 | 2 | 8 | 0 |
| MJUP | 4 | 7 | 0 | 0 | 11 | 0 |
| NAP(W) | 0 | 0 | 13 | 8 | 21 | 1 |
| JI | 1 | 1 | 1 | 0 | 3 | 1 |
| PML (Council) | 6 | 0 | 2 | 0 | 8 | 0 |
| PDP | 4 | 0 | 0 | 0 | 4 | 2 |
| Others | 1 | 1 | 0 | 2 | 4 | 1 |
| Ind | 28 | 14 | 6 | 5 | 53 | 7 |
| **Total seats** | **180** | **60** | **40** | **20** | **300** | **300** |

*Source:* http://www.elections.com.pk/contents.php?i=7#Party. Accessed on 1 November 2014.

Secretary respectively. Mujibur Rahman was arrested again in the course of the national presidential elections but, on his release, he once again resumed his agitation. On 5 February 1966, at the National Conference of Opposition Parties at Lahore in Pakistan, Mujibur Rahman placed the historic 6-point charter of demands for East Pakistan (see Appendix 1). On 1 March 1966, Mujibur Rahman was elected the President of the Awami League and began a vigorous campaign to create public opinion in favour of this charter. On 3 January 1968, the Pakistani government launched the ill-famed Agartala Conspiracy Case. Mujibur Rahman and thirty-four other Bengali civil and military officers were accused of trying to destroy Pakistan in collusion with Indian agents. It was alleged that their objective was to destroy Pakistan by creating East Pakistan as a sovereign independent country. Mujibur Rahman was arrested and, in protest against this arrest, the Central Students Action Council launched a massive movement across East Pakistan demanding his release and the withdrawal of the case against him. Under pressure of public opinion, on 22 February 1969, the Pakistani government was forced to withdraw the case and release all those arrested, including Mujibur Rahman.

Mujibur Rahman was given a massive, million-people-strong civic reception at Race Course Maidan on 23 February and was formally declared 'Bangabandhu'. On 10 March, he attended the Round Table Conference of all parties convened by President General Ayub Khan at Rawalpindi and pressed for the acceptance of his demands. He declared that public agitation and mass dissension could not be contained unless East Pakistan's demands were accepted immediately. On the central government's refusal, Mujibur Rahman returned to Dacca on 14 March.

After the collapse of the Round Table Conference, General Ayub Khan resigned as President, handing over to General Yahya Khan, Commander-in-Chief of the Pakistan Armed Forces.

On 25 March 1969, Pakistan went back to military rule.

Though General Yahya Khan tried to quell the massive public agitation, there was no alternative but to restore democracy and hold elections. It was in this scenario that a politically volatile Pakistan held its first free general elections on 7 December 1970. General Yahya Khan declared elections in 300 constituencies of the Pakistan National Assembly (PNA) in both East and West Pakistan as also in the provincial assemblies. Proportional to the regional demographic, 162 of the 300 seats to the PNA were allocated to East Pakistan, with the remaining 138 seats to West Pakistan. The results were unambiguous. The Awami League under the leadership of Mujibur Rahman captured 160 of the 162 seats of East Pakistan, thus getting an absolute majority in the PNA. It fared even better in the provincial elections, and got 288 out of 300 seats in East Pakistan.[16]

The logic of free and fair elections demanded that Mujibur Rahman be invited to form the government. This logic, however, faced stiff opposition. Though General Yahya Khan had promised to restore democracy, the dynamics of Pakistani politics, the overwhelming control of the army and the entrenched vested interests (of the army, industrialists and upper bureaucracy) did not allow democratic processes to be followed. Zulfikar Ali Bhutto, leader of the Pakistan People's Party, which got more than 80 seats in West Pakistan, demanded parity between East and West Pakistan by way of a coalition between the largest party of East Pakistan, the Awami League, and the largest party of West Pakistan, the Pakistan People's Party, thus ignoring the first principle of a democratic government. Bhutto travelled to Dacca with this proposal on 27 January 1971, and held discussions with Mujibur

---

[16]'Election Statistics of Pakistan', *Pakistan Election*, www.elections.com.pk, accessed on 6 November 2014.

Rahman over the next three days.[17] The talks failed. Bhutto then put forth the demand that power be transferred to the two majority parties in their respective regions: that is, to the Awami League in East Pakistan and to the Pakistan People's Party in West Pakistan. Mujibur Rahman dismissed this demand too, declaring that it was irrational and unprincipled. General Yahya Khan, under pressure from Bhutto and the strong anti-Bengali lobby active in West Pakistan, indefinitely postponed the session of the PNA scheduled to be held from 3 March 1971. And, as soon as he made this announcement, East Bengal erupted in protest.

On 7 March, at a massive public meeting at the Dacca Race Course Maidan, Mujibur Rahman appealed to all Bengalis to unite in the struggle for liberation: 'This struggle of ours is the struggle for our total freedom…You convert each house into a fort; whatever you have at your hand, you confront the enemies with that. We have given enough blood and we will give much more. We will liberate ourselves. Inshallah.'

From 7 March itself, Mujibur Rahman took over the administrative responsibilities of East Pakistan, calling for total non-cooperation with the national government led by General Yahya Khan. In fact, from 7-25 March, there were two governments in East Pakistan: the de jure government led by General Yahya Khan and the de facto government led by Mujibur Rahman. Faced with this emergent situation, General Yahya Khan travelled to Dacca to break the deadlock and discuss the demand of transfer of power with Mujibur Rahman, as did Zulfikar Ali Bhutto. However, the military junta, the real power-to-be in Pakistan, had no intention of accepting Mujibur Rahman's demand. In the name of discussion, the period between 16 and

---

[17]Nitish K. Sengupta, *Land of Two Rivers: A History of Bengal from the Mahabharata to Mujib* (New Delhi, 2011), p. 546.

24 March was utilized to transport military might—forces and equipment—from West Pakistan to East Pakistan.

On 25 March, General Yahya Khan declared that his discussion with Mujibur Rahman had failed to arrive at a conclusion. From 9 p.m. that night, the Pakistani army cracked down on the people of East Pakistan. They attacked Dacca University, Pilkhana EPR Headquarters and Rajarbagh Police Headquarters. Anticipating his imminent arrest, Mujibur Rahman, on the same night, declared:

> This may be my last message. From today Bangladesh is independent. I call upon the people of Bangladesh wherever you might be and with whatever you have, to resist the army of occupation to the last. Your fight must go on until the last soldier of the Pakistan occupation army is expelled from the soil of Bangladesh and final victory is achieved.

This declaration was conveyed throughout East Pakistan through wireless, telephone and telegram. Mujibur Rahman was arrested on the night of 25-26 March at 1.30 a.m. and taken to the army headquarters at Dacca, where he was confined for three days after which he was flown to West Pakistan. On 26 March, General Yahya Khan banned the Awami League and condemned Mujibur Rahman as a traitor.

On 10 April, a government-in-exile with Mujibur Rahman as its President (in absentia) was declared, and this revolutionary government took oath on 17 April at a place called Baidyanathtala in Meherpur in the Kushtia district of East Pakistan (this place later came to be known as Mujibnagar). Syed Nazrul Islam, Vice President, was sworn in as the acting President with Tajuddin Ahmad as Prime Minister (see Appendix 2 for Tajuddin Ahmad's press statement).

The following months saw a massive violation of basic human rights in the form of blood-chilling atrocities, genocide and mass rape, resulting first in the displacement and uprooting of more than ten million people from East Pakistan to adjacent India and then a heroic, and successful, struggle for independence. After the thirteen-day India-Pakistan war, Pakistan's General Niazi, along with more than 91,000 officers and soldiers, surrendered to the joint command of India and Bangladesh's Mukti Bahini (Liberation Army) on 16 December 1971.

•

Many of us were passionately concerned about the events that were unfolding then. The plight of millions of homeless people crossing the border seeking refuge in the neighbouring states of India stirred the hearts of our people as we felt the anguish of this hapless multitude.

The nature of India's response to the situation in East Bengal was a result of a number of factors, not least among which was the 'Indira wave' which brought Indira Gandhi resoundingly back to power in the March 1971 general elections.

> India had not had a strong Prime Minister to deal with recalcitrant elements in both her own party and the opposition since the pre-1960 Nehru era, and Mrs Gandhi proved as adept and adaptable as her father in using her power base in formulating and implementing policy—especially foreign policy in the context of regional developments in 1971.[18]

Further, India had a history of standing up for the protection of human rights. In fact, as early as 1949, Pandit Jawaharlal Nehru, the first Prime Minister of India, stated that 'where freedom is

---

[18] Richard Sisson and Leo Rose, *War and Secession: Pakistan, India and the Creation of Bangladesh* (New Delhi, 1990).

menaced, or justice threatened or where aggression takes place, we cannot be and shall not be neutral'. Indira Gandhi followed this lead, and unhesitatingly translated the vision of Pandit Jawaharlal Nehru into action by extending Indian support to the people of Bangladesh.

The other, more immediate, reason was the enormous influx of refugees into the Indian states of West Bengal, Assam, Meghalaya and Tripura.

> The theme of economic burden had become prominent in both Indian domestic and international calculations... The official estimates for supporting several million refugees in camps that had to be constructed and maintained for this purpose were astronomical in terms of India's resources, threatening a serious disruption of the government's budget allocations for development programmes and cutting deeply into the country's substantial, but painfully acquired, grain surplus.[19]

The economic burden was not the only factor of concern to India. The developments in East Pakistan raised a different kind of problem for the Government of India in the northeastern hill states of Tripura and Meghalaya. In both states, but particularly in Tripura, the sudden influx of two to three million refugees threatened the internal stability of complex tribal political systems by seriously distorting the tribal–non-tribal population ratio to the former's disadvantage and, in the process, raising new issues and problems in what had comparatively been quiescent areas.[20]

Indira Gandhi keenly watched the developments in East Pakistan. On 25 March, she issued an order for India's border

---

[19]Richard Sisson and Leo Rose, *War and Secession: Pakistan, India and the Creation of Bangladesh* (New Delhi, 1990).
[20]Ibid.

with East Pakistan to be kept open so as to allow refugees safe passage into India. Not only that, she also emphasized that East Pakistan's leaders were to be received in India and taken to safety. On 30 March, Indira Gandhi moved a resolution in both Houses of Parliament on the happenings in East Pakistan, and outlined the approach of the Government of India:

> This House expresses its profound sympathy for and solidarity with the people of East Bengal in their struggle for a democratic way of life. Bearing in mind the permanent interests which India has in peace, committed as we are to uphold and defend human rights, this House demands immediate cessation of the use of force and the massacre of defenceless people... This House records its profound conviction that the historic upsurge of the 75 million people of East Bengal will triumph. The House wishes to assure them that their struggle and sacrifices will receive the wholehearted sympathy and support of the people of India.[21]

On 15 June, during the budget session, I initiated a discussion on the floor of the Rajya Sabha, suggesting that India should accord diplomatic recognition to the Government of Bangladesh in exile in Mujibnagar. When a member sought my suggestion on how to tackle the problem, I responded by saying: 'I am talking of a political solution which means categorically recognizing the sovereign democratic Government of Bangladesh. Political solution means giving material help to the democratic, sovereign Government of Bangladesh...' I reminded the House of the many instances in world history when intervention on similar grounds had taken place.

---

[21] *Select Speeches of Indira Gandhi: The Years of Endeavour: August 1969-August 1972* (New Delhi: Ministry of Information and Broadcasting, 1975), p. 525.

The exhortations within India as well as in Parliament notwithstanding, Indira Gandhi set forth on a tour of the West—Europe and USA—to energise world opinion to the cause. This was in spite of US' slant towards Pakistan evident in Kissinger's early comment that in the event of hostilities between Indian and Pakistan over Bangladesh, the US would not support India. All these efforts, in India and abroad, were made with the intention of stalling the prospect of war. An intensive diplomatic campaign got under way...with Foreign Minister Swaran Singh, several other cabinet ministers, and the highly respected 'independent' Jayaprakash Narayan leading missions to key countries in Eastern and Western Europe, North America and Asia. The message carried by all these missions was the same—the need to pressure the Pakistan government into offering a political solution in East Pakistan acceptable to the Awami League if peace and stability were to be preserved in South Asia... If New Delhi had had any illusions about the utility of international pressure upon Pakistan when these missions set out, these had disappeared by the time the last of them returned in early July... A second wave of diplomatic missions were sent out in September, but this time primarily to Latin American and African countries to brief them on the position India would press at the UN General Assembly session starting October and prepare them for the direct use of military force by India.[22]

I got a lot of recognition from Indira Gandhi when she sent me abroad to build an atmosphere of support for India's position on this issue. As a member of the Indian delegation to the 59th

---

[22]Richard Sisson and Leo Rose, *War and Secession: Pakistan, India and the Creation of Bangladesh* (New Delhi, 1990).

conference of the Inter-Parliamentary Union (2-10 September 1971), we took the opportunity to explain the situation to the large number of country delegates present and urged them to prevail upon their governments to speak out against the violation of human rights in East Pakistan. I was then sent to the United Kingdom and the then Federal Republic of Germany with a similar mandate.

■

On 3 December 1971, at twilight, Pakistan launched pre-emptive air strikes against India.

> Border battles between India and Pakistan have erupted into full-scale war. Jets from West Pakistan have attacked at least four Indian airports, with reports [stating that] eight airfields have been struck... Initial reports of the Pakistani air attacks were unclear but both capitals confirmed the Indian airports of Amritsar, Pathankot, Avantipur and Sringar were hit... The Indian Government has declared a state of emergency.[23]

And thus started the thirteen-day war between India and Pakistan, pitting Pakistan against the joint forces of the Indian Army and Bangladesh's Mukti Bahini. The war was won swiftly. After the surrender of the Pakistani forces on 16 December 1971 at Dacca Race Course Maidan, Indira Gandhi announced in the Lok Sabha:

> Mr Speaker, Sir, I have an announcement to make which I think the House has been waiting for sometime. The West Pakistan Forces have unconditionally surrendered in Bangla Desh. The instrument of surrender was signed in Dacca at 16.31 hours at IST today by Lt. Gen. A.A.K. Niazi on

---

[23]'1971: Pakistan intensifies air raids on India', *BBC News*, 3 December 1971.

behalf of the Pakistan Eastern Command. Lt. Gen. Jagjit Singh Aurora, GOC-in-C of the Indian and Bangla Desh forces in the Eastern Theatre accepted the surrender. Dacca is now the free capital of a free country.[24]

Indira Gandhi took a tremendous risk by steadfastly supporting the liberation struggle of East Pakistan, particularly given the perils of getting involved in a major conflict with Pakistan and its supporters—the United States and China. She stood steadfast in the face of tremendous US pressure and posturing from China, proving that she was a leader with nerves of steel, fully equipped and able to carry on her father's legacy. With single-minded nationalist diplomacy, Indira Gandhi took India to victory—a war won in spite of the odds—a unique moment in India's military history.

---

[24] *Lok Sabha Debates,* Vol. X, 16 December 1971.

CHAPTER TWO

# THE MIDNIGHT DRAMA:
# DECLARATION OF THE EMERGENCY

A few minutes before midnight on 25 June 1975, the President of India, Fakhruddin Ali Ahmed, proclaimed a 'State of Emergency' under Article 352 of the Constitution. I was in Calcutta for my Rajya Sabha election, scheduled for 26 June, and got to know of this development on the morning of the 26th. Indira Gandhi asked me to return to Delhi as soon as the election was over and meet her at the earliest. D.P. Chattopadhyaya—who was then the Minister of State for Commerce and also in Calcutta for the Rajya Sabha election—told me he had received similar summons from Delhi.

I got to the assembly building at about 9.30 a.m. It was teeming with state legislators, ministers and political leaders, some with questions and others with conspiracy theories. Some went to the extent of suggesting that, a la Mujibur Rahman of Bangladesh, Indira Gandhi had abrogated the Constitution and usurped power for herself, with the army in tow. I corrected these prophets of doom, saying that the Emergency had been declared according to the provisions of the Constitution rather than in spite of it. I argued that if the Constitution had indeed been abrogated, why would the Rajya Sabha election take place at all? The logic worked and people started to see reason. Around 11 a.m., Siddhartha Shankar Ray—the then Chief Minister of West Bengal—returned to Calcutta from Delhi and called me to his chamber. I met him there along with D.P. Chattopadhyaya and a couple of state ministers, one being Abdus Sattar, and discussed the developing scenario. Siddhartha babu briefed us about the happenings in Delhi the night before.

It is believed that Siddhartha Shankar Ray played an important role in the decision to declare the Emergency: it was his suggestion, and Indira Gandhi acted on it. In fact, Indira Gandhi told me subsequently that she was not even aware of the constitutional provisions allowing for the declaration of a state of Emergency on grounds of internal disturbance, particularly since a state of Emergency had already been proclaimed as a consequence of the Indo-Pak conflict in 1971.

According to Siddhartha Shankar Ray's deposition before the Shah Commission (set up by the Janata government to investigate the 'excesses' of the Emergency), he was summoned to Indira Gandhi's residence on the morning of 25 June 1975. He reached 1 Safdarjung Road and met Indira Gandhi, who said that she had received a slew of reports indicating that the country was heading into a crisis. She told him that in view of the all-round indiscipline and lawlessness, some strong corrective measures needed to be taken. Siddhartha babu told the Shah Commission that Indira Gandhi had, on two or three previous occasions, told him that India needed some 'shock treatment' and that some 'emergent power or drastic power' was necessary. He recalled to the Shah Commission that on one such occasion (before the announcement of the Allahabad High Court judgement on 12 June 1975), he had told her that they could take recourse to the laws already on the statute books, and cited to her the success with which he had tackled the law and order problems of West Bengal within the framework of the law. According to Siddhartha babu, Indira Gandhi then read out intelligence reports of Jayaprakash Narayan's public meeting scheduled for that evening. The reports indicated that he would call for an all-India agitation to set up a parallel administration network as well as courts, and appeal to policemen and those in the armed forces to disobey what were supposed to be illegal orders. Indira Gandhi, he maintained, was firm in the understanding that India was drifting towards chaos and anarchy. Siddhartha babu then asked Indira Gandhi for some time to consider the possible courses of action, and returned later that evening, at about 5 p.m., to tell her that she could consider,

> ...if she so desired, Article 352 of the Constitution for the purpose of imposing internal emergency [whereupon] she asked Shri Ray to go along with her to the President immediately... She gave to the President a summary of what she had told Shri Ray with regard to the facts, that the President heard her for about twenty minutes to half an hour and then asked Shri Ray as to what were the exact words in the Constitution, that the President then told the Prime Minister to make her recommendation...[25]

Siddhartha babu had been very close to Indira Gandhi ever since the days of the Congress split in 1969, and was at one point regarded as one of her most influential advisors. Indira Gandhi would seek his advice on diverse matters. As a member of the CWC and the Central Parliamentary Board, Siddhartha babu had considerable influence over the decision-making process of the organization and administration. His voice was prominent at the meetings of the National Development Council and at the

---

[25]Shah Commission, interim report.

conferences of chief ministers. He had a say in Congress policies at the national level from the early 1970s till the end of 1975. In matters relating to West Bengal, his was the decisive voice. So, it is not surprising that he was privy to considerable information, as the following incident indicates.

At the AICC session at Delhi in August 1974, Siddhartha babu told me of an imminent cabinet reshuffle, indicating some of the potential changes. As my diary entry for the day reminds me, he revealed to me that I would get a better portfolio/assignment. His information proved to be correct, as was evident in the reshuffle of October 1974 (when I was made Minister of State for Finance).

Interestingly, though not surprisingly, once it was declared, there were a whole host of people claiming authorship of the idea of declaring the Emergency. And, again not surprisingly, these very people took a sharp about-turn when the Shah Commission was set up to look into the Emergency 'excesses'. Not only did they disown their involvement, they pinned all the blame on Indira Gandhi, pleading their own innocence. Siddhartha babu was no exception. Deposing before the Shah Commission, he ran into Indira Gandhi— draped in a crimson saree that day—in the Commission Hall and tossed a sprightly remark: 'You look pretty today.'

'Despite your efforts,' retorted a curt Indira Gandhi.

Kasu Brahmananda Reddy, the then Home Minister, told the Shah Commission that he was summoned to the Prime Minister's residence at about 10.30 p.m. and was told that on account of the deteriorating law and order situation, it was necessary to impose an internal Emergency. He informed Indira Gandhi that the powers already available under the existing Emergency could be availed of to deal with the situation, but was told that while this possibility had been examined, the declaration of an internal Emergency was considered necessary. Brahmananda Reddy told the Commission that he then signed a letter to the President of the Republic and appended the draft proclamation of Emergency for the President's assent with this letter. The letter signed by Brahmananda Reddy was on a plain sheet of paper and not on the letterhead of the Home Minister of India.

The letter sent to the President recommending the proclamation of Emergency by Prime Minister Indira Gandhi is reproduced on the following page. According to the Commission's report, a copy of the letter was made available to them from the file in the President's office (for further information on Indira Gandhi's rationale for declaring the Emergency, see her letters to the Shah Commission, some of which are reproduced in Appendix 3).

A large number of ministers and bureaucrats appeared before the Shah Commission. Evidence recorded by the Commission indicated that the decision of declaring an internal Emergency was taken by Prime Minister Indira Gandhi alone and that the cabinet was not taken into confidence. The proceedings of the Shah Commission were peculiar. Suffice it to say that it seemed that the Commission was collecting materials and information only to substantiate a pre-conceived conclusion.

■

Before the midnight drama of 25-26 June 1975, the country had been passing through a difficult phase. The Bangladesh war of 1971 had had a serious impact on the Indian economy, and the oil crisis of 1973 added to its troubles. India's foreign aid climate deteriorated significantly as some member countries of the Aid India Consortium adopted an indifferent attitude towards India's balance of payments problem. Prices soared: September 1974 witnessed a steep rise in the wholesale price index, touching 33.33 per cent. Smuggling and profiteering created an environment of frustration and restlessness. Industrial unrest increased, culminating in the railway strike of 1974, dealing yet another severe blow to the economy.

TOP SECRET

Prime Minister of India
New Delhi, June 25, 1975

Dear Rashtrapatiji,

As already explained to you, a little while ago, information has reached us which indicates that there is an imminent danger to the security of India being threatened by internal disturbance. The matter is extremely urgent.

I would have liked to have taken this to Cabinet but unfortunately this is not possible tonight. I am, therefore, condoning, or permitting a departure from the Government of India (Transaction of Business) Rule 1961 as amended up-to-date by virtue of my powers under Rule 12 thereof. I shall mention the matter to the Cabinet first thing tomorrow morning.

In the circumstances and in case you are so satisfied, a requisite Proclamation under Article 352(1) has become necessary. I am enclosing a copy of the draft proclamation for your consideration. As you are aware, under Article 352(3) even when there is an imminent danger of such a threat, as mentioned by me, the necessary Proclamation under Article 352(1) can be issued.

I recommend that such a Proclamation should be issued tonight, however late it may be, and all arrangements will be made to make it public as early as possible thereafter.

With kind regards,
Yours sincerely,

(Sd/- Indira Gandhi)

*Source:* Shah Commission, interim report.

The government's attempt to nationalize the wholesale trade in foodgrains failed and added to the confusion. While nationalization in sectors such as coal mining created confidence in the minds of the working class, these measures extracted their own pound of flesh from the Indian economy. It was against this backdrop that Jayaprakash Narayan (JP) started his movement against corruption. People supported his call because the sky-rocketing inflation and the lack of goods and services had already affected them adversely. This picture is well highlighted by Y.B. Chavan's budget statement of 28 February 1974.

> During the last three years conditions have not been favourable; in fact, they have been far from normal in many ways. In each of these years, we had to face new challenges of extraordinary dimensions. We have tried to meet these challenges to the best of our ability. I shall, however, readily admit that, because of the unusually severe strains caused by a combination of certain national and international factors beyond our control, progress in achieving our objectives has fallen short of expectations.[26]
>
> ...I would like to state frankly that in the coming financial year, the economy will be faced with even more challenges. Its strength and adaptability will be severely tested. The steep rise in the prices of crude oil and also some other commodities has turned the terms of trade sharply against us and has rendered our tasks exceptionally difficult. Recent developments must, however, be viewed in a wider historical perspective. Nowhere in the world has the process of social and economic change been smooth or free from ups and downs.[27]

---

[26]Para 2, Part A of the budget speech, 1974.
[27]Para 3, Part A of the budget speech, 1974.

...As the House is aware, the government has been deeply concerned about the acute inflationary pressures that have prevailed in the economy during the last two years. The measures that have been adopted to deal with these inflationary pressures are well known to the Hon. Members. It is a matter of deep regret to me that, despite these measures, prices have continued to rise. The House will appreciate that pressure on prices was inevitable as a result of the unsatisfactory performance in the field of agricultural production in two successive years, 1971-72 and 1972-73. The steep fall of 9.5% in agricultural output in 1972-73 was bound to upset the delicate balance between demand and supply. Because of a much sharper increase in international prices, the substantial imports of food-grains we arranged were also unable to exercise a stabilizing influence on domestic prices. Even with a more normal kharif crop in 1973, the pressure on prices has not abated in view of other inflationary forces at work in the economy... It appears certain that the national income in 1973-74 will record a significant growth; this will help to neutralize the unsatisfactory behaviour of national income in two previous years. It is, however, a matter of deep concern to us that in the Fourth Plan our overall rate of growth has been much lower than the Plan target. It is a matter of deep regret that the upsurge in industrial production that was evident in 1972 was not sustained in 1973. The available indications suggest that there was hardly any increase in the rate of growth of industrial production in 1973. It will be a major objective of our economic policy to revive the tempo of industrial activity in 1974. To secure an adequate rate of growth is the challenge that we face in the Fifth Five Year Plan.[28]

The fact that Y.B. Chavan had to present new taxation proposals before the Lok Sabha on 31 July, just five months after the presentation of the regular budget for 1974–75, is indicative of the depth of the crisis. If this was not extraordinary, what else was? Apart from the new taxation proposals, the government also introduced certain austerity measures such as impounding a part of the dearness allowance and dividend in an effort to contain money supply. These mid-year proposals were to yield approximately Rs 210 crore for the whole year. Chavan observed:

> The basic objective of the three recent Ordinances, involving temporary restrictions on declaration of dividends, immobilization of 50% of additional Dearness Allowance and of increase in wages and salaries, and compulsory deposit by income-tax payers in [the] higher income group is to reduce the pressure on demand and decelerate the rate of growth of money supply. In any appraisal of these measures we must not lose sight of the narrow options open to the government. In the present situation, the only other feasible course of action could be a drastic cut in all developmental expenditure. This would entail severe adverse effects on the future growth of the economy.[29]

In October 1974, there was a change in the Ministry of Finance. Chavan was moved to External Affairs and his deputy, K.R. Ganesh, was moved to the Petroleum Ministry. C. Subramaniam and I were brought into the Ministry of Finance, and I was charged with the Department of Revenue and Expenditure. From

---

[28]Paras 4 and 5, Part A of the budget speech, 1974.

[29]See indiabudget.nic.in/bspeech/bs197475(july).pdf. Accessed on 1 November 2014.

10 October 1974 till the time the Janata Party came to power (24 March 1977), this team was responsible for managing the country's finances.

In his budget speech of 1975-76, C. Subramaniam echoed Chavan's sentiments:

> It is unnecessary for me on this occasion, to recount in detail, the variety of factors, both external and internal, which have interfered with the orderly implementation of our development plans and strategies in recent times. The virulence with which inflation has been spreading and its devastating impact across national boundaries continues to impose on developing countries such as India burdens and hardships which we have been ill-equipped to withstand. The impact on the living standards of our people and on the pattern of real income within the country has been serious enough. What is even worse is the persistent rise in prices which has eroded the capacity to save and thus imposed a painful constraint on the flow of investible resources so urgently needed to sustain our plans for a better future.[30]

One can reasonably argue, therefore, that the Indian economy was in a bad shape in the three to four years prior to the imposition of Emergency. And even if the political unrest which led to the declaration of the Emergency overshadowed the economic aspects, there is no denying the fact that economic hardships—high prices, non-availability of goods and lack of services—had prepared the ground for political unrest.

■

---

[30]Para 1.3, Part A of the budget speech, 1975.

A political realignment—in the country and within the Congress Party—began unfolding in the late 1960s. Indira Gandhi's left-of-centre economic stance was disliked by the conservatives in the Congress leadership, popularly known as the 'syndicate'. This group had started asserting itself after the death of Jawaharlal Nehru; their claim was that their seniority and experience counted for more than that of the political 'novice', Indira Gandhi. These prominent Congress leaders—K. Kamaraj, S. Nijalingappa, Atulya Ghosh, S.K. Patil, Biju Patnaik, C. Subramaniam and Neelam Sanjiva Reddy—formed an informal group with the idea of pressuring Indira Gandhi to act on their advice. Their plan, however, did not succeed. Most of these leaders were defeated in the general elections of 1967, and the Congress failed to form governments in West Bengal, Bihar, Orissa, Tamil Nadu and Kerala. Before the elections, a number of prominent Congress leaders from these states had been expelled from the party, and some of them (Ajoy Mukherjee and Professor Humayun Kabir in West Bengal, Mahamaya Prasad Sinha in Bihar, and Pabitra Mohan Pradhan in Orissa) formed regional outfits which fought the general elections of 1967, thus playing a crucial role in defeating the Congress in these states. As we know, later, Chaudhary Charan Singh in Uttar Pradesh and Govind Narayan Singh in Madhya Pradesh defected from the Congress, causing the fall of the Congress governments in these two states too.

Going into the 1967 elections, the Congress was hampered by a number of factors. Foremost was the fact that they were now facing an election without the leadership of Nehru, who had ably led the party in previous general elections. In addition, these elections were being held in the immediate aftermath of the devaluation of the Indian rupee in 1966 and at a time when the food crisis was at its worst (the fruits of the Green Revolution would start accruing only after 1969).

The level of general dissatisfaction manifested itself when the ruling Congress lost 78 seats in the Lok Sabha and, at 283, came perilously close to the half-way mark. The gainer was the Swatantra Party, an extreme right-wing party, which got 44 seats and ended up as the second largest party in the Lok Sabha.

Indira Gandhi's election as the leader of the Congress Parliamentary Party was also not a smooth affair. In the election held after the death of Lal Bahadur Shastri, she had a strong opponent in Morarji Desai. While she won comfortably, Morarji Desai got 169 votes—not a small number by any count—as a result of which he had to be accommodated as the Deputy Prime Minister (with charge of the Ministry of Finance) after the 1967 general elections.

■

Even as the government was settling down to the newly-formed equations in Parliament, and the states it had lost, it was faced with a crisis when the judiciary took on the Parliament.

Most unexpectedly, nearing the end of his tenure as Chief Justice of India, Koka Subba Rao, delivered a bombshell of a judgement (by a 6 to 5 majority) in the Golak Nath case. While the central government was still trying to understand the nuances of this historic judgement—which pronounced that the Parliament was not competent to amend the Fundamental Rights enshrined in the Constitution—there was an even more surprising development. On 12 April 1967, the day after he retired, Subba Rao, supported by opposition parties, announced his candidature for the post of President of India, to contest against Congress nominee Dr Zakir Hussain. Many eyebrows were raised.

The central government suddenly found itself hamstrung and unable to carry forward its left-of-centre developmental agenda, which required constitutional amendments. With many states now ruled by opposition parties, and a divided Congress Party to contend with, it became almost impossible to pass amendments and carry forward the agenda for reforms.

After Indira Gandhi's solid victory in the subsequent general elections of 1971, she was able to action the 24th Amendment to the Constitution, thus wiping out the effect of the Golak Nath judgement. But the fact is that with the Golak Nath case, the seeds of confrontation between the government and the judiciary were sown, and later pronouncements only went on to harden the attitudes of the judiciary.

The politics of the fourth Lok Sabha was fraught with pressures, from outside the party as also from within. Indira Gandhi knew that in order to consolidate the party's position, it was essential to have left-of-centre and pro-people policies.

And, in this scenario, Indira Gandhi started asserting herself. She set about mobilizing the rank and file of the Congress around her and, being the only leader with mass appeal, struck a chord with a large number of Congress workers. She criticized the conservative opposition within the party and emphasized that unless pro-people programmes were undertaken and implemented vigorously, the gulf between the Congress government and the common masses would not be bridged. Indira Gandhi's differences with the old guard of the Congress were mainly on economic policy. Most of these leaders, who had spent long years in administration, either at the state level or at the centre, had become used to the status quo and were reluctant to adopt any radical changes. Indira Gandhi, on the other hand, was convinced of the need for radical changes in Congress's economic policies: bank nationalization, abolition of privy purses, land reforms, and legal and other administrative measures to prevent the concentration of economic power in the hands of a few. The 10-point programme articulated by her reflected her radical and pro-poor stance.

Overriding Morarji Desai, the then Deputy Prime Minister and Minister of Finance, she personally took charge of the Finance Ministry and vigorously set forth on her pro-left socio-economic agenda: fourteen scheduled commercial banks were nationalized to prevent the monopoly of economic power in the hands of a few; the Monopoly and Restrictive Trade Practices (MRTP) Act was passed and privy purses were abolished, among other reforms.

Bank nationalization was actioned in 1969, though in the face of stiff opposition. The Ordinance on Bank Nationalization was promulgated on 19 July 1969 with the nationalization of fourteen commercial banks with a deposit of over Rs 50 crore. With this bold and decisive action, Indira Gandhi once again assumed the initiative and occupied centre stage.

Immediately after this Ordinance was promulgated, a writ was filed in the Supreme Court. This was a test for the government before the Supreme Court. The entire nation watched as the Supreme Court, on 10 February 1970, threw out the Ordinance as invalid. Indira Gandhi took it as an affront and gave it a political twist to show that big businesses were crushing the common man's interest which she was aiming to champion by her pro-poor and 'garibi hatao' policies.

July 1969 was a turning point for the Congress. Zakir Hussain passed away in May 1969, and the President's post fell vacant. The Congress Parliamentary Board, dominated by the 'syndicate', proposed the name of Neelam Sanjiva Reddy (six in favour, with four in favour of Indira Gandhi's candidate, V.V. Giri). Indira Gandhi fought this tooth and nail, fearing that the syndicate's choice might hamper her functioning as Prime Minister. She demanded, rightly that, as the Prime Minister, her vote should count for more—as the Prime Minister commanded the majority support of Members of Parliament which comprised half of the total votes in the collegium for presidential elections. She exhorted a conscience vote. The result: the official candidate of the Congress, Sanjiva Reddy, was defeated by her nominee, V.V. Giri. The consequent face-off resulted in the then Congress President, S. Nijalingappa, on behalf of the 'syndicate', expelling Indira Gandhi from the party. Indira Gandhi stood her ground—'it is presumptuous on the part of this handful of men to take disciplinary action against the democratically elected leader of the people'—and thus came the formal split in the Indian National Congress in November 1969. Indira Gandhi's Congress came to be known as the Congress (R) while the 'syndicate' Congress was known as Congress (O).

After the split, the Congress Party lost its majority in both the Lok Sabha and the Rajya Sabha. The official Congress Party—Congress (O)—asked the Lok Sabha and Rajya Sabha to elect a new leader of the Lok Sabha, replacing Indira Gandhi. But a majority of Congress MPs chose her as their leader, and so she remained in power. Deputy Prime Minister Morarji Desai was elected leader of Congress (O). Indira Gandhi managed to continue in power for almost a year with the support of the Left parties as well as the DMK of Tamil Nadu, led by M. Karunanidhi. While her radical programmes made her popular among the masses, she earned the ire of veteran Congress leaders who described her as a 'fellow traveller of the communists'.

This was the scenario when Indira Gandhi called for mid-term elections in December 1970. The Congress (O), along with the Jana Sangh, the Swatantra Party and the Bharatiya Kranti Dal (BKD; led by Charan Singh), formed a coalition to contest the elections. This combination was known as the 'grand alliance' and their slogan was 'Indira hatao' (remove Indira). Indira Gandhi met the challenge by reaching an understanding with parties like the CPI and the DMK.

Indira Gandhi won by a landslide, getting more than a two-thirds majority in the Lok Sabha. Her party swept the 'Hindi belt' in northern India, and won spectacularly even in those states where Congress (O) stalwarts were personally leading the electoral battle—Karnataka (S. Nijalingappa), Gujarat (Morarji Desai) and Andhra Pradesh (Neelam Sanjiva Reddy). Faring well even in the states of West Bengal and Tamil Nadu, Indira Gandhi emerged as the most powerful victor in the electoral battle of 1971.

After the thumping majority she got in March 1971, Indira Gandhi was able to introduce the 25th Amendment (passed on 20 April 1972). According to this, the jurisdiction of courts to determine the adequacy of compensation on the acquisition of property was taken away. A new clause was added that no law which declared that it was giving effect to the principles in clauses (b) and (c) of Article 39 would be called into question on the ground of inconsistency with fundamental rights. In addition, the Golak Nath as well as the bank nationalization judgements were 'corrected' through constitutional amendments.

■

The logical next step in the pro-people and left-of-centre agenda was to do away with the privileges of rulers and ICS officers.

Prior to 15 August 1947, princely rulers were sovereign though their sovereignty was subject to the paramountcy of the British Crown. This paramountcy lapsed on 15 August 1947 because of the Indian Independence Act, 1947, as a result of which these rulers became absolute sovereigns. Under the law they were free to accede to either of the two dominions—

India or Pakistan—or remain independent. As it happened, the princely states adjoining India merged with India. After their merger these princely rulers had no sovereign powers; they had only such rights and privileges as were recognized or created under the covenants entered into by them with the Government of India and those embodied in the nation's Constitution. With the Constitution coming into force, all princely states which had merged with India (as also their subjects) became citizens of India, with all the rights and duties of citizens of this country.

From about 1967, there was a move in the ruling party to abolish the privy purses guaranteed to the princely states under the Constitution as well as the covenants and agreements recognized in Article 363. Consequently, the 26th Amendment Bill was moved in the Lok Sabha on 2 September 1970, to delete certain provisions of the Constitution relating to the guarantees given to the princely rulers. This Bill was passed in the Lok Sabha but failed to get the requisite majority in the Rajya Sabha. The motion for consideration of the Bill was rejected on 5 September 1970. The same evening, the Union Cabinet met and decided to advise the President to withdraw the recognition and the purses and privileges guaranteed to the rulers of the princely states. On the same night, the President, who was in Hyderabad, purporting to act under clause (22) of Article 363 of the Constitution, signed an Instrument withdrawing the recognition till now granted to princely states. After obtaining his signature, the document(s) were flown to Delhi the same night and the impugned orders issued on 6 September 1970. On the strength of these orders, the Government of India asserted that all princely rulers had been de-recognized and, consequently, none of them were now entitled to the rights and privileges till now available to them.

Expectedly this matter was taken to the Supreme Court, where a special bench of eleven judges, headed by Justice J.C. Shah, was constituted for its hearing. Madhav Rao Scindia of Gwalior was the principal mover of the writ (15 December 1970) to challenge the vires of the Ordinance. The judgement pronounced on 15 December 1970 went in favour of the petitioner and read as follows:

### Order

In accordance with the opinion of the majority the Petitions are allowed and writs will issue declaration that the orders made by the President on September 6, 1970, challenged here, were illegal and on that account inoperative and the petitioners will be entitled to all their pre-existing rights and privileges including the right to privy purses, as if the orders have not been made. The petitioners will get their costs of the petitions. One hearing fee in those petitions in which the petitioners have appeared through the same counsel.

Petitions allowed

The only dissenting judge was A.N. Ray, whose order was in favour of abolition of privy purses, and according to him:

- Recognition of Rulership is not a legal right. It is not a right to property. Privy Purse is not a legal right to property. There is no fundamental right to Privy Purse. There is no fundamental right to Rulership.
- A series of decisions of this Court have held that Article 363 is a bar to rights to Privy Purse, personal rights and privileges, recognition of Rulership from being agitated in courts. These decisions have spoken the words of the Constitution.

- The petitions, therefore, fail and are dismissed. Each party will pay and bear its own costs.

In fact, the judgement in the privy purses case provided the signal to Indira Gandhi to dissolve the fourth Lok Sabha and go in for a mid-term poll, which she won with a large mandate.

Thus, it may be observed that in this confrontation, the Parliament trumped the judgement of the Supreme Court, delivered by an eleven-member bench. But, finally, in April 1973, in the Kesavananda Bharti case, the Supreme Court decided that the ruling in the Golak Nath case was wrong, and that the Parliament had the power of amendment but it could not alter the basic structure of the Constitution.

The sum total of this face-off was that while the state always had the larger national interest in mind, the courts always chose the rights of the individual above all else.

While history remains confined to books, the impact of those years is still being felt.

■

The foundations of the perceived mistrust of the judiciary had been laid by the judgement in the Golak Nath case in April 1967. And while Indira Gandhi wanted to go ahead with her reforms agenda, all her efforts appeared to be stymied by the judiciary. Of course, the Golak Nath judgement was well reasoned, but appeared to be too close for comfort.

Indira Gandhi's landslide victory in 1971 gave her a stronger mandate to deal with the issue, giving as it did an upper hand to the political executive. This is when murmurs of a committed judiciary also began to be heard. In the post-1971 dispensation, most of the decisions in such matters came to be taken by the troika of H.R. Gokhale, Minister for Law; S. Mohan Kumaramangalam, Minister for Steel; and S.S. Ray, Minister for Education; all of whom were legal luminaries. Some of the judicial appointments made at that time definitely had their stamp. Nobody was openly critical, but there was a certain degree of uneasiness amongst the judges regarding some of these appointments. Matters also came to be discussed in Parliament, particularly during the debate on the 24th Amendment. The situation escalated to such an extent that the Chief Justice of India, S.M. Sikri, took umbrage at certain pronouncements in the debate and protested to the Prime Minister, even while the crisis with East Pakistan was at its peak. That Indira Gandhi replied without much delay, despite the war with Pakistan, only went to show the seriousness she attached to the whole affair. A copy of her reply is reproduced later in this narrative. It was not only a terse policy statement, but can also be seen as an assertion of the political executive.

The legacy of Indira Gandhi's first term, which was over in March 1977, continued well into her second tenure which commenced in January 1980. P. Shiv Shankar had taken over as the Law Minister and, in his bid to pack the superior judiciary, a clever device was resorted to, which took the shape of the following letter:

Ministry of Law, Justice and
Company Affairs, India
New Delhi-110 001.

March 18, 1981

My dear—

It has repeatedly been suggested to [the] Government over the years by several bodies and forums including the States

Reorganisation Commission, the Law Commission and various Bar Associations that to further national integration and to combat narrow parochial tendencies bred by caste, kinship and other local links and affiliations, one third of the Judges of a High Court should as far as possible be from outside the State in which that High Court is situated. Somehow, no start could be made in the past in this direction. The feeling is strong, growing and justified that some effective steps should be taken very early in this direction.

2. In this context, I would request you to:

(a) Obtain from all the Additional Judges working in the High Court of your State their consent to be appointed as permanent Judges in any other High Court in the country. They could, in addition, be requested to name three High Courts, in order of preference, to which they would prefer to be appointed as permanent judges; and

(b) Obtain from persons who have already been or may in the future be proposed by you for initial appointment their consent to be appointed to any other High Court in the country along with a similar preference for three High Courts.

3. While obtaining the consent and the preference of the persons mentioned in paragraph 2 above, it may be made clear to them that the furnishing of the consent or the indication of a preference does not imply any commitment on the part of the Government either in regard to their appointment or in regard to accommodation in accordance with the preferences given.

4. I would be grateful if action is initiated very early by you and the written consent and preferences of all Additional

Judges as well as of persons recommended by you for initial appointment are sent to me within a fortnight of the receipt of this letter.

5. I am also sending a copy of this letter to the Chief Justice of your High Court. With regards.

Yours sincerely,
Signed

(P. Shiv Shankar)

To:

1. Governor of Punjab
2. Chief Minister (By name) (Except North Eastern Sates)

Earlier, during the Emergency, a large number of judges had been transferred to other High Courts, so much so that in one instance sixteen judges had been transferred on a single day. These transfers had generally been seen as the executive's attempt to pressurize the judiciary to tow its line. The notorious Additional District Magistrate Jabalpur's case also happened during this period, where the judiciary seemed to bend to follow the Emergency's provisions of detention.

P. Shiv Shankar's letter expectedly drew a severe reaction from senior advocates and was seen as gross interference with the independence of the judiciary, reminding people of the days of the Emergency. This also set off a chain of events which finally culminated in the three cases decided by the Supreme Court. Apprehensive of repeated onslaughts from the executive, the judiciary tried to insulate itself from executive interference in either transfers or appointments to the higher judiciary. How the pendulum swung from one side to the other, between the first judge's case and the third, is narrated in Indira Gandhi's letter to the Chief Justice of India in December 1971.

*Indira Gandhi's letter to the Chief Justice*

December 18, 1971

Dear Chief Justice,

I have your letter of December 3, 1971. As you know I was away on that date. You are also aware of the events which took place which kept us all so fully occupied. I am, therefore, taking the earliest opportunity to write to you.

I am glad that you wrote to me because it enables me to clear some of the apprehensions which you have expressed. Your brother judges and you have taken exception to some observations made by the Minister of Law and Justice in the course of the cut and thrust of a debate in Parliament. You know him well. You also know my other cabinet colleagues Shri Mohan Kumaramangalam and Shri Siddhartha Shankar Ray. They have all been brought up to respect the Judiciary. You need have no doubt whatever that the government and the country as a whole will always uphold the dignity of the courts including the highest court in our land.

Our country is going through profound social, political and economic transformation. Such transformation took place in Europe and America through violence, revolutions and upheavals. In India we are trying to achieve the same results by arguments. Therefore there are bound to be moments of conflict between Parliament and Judiciary or the Judiciary and the Executive. These are inherent in any living and evolving society. I do not have to recall the moments of such conflict in the United States and Britain. Despite these conflicts institutions have grown and taken deep roots. We can derive some satisfaction from the fact that for nearly a quarter of a century we have avoided excesses and have resolved differences arising out of the divergent visions of the Law and the justice without undermining their dignity and prestige.

I remember Bentham's wise remarks that when the Judge had made his decision he was 'given over to criticism'. As you know most of the constitutional amendments putting a particular interpretation on certain Articles of the Constitution. Inevitably the merits or otherwise of such judgements have been debated at length during the passage of successive constitution amendment bills. This in itself is a measure of the high regard of Parliament and the Government for the Judiciary.

I hope that you and your brother judges will see the conflict of arguments, debates, discussions in Parliament in a wider context and not as (in) any adverse conclusions.

So far as I can make out, ministers participating in the debate did not say anything which had not already been said on many earlier occasions in Parliament. In the course of the debate on the Fourth Constitution Amendment one of your own distinguished colleagues Shri Justice Hegde when he was a member of parliament made certain observations, without, I am sure, intending to affect the prestige and authority of the Supreme Court. The portion referred to by you was in fact a quotation from this speech.

I personally have no doubt whatsoever that as our nation moves forward and our society gains inner cohesion and sense of direction all our great institutions, Parliament, Judiciary and Executive, will reflect the organic unity of our society. Legal stability depends as much upon the power to look forward for necessary adjustment and adaptation as to look backward for certainty. We have all to guard against the danger of substituting those inarticulate major premises of social and economic thinking of which we as individuals might happen to approve at a given time for the will of the people as reflected in Parliament. The needs and grievances of the people in a democracy cannot be met by repression of their manifestations but by remedying the causes which underlie them.

I should like to reassure you and your brother judges of our abiding respect for the courts and their vital role. Their nation expects them to maintain their high tradition of impartiality and to act according to their rights, without fear or favour. If there are ever any moments when you feel like writing to me, please do not hesitate to do so.

With regards,

Yours sincerely,
Signed
(Indira Gandhi)

Hon'ble Shri S.M.Sikri
Chief Justice of India
5, Hastings Road,
New Delhi.

This letter shows the strained relationship that existed between the judiciary and the executive; even the Chief Justice of India had to complain to the Prime Minister in writing.

■

As we have seen, in December 1971, India was forced to contend against Pakistan in the wake of the genocide in the then East Pakistan, and the consequent migration of ten million refugees into India. Pakistan's subsequent surrender to the joint forces of Bangladesh's Mukti Bahini and the Indian Army further enhanced Indira Gandhi's prestige within the country and outside. Possibly as a result, her party continued its successful run into the state assembly elections of 1972, with the most spectacular victory being the return of the Congress to power in West Bengal by routing the Left. However invincible she may have appeared to be in these electoral battles, the performance of her party in the state assembly elections in Uttar Pradesh and Orissa in 1974 was not all that impressive. In 1973, the party lost a couple of by-elections, too.

Allegations of corruption were brought against some government personnel, as well as some Members of Parliament and state assemblies. It was made to appear that persons holding high offices were either corrupt or shielding those who were corrupt. It is then, as I have mentioned in passing, that Jayaprakash Narayan launched the 'bhrashtachar hatao' (remove corruption) movement. Many political parties (mainly those of the right) grabbed this opportunity and jumped on to the 'anti-corruption' bandwagon. They realized that, left to themselves, they would run out of steam in any electoral battle against Indira Gandhi. Their only hope was JP. Their charter of demands 'called for elections to be held in Gujarat and Bihar and formalized the spirit of "Total Revolution" with the list of demands (for reforms leading to greater social justice, respect for civil liberties, electoral reform, anti-corruption measures, etc.).'[31] Intimidation, coercion, strikes, bandhs and gheraoes became rampant. People, already frustrated with the depressing economic situation and reeling under escalating market prices, did not resist this movement.

---

[31]Christophe Jaffrelot, *The Hindu Nationalist Movement and Indian Politics: 1925 to the 1990s* (New Delhi, 1996).

And this is when the Allahabad High Court delivered its judgement (12 June 1975) on the petition filed by Raj Narain (a socialist leader) challenging the validity of Indira Gandhi's election in 1971 from the Rae Bareli constituency where Indira Gandhi had defeated him and others by a huge margin. Raj Narain's petition alleged electoral misconduct. Justice Jagmohan Lal Sinha, in his judgement, ordered:

> In view of my findings…this petition is allowed and the election of Indira Nehru Gandhi, respondent No. 1, to the Lok Sabha is declared void… The respondent No. 1 accordingly stands disqualified for a period of six years from the date of this order as provided in section 8A of the Representation of People Act… The operation of the said order is accordingly stayed for a period of 20 days. On the expiry of the said period of twenty days or as soon as an appeal is filed in the Supreme Court, whichever takes place earlier, this order shall cease to carry effect.

The Allahabad High Court judgement intensified political activity across the country and the subsequent period became politically turbulent—leading ultimately to the Emergency being declared on 25 June 1975.

# CHAPTER THREE

# JAYAPRAKASH NARAYAN'S OFFENSIVE

The Allahabad High Court held Indira Gandhi to be guilty of malpractice during her 1971 electoral contest in Rae Bareli. While the court found her guilty on two technical grounds—taking assistance of government officers to construct rostrums and supply power for loudspeakers at two election rallies and taking the assistance of Yash Pal Kapoor, a government official, for furthering her election prospects—it acquitted her of the other charges. That is, she did not exceed the prescribed ceiling on election expense; did not bribe voters with gifts and free conveyance; her use of air-force aircraft and helicopters during the election was not corrupt practice; and the use of the cow and calf symbol did not amount to an exploitation of voters' religious sentiments. This being the case, it became clear that Indira Gandhi's election was declared void because of a legal technicality. No one would seriously believe that her victory by a substantial margin could not have come without the services of Yash Pal Kapoor or the construction of rostrums and power supply to loudspeakers by government officers. A Western newspaper commented that the judgement was too severe, akin to giving out a death sentence to someone for violating traffic rules.

The day after the judgement (that is, on 13 June 1975), JP thundered from Patna, 'Mrs Gandhi's failure to bow to the High Court verdict would not only be against the law as found by the Allahabad High Court, but against all public decency and democratic practice.' On the same night, opposition leaders sat on a dharna outside Rashtrapati Bhawan demanding her resignation as Prime Minister. The President, V.V. Giri, was in Kashmir at the time. The dharna went on till he returned on 16 June and heard their demands. In the meantime, opposition parties other than the CPI decided to observe a 'Resignation Demand Week'.

The reaction of the Congress to these tactics was unambiguous. A large number of Congress MPs called on Indira Gandhi to express their solidarity and pledged loyalty to her leadership. The Congress decided to meet the challenge in two ways: (*a*) a plea for an absolute 'stay' on the order of the Allahabad High Court was filed on 23 June to the vacation judge, Justice V.R. Krishna Iyer, of the Supreme Court; and (*b*) a public meeting was organized in Delhi at the Boat Club on 20 June.

The rally at the Boat Club was a mammoth one, with one estimate putting it at fifteen lakh people from almost every part of the country. To the people assembled at the rally, Indira Gandhi made an emotional appeal to protect India's endangered democracy. She pointed to conspiracies hatched by some opposition parties in the name of 'the rule of law' but which had the sole purpose of removing her. She observed, 'The question is not whether I live or die, but one of national interest.'

Meanwhile, the Congress Parliamentary Party convened a meeting on 18 June where Indira Gandhi said: 'My continuance does not depend on what the opposition demands but on what my own party and the people want.' A resolution, proposed by Jagjivan Ram and seconded by Y.B. Chavan, affirmed complete confidence in Indira Gandhi and declared her continued leadership as Prime

Minister to be 'indispensable for the nation'. Dev Kanta Barooah, the then Congress President, made his oft-quoted remark, 'India is Indira, Indira is India.' He further observed: 'The judgement in no way diminishes the moral authority of the Prime Minister and that the firm desire of the people provides the justification for her continuance in the [sic] office. We have lost a battle. We must prepare to win the war.'

The element of sycophancy notwithstanding, such was the mood of Congressmen in those days. They had to fight to survive, and for them there was no leader other than Indira Gandhi who could lead them to victory. Her ability to rake in votes for the Congress remained undisputed.

But the opposition was determined not to lose this opportunity. Expectedly, therefore, JP retorted, 'The point at issue is not whether Congress MPs have faith in Smt. Gandhi's leadership, but whether there is rule of law in the country and whether it applies to everyone, high or low.' Thus the opposition continued to agitate and demand her resignation. It was then that Indira Gandhi got the much-awaited conditional stay from the Supreme Court. Justice Krishna Iyer observed, 'I propose to direct a stay substantially on the same lines as have been made in earlier similar cases, modified by the compulsive necessities of this case.' He held, 'The High Court's finding until upset, holds good, however weak it may ultimately prove.' As the appeal was likely to be disposed of in two or three months, there were advantages in the continuance of the same team dominated by the presence of the key personality within the Council of Ministers.

Justice Krishna Iyer's stay order was not entirely in Indira Gandhi's favour. She was allowed to continue as Prime Minister but, as far as the Parliament was concerned, while she could participate in the debates of the House, she was not allowed to vote on any issue or draw a salary.

The opposition parties could have decided to wait for the final judgement of the Supreme Court, but they did not do so. In fact, in its judgement of 7 November 1975, the Supreme Court constitution bench comprising Chief Justice A.N. Ray, Justice H.R. Khanna, Justice K.K. Mathew, Justice M.H. Beg and Justice Y.V. Chandrachud acquitted her of the charges on which she had been found guilty by the Allahabad High Court. The unanimous judgement upheld her election from Rae Bareli. However, the opposition parties didn't even wait for the expiry of the period of the absolute stay of twenty days granted by the Allahabad High Court, and the conditional stay granted by Supreme Court Justice Krishna Iyer.

■

Battle lines were drawn and both sides geared up. On 25 June 1975, JP addressed a massive rally at Ramlila Maidan, Delhi, at which he announced a programme of civil disobedience. He repeated his exhortation to the police and the army to disobey 'illegal' orders, challenging Indira Gandhi to bring charges against him if she thought he was preaching treason. He asked students 'to walk out of classrooms and walk into jails'. He suggested to the Chief Justice of India, A.N. Ray, that it would not be in his personal interest to sit on the division bench of the Supreme Court which would hear Indira Gandhi's appeal, as he was obliged to the Prime Minister for his appointment. 'This is India. There can't be a Mujib [Mujibur Rahman of Bangladesh] here,' declared JP. The reference was to Mujibur Rahman's role in converting Bangladesh from a parliamentary to a presidential system, and to a one-party (Bangladesh Krishak Sramik Awami League) system.

JP's histrionics clearly highlighted that the opposition's sole aim was to get Indira Gandhi to resign—wanting her out even before the final decision of the Supreme Court. Restoration of the rule of law was then clearly not the issue, as it still prevailed in the country. The Prime Minister was entitled to continue in office and she did so according to the law of the land. By behaving in this manner, the opposition was denying the Prime Minister the legal rights available to ordinary citizens of India.

It would perhaps be relevant to mention here that there were others, too, who felt that she should resign. Shortly after the declaration of the Emergency, I had the privilege of meeting the then Finance Minister of Bangladesh, Tajuddin Ahmad, in Delhi. We had a closed-door meeting after a lunch I hosted for him. Citing the example of Gamal Abdel Nasser in Egypt, Tajuddin surmised that Indira Gandhi's image may not have taken such a battering had she stepped down after the Allahabad High Court judgement. Nasser had resigned after Egypt's defeat at the hands of Israel, withdrawing it following a massive upsurge of Egyptian public opinion in his favour. His image had remained intact.

I pointed out to Tajuddin the situational dissimilarities in this comparison. Here, a persistent campaign of agitation was being built up to remove Indira Gandhi, and the Allahabad High Court judgement had merely provided her opponents with a useful handle. I could not tell if he was convinced. But this issue figured in the minds of other foreign leaders, too, many of whom could not accept that the only answer was to declare a state of Emergency.

In a letter written from jail, JP wrote that he was appalled at press reports of Indira Gandhi's speeches and interviews, and added, 'The very fact that you have to say something every day to justify your action implies a guilty conscience.' The letter went on to state, 'Having muzzled the Press and every kind of public dissent, you continue with your distortions and untruths without fear of criticism or contradiction. If you think in this way you will be able to justify yourself in the public eye and [bring] down the opposition to political perdition you are…mistaken.'[32] He flatly denied the charges that there was a plan to paralyze and destabilize the government. He maintained that, in a democracy, people did have the right to ask for the resignation of an elected government if it became corrupt and/or had been misruling. And if there was a legislator who persisted in supporting such a government, he, too, must go, so that the people might choose a better representative.

JP pointed to the mammoth anti-government rallies and processions in Patna, the thousands of constituency meetings held all over the state, the three-day Bihar bandh and the 'largest ever' meeting held at the Gandhi Maidan on 18 November 1974, citing them as convincing measures of the people's will. He maintained that in Bihar the government was given a chance to settle issues across the table, but it preferred the method of confrontation with unparalleled repression. It was no different in Uttar Pradesh. In both cases, JP claimed, the state governments rejected the path of negotiation, and chose one of strife. Thus, he insisted, '…the plan of which you speak, the plan to paralyze the government, is a figment of your imagination, thought up to justify your totalitarian measures.'

If there was a plan, he stated, it was a simple, innocent and short-term plan: to continue the agitation till the Supreme Court decided on Indira Gandhi's appeal. The plan was announced at the Ramlila Maidan on 25 June 1975: select people would do satyagraha in front of (or near) Indira Gandhi's residence with the demand that she step down till the Supreme Court verdict on her appeal. The plan was to extend the agitation to other states subsequently.

---

[32]Reprinted in the *Far Eastern Economic Review*, 20 February 1976.

In his letter, JP went on to say,

I do not see what is subversive or dangerous about it. In a democracy, the citizen has an inalienable right to civil disobedience when he finds that other channels of redress or reform have dried up... Even that programme of *satyagraha* would not have occurred to the Opposition had you [Mrs Gandhi] remained content with quietly clinging on to your office. But you did not do it. Through your henchmen you had rallies and demonstrations being organized in front of your residence begging you not to resign. You addressed these rallies and justifying your stand, advanced spurious arguments and heaped calumny on the head of the Opposition... When such despicable happenings were taking place every day, the Opposition had no alternative but to counter the act of mischief. And how did it decide to do it? Not by rowdyism but by orderly *satyagraha*, self-sacrifice.

Disputing the charge made against him of trying to brew trouble within the armed and police forces, JP stated that all he had done was to make the men and officers of the forces conscious of their duties and responsibilities. He maintained that all his exhortations were within the ambit of law, the Constitution, the Army Act and the Police Act.

JP's letter concluded with: 'You seem to act swiftly and dramatically only when your [Mrs Gandhi's] personal position is threatened. Once that is assured, the drift begins again. Dear Indira Gandhi, please do not identify yourself with the nation. You are not immortal, India is.'

This letter, according to D.R. Mankekar, did not see the light of the day till the Emergency was lifted. While I had no personal knowledge of this letter, and came to know of it only when his book, *Decline and Fall of Indira Gandhi,* co-authored by Kamla Mankekar,[33] was published, I propose to analyse, its contents in the context of the development which took place before the declaration of the Emergency.

JP had contended that if a government was corrupt, people, through agitation, could demand its resignation. While I do not debate that point, my contention is that such charges of corruption must be factually substantiated rather than be based on supposition. Not a single charge of corruption was established against those whom the opposition implicated as corrupt. Not even the scores of commissions set up during the Janata regime could establish these charges. If the opposition's allegations were based on facts, would this be the case?

Second, which democracy in the world would permit a change of a popularly and freely elected government through means other than a popular election? Can parties beaten at the hustings replace a popularly elected government by sheer agitation? Was it not prudent for those who were determined to change the government to wait till the elections which were but round the corner? Does the rule of law mean that the remedies available to the common man are to be denied to someone holding an elected office? Why did the opposition want Indira Gandhi to resign even before the appeal was heard by the Supreme Court? Is it not a fact that the Supreme Court permitted Indira Gandhi to continue as Prime Minister *against a conditional stay*? How could anybody replace her when the overwhelming majority of Congress MPs—with a two-thirds majority in the Lok Sabha—resolved that Indira Gandhi should continue as the party's leader in Parliament and thereby as the Prime Minister of India? How does the issue of morality at all

---

[33]D.R. Mankekar and Kamla Mankekar, *Decline and Fall of Indira Gandhi* (New Delhi, 1977).

arise when allegations causing Indira Gandhi to lose the Allahabad High Court election suit were of a technical nature and no charges of moral turpitude could be established against her?

■

A closer analysis of the situation provides the answer. Without a doubt, JP was spearheading the strategy of the opposition. The fact that opposition parties accepted his leadership and joined his total revocation movement had little to do with ideological conviction. With no one among them to measure up to Indira Gandhi's political charisma, they needed a moral authority to provide them strength. And who better than JP to do this at the time? Without JP, this movement would not have been so powerful; it would not have attained the dimension it did without JP, evident in the tremendous popular response it received even before the Emergency was declared. The fact that the Congress was defeated in the Gujarat assembly elections in 1975 was mainly on account of this movement.

I did not know JP. I met him only once in 1974 at the Gandhi Peace Foundation along with C.M. Stephen. Krishna Kant had organized this meeting. We talked about the Naxalite movement, and I was impressed by his personality and his genuine approach to this emotional and sensitive issue. I found him to be far above petty political games; he truly wanted to restore moral values in Indian politics and hence expected everyone, including those in the ruling party, to follow his advice. I have reason to believe that he was more than justified in having such expectations. He was a rare Indian politician who didn't clamour for office or power in spite of having it within his reach; he was a man who could have succeeded Nehru as the second most popular man on the Indian political stage. How could such a man not see through the opportunism of the opposition parties?

However, rationally speaking, I could not support the movement. To me it appeared to be directionless. It was contradictory in that it was a movement fighting against corruption yet composed of people and parties whose integrity was not above board. Not only personalities, but organizations too joined the movement to further their own interests. The opposition parties were no exception.

This drama had one more, not so evident, aspect. It was believed that the tradition-bound Indian people would expect Indira—the daughter of Nehru—to avoid confrontation with JP—a friend of Nehru—particularly in view of his stature. He was like a father figure whose views you may not accept but whose advice and strong feelings you could not ignore. However, this did not happen.

■

This movement launched by the opposition parties went on even after the arrest of a large number of leaders and workers of various political parties. Though the press was censored during the Emergency, hesitations, doubts and strident criticism were voiced through a variety of other channels. Opposition MPs used the floor of the House to vociferously express their concerns (see Appendix 4 for extracts of some speeches in Parliament). The communist parties, who were less equivocal in the House, possibly due to the rightist component (parties such as the Jana Sangh) within the JP movement, put together a vociferously critical manifesto (see Appendix 5 for extracts). In addition, leaders of the non-CPI opposition parties sent two representations to the President of India on 5 August 1975—one related to jailed political prisoners and another related to the proposed legislation for the amendment of election laws (see Appendix 6). The Lok Sangharsh Samiti, which was constituted to carry on the agitation under JP, wrote a letter to the Prime Minister after the satyagraha movement was launched against the Emergency.

Referred to as the darkest period in independent India's history, the after-effects of the Emergency have significantly influenced subsequent events. So much so that the country has been debating this action even years after its imposition and withdrawal.

■

As we know, the Janata Party government which came to power after the Emergency set up an inquiry commission with Justice J.C. Shah as Chairman. After examining the circumstances under which the Emergency was declared, the Shah Commission concluded that it was an action of 'excess' not warranted by facts and was the action of a sole individual (Indira Gandhi) to protect her personal interests. A number of published books, too, held this view.

In his book, *An Eye to India,* David Selbourne[34] argued that the seed of the 'emergency aberration' was embedded in the Indian system itself. He did not believe that India could successfully launch and practise a system of parliamentary democracy. Like most European commentators of his ilk he, too, believed that without Western patronage, the Indian democratic system would necessarily be deficient.

For, the emergency was a part of continuance in the history of India since independence. It is a history which cannot be perceived as a simple trilogy, that is, as a pre-emergency democracy (the world's largest), as emergency dictatorship

---

[34]David Selbourne, *An Eye to India* (New Delhi, 1977).

and a post-emergency democratic restoration. Moreover, the emergency served as no previous sequence of events has done in modern India to make manifest the nature of the Political Economy of India, the nature of the State and the condition of the Indian people. Finally, the Indian emergency, as a response to political and economic crisis, constitutes a paradigm case, an object lesson, whose implications cannot be confined to India.

In his book, *The Judgement,* Kuldeep Nayar[35] admits that he collected information from various persons, including those in the administration. He claims to have remained objective, but his immediate reaction to the Emergency was that 'a nation had been trussed and gagged'. He himself was detained during the Emergency and it was not easy for him to remain 'objective', much as he would have us believe otherwise.

In their book, *Decline and Fall of Indira Gandhi,* D.R. Mankekar and Kamla Mankekar state:

This book presents the scenario of a grave tragedy of the inscrutable hand that gave a twist to the destinies of this country, and of the haughty who was convinced of her infallibility, popularity and immortality and then stepped on to her downfall. The document of this drama assumes the character of a catharsis.

The Emergency was a crucial phase in our parliamentary democracy. The declaration, its operation and, finally, its withdrawal had a profound impact on India's political structure as I have mentioned earlier. Those who had been sceptical of a parliamentary democracy succeeding in India became gleeful at

---

[35]Kuldeep Nayar, *The Judgement: Inside Story of the Emergency in India* (New Delhi, 1977).

the thought that they had been proven correct. Those who had bought into the idea of democracy and were enchanted by the Constitution of India and the successful execution of electoral democracy since 1952 were rudely shocked.

I will discuss the impact of the Emergency on domestic politics in the subsequent narrative. As this point in the book, it will be sufficient to say here that many of us who were part of the Union Cabinet at that time (I was a junior minister) did not then understand its deep and far-reaching impact. While there is no doubt that it brought with it some major positive changes—discipline in public life, a growing economy, controlled inflation, a reversed trade deficit for the first time, enhanced developmental expenditures and a crackdown on tax evasion and smuggling—it was perhaps an avoidable event. Suspension of fundamental rights and political activity (including trade union activity), large-scale arrests of political leaders and activists, press censorship, and extending the life of legislatures by not conducting elections were some instances of the Emergency adversely affecting the interests of the people. The Congress and Indira Gandhi had to pay a heavy price for this misadventure.

# CHAPTER FOUR

# PUTTING THE HOUSE IN ORDER: ACTIONING REFORMS

As I have mentioned earlier, I was in Calcutta on the day the Emergency was declared and returned to Delhi by an evening flight on 26 June 1975.

I set about my job in earnest and launched a battle against economic offences as I had been instructed. On 27 June, at a meeting with senior revenue officials—Chairman, Direct Taxes; Chairman, Customs and Central Excise; Director, Revenue Intelligence; Director, Enforcement; and the Finance Secretary, along with a few others—I emphasized that the fight against economic offences had to be further strengthened in the wake of the new developments. We discussed the economic and enforcement measures needed to tackle the problem, after which I asked the officers to identify the legislative or administrative support necessary to pursue our agenda.

An Ordinance was promulgated by the President on 1 July 1975, effectively amending the COFEPOSA, or the Conservation of Foreign Exchange and Prevention of Smuggling Activities Act. The COFEPOSA had been enacted in 1974 to deal with smugglers and foreign exchange racketeers. However, since 1974, when preventive detention was adopted as a measure to nab the big fish and bring them to book, some deficiencies had come to light. The one main difficulty was that the high courts started releasing detainees if even one of the many grounds of detention was found invalid. This came to light when the Delhi High Court delivered its judgement, in April 1975, on the detention (under this Act) of five suspected smugglers. The High Court released two—Sukar Narain Bakhia and Yusuf Patel. The implication of the judgement was that if just one of the many grounds on which a person was detained was found invalid, he could be released. As a result, a large number of similar appeals were subsequently filed before the Delhi High Court, and this weakened the government's resolve to tackle the problem. This loophole and other shortcomings of the Act were plugged by an amendment to COFEPOSA, and the Act was made stronger to deal with the situation adequately. Now, a detention order could not be deemed invalid or inoperative merely because one or some of the grounds were found to be not maintainable.

A Cabinet Committee—consisting of Om Mehta, Minister of State for Home Affairs; Dr Sarojini Mahishi, Minister of State for Law and Justice; and I—was constituted to deal with smuggling and other economic offences, and we first met on 2 July 1975. The Cabinet Committee issued three directives:

- Immediate arrest of smugglers ordered to be detained but yet absconding. With the aim of tracing and arresting them, appropriate instructions were to be issued to state governments, and photographs of the proclaimed offenders were to be published and orders for the attachment of their properties issued;
- Jailed smugglers were to be treated in accordance with the prescribed rules; no unauthorized concessions were to

be allowed to them. [This instruction became necessary as there were reports of some smugglers carrying on their activities from jail in connivance with jail officials. Questions were also raised in Parliament to this effect.]

- The confiscated boats [a significant amount of smuggling took place between the Gulf and coastal Maharashtra and Gujarat] were to be put to immediate use in anti-smuggling operations. Recruitment of the requisite crew was thus sanctioned.

Consequently, during night-long operations over 2-3 July 1975, as many as twelve top smugglers were arrested in Bombay, Delhi and Madras. The arrested persons included those who had been released by the Delhi High Court in April 1975. This was the beginning and, during the period of the Emergency, a large number of economic offenders were detained. While a few may have been detained unjustly, most were, without doubt, held for activities that were inimical to the interests of law-abiding citizens.

I addressed a press conference in Calcutta to explain the new measures aimed at controlling economic offences. According to a report that appeared in *Business Standard* (9 July 1975, quoting PTI):

Stringent measures are being taken to effectively curb smuggling activities and other economic offences in the country as a follow-up of the new economic programmes announced by the Prime Minister, the Union Minister of State for Finance Pranab Mukherjee said in Calcutta on Tuesday, reports PTI. Mr Mukherjee said that the anti-smuggling operations would be intensified and with this end in view, top level meetings would be held in five smuggling-prone centres in the country. The five centres are: Calcutta, Bombay, Madras, Ahmedabad and Cochin... The Minister said 243 smugglers against whom detention orders had been issued were absconding throughout the country including 51 in West Bengal. Of them, action had already been initiated against 107 smugglers to attach their property after declaring them as proclaimed offenders. In the first week of July 1975, goods worth Rs 5 lakhs were seized. Against 82 detention orders issued under COFEPOSA, 44 persons were arrested while 12 were absconding. In the case of 16 others, writ petitions were pending in the High Court in Calcutta, Mr Mukherjee said.

Though the action plan for rounding up absconding smugglers was executed, we came up against a few roadblocks. Attaching their property with the aim of compelling them to surrender proved to be difficult. It was found that the smugglers did not hold the property in their own names—that is, most of their fixed assets were benami, or unaccounted for, in terms of title. Not only that, given the resources at their command, some of them could avail of the best legal and medical services to avoid detention on health grounds. At times, even after detention, there were kingpins who had to be released on health grounds on account of certificates issued by eminent medical practitioners. During this entire phase we had to contend with these problems, constantly trying to plug loopholes.

Another legislation was passed by both Houses of Parliament in January 1976 for confiscating the properties belonging to smugglers: the SAFEM (FOPA), or the Smugglers and Foreign Exchange Manipulators (Forfeiture of Property Act). While speaking on the issue in Parliament, I emphasized that the legislation would send a clear message to smugglers and foreign exchange manipulators that they would no longer be able to enjoy their tainted money. It had been framed so as to ensure that habitual offenders failed to hoodwink the law. The main feature of the legislation was that if one half of the investment in a property remained unproven, options would be given to the persons affected to pay a fine in lieu of confiscation, with this fine being equal to one and one-fifth of the value of the unexplained investment. I explained that the legislation empowered the government to deprive smugglers and foreign exchange manipulators of their ill-gotten properties, and was to be administered by senior central government officers, not below the rank of a joint secretary. Competent authorities were to be situated at important places like Calcutta, Bombay, Madras and Ahmedabad. An appellate authority was to be established under a retired judge of the Supreme Court or high courts or a person eligible to be appointed as a judge. There could only be one appeal against the order of forfeiture by the competent authority to this appellate body. After the Ordinance was issued, the Revenue Department started collecting information on the properties of the smugglers; in Bombay, such information was collected for nearly a thousand people.

The success of these interventions notwithstanding, we realized that anti-smuggling operations could never be successful so long as there existed a huge gap between the demand and supply of consumer goods, some of these being synthetic fibres, clothing and watches. We decided to increase the production of such items; duties on man-made fabrics manufactured in the country were suitably adjusted so as to increase indigenous production; and HMT (Hindustan Machine Tools, a government undertaking which manufactured watches) was encouraged to set up new units to produce more watches.

Curbing the smuggling of gold was not that easy. While seizures under the Gold Control Act had increased significantly, this area remained a problem. Given the lack of social security, gold has always been the asset of choice in India. The continuous appreciation of the value of gold in the country thus acted as an incentive for gold smuggling. During the late 1960s, Morarji Desai tried to combat the rising demand for gold by passing the Gold Control Act, but the legislation failed in its endeavour and, instead, created business problems for goldsmiths. The long and short of the matter was that gold continued to be smuggled into India. Though India had two gold mines in Karnataka, our indigenous gold production was not more than ten to twelve tonnes a year. So the problem couldn't be tackled by increased indigenous production either.

The issue with gold notwithstanding, some of these measures had a salutary effect on curbing smuggling activities in India. News received from intelligence sources pointed to the accumulation of huge quantities of stocks of various items in places like Dubai and Hong Kong, from where goods were regularly smuggled into India.

COFEPOSA, though not repealed, became inoperational during the three-year rule of the Janata and the Lok Dal. In fact, the Janata Party Finance Minister, H.M. Patel, went to the extent of suggesting that he was not interested in the departments (income tax or others) within the Ministry of Revenue conducting tax raids as, according to him, 'the raids were politically motivated'. As a result of this attitude, the war against economic offenders initiated before the Emergency and strengthened during this period could not be carried to its logical conclusion.

•

After taking over as Minister of State for Finance in December 1975, I carried on with the work initiated by my predecessor, K.R. Ganesh. The income tax department was instructed to bring new assessees within the tax net, an instruction based on the knowledge that a large number of professionals and self-employed persons were avoiding tax. As 'survey-search-seizure' intensified, many people who had so far avoided paying tax volunteered to disclose their concealed income and were brought within the tax net. The provision of voluntary disclosure was made an in-built feature of the tax system by amending the tax laws (direct). In 1974-75, the number of professionals and self-employed persons brought under the tax net touched 1,33,642. Of these, 1,08,012 were new assessees belonging to the professional classes: lawyers (78,638); chartered accountants (11,243); doctors (8,366); engineers (15,278); contractors (6,981); and architects (2,724). Given the significant increase in the number of tax payers, there was a resultant increase in tax revenue too.

■

We then focused on simplifying the procedure of remittances from abroad. A large number of non-resident Indians sent money to relatives in India mostly through clandestine routes: smugglers collected foreign exchange from people abroad and paid their relatives in India in the local currency, with transactions carried out at higher exchange rates. In fact, they built a parallel banking system to fund smuggling and ran it efficiently. Our task was to demolish this arrangement and, with this aim, a large number of branches of Indian banks were opened abroad in localities with high concentrations of Indians. Remittance procedures were simplified in consultation with the Reserve Bank of India (RBI) and operators of this unauthorized banking system were nabbed under the Preventive Detention Act. To encourage the receipt of foreign exchange through regular channels and to ensure that part of the investable surplus of non-resident Indians went into Indian banks, two deposit schemes were introduced. Non-resident

Indians could deposit foreign currency—US dollars and British pounds—in Indian banks and they could get back their money, both the principal and the interest, in foreign currencies. Higher rates of interest were provided for these accounts. Alternatively, such depositors could also choose a plan of receiving Indian rupees against their foreign currency deposits. Both these deposit schemes had a lock-in period to avoid speculation. Additionally, concessions were given to non-resident Indians investing in India, including in real estate. These measures were taken to ensure that the money to fund smuggling activities was not available. They also helped India's meagre foreign exchange reserves to swell. From October 1974 to November 1975, that is, in fourteen months, remittances through legal channels increased by Rs 441 crore. From an average of Rs 41 crore per month before the crackdown, remittances spiralled to Rs 67 crore per month. In the post-Emergency period, foreign exchange reserves increased by 144 per cent and 93 per cent, respectively, in two years against 5 and 21 per cent, respectively, in the two years before the Emergency.

Our strategy to tackle economic offences started yielding results. The raids and searches by the income tax department made life difficult for tax evaders and black money operators. A total of 2,029 income tax raids were conducted during the financial year of 1974-75, with 1,523 more between April and November 1975. Assets seized during this period were valued at Rs 17 crore and Rs 14 crore respectively. In short, an environment was created where tax dodgers had to spend sleepless nights.

It was in this scenario that a group of top industrialists met me and suggested that the government consider giving tax dodgers the chance of voluntarily disclosing their concealed income and wealth. The influential Congressman Rajni Patel was a strong advocate of this scheme. I was initially disinclined—I not only agreed with the Wanchoo Committee report that such an action seemed to reward dishonesty at the cost of honest taxpayers, but also knew that there would be an unfavourable public reaction—but as my officers thought the suggestion viable I asked them to study its feasibility and put together a report on the results of similar schemes introduced earlier. Similar schemes had been introduced on three occasions in the past—during the tenures of C.D. Deshmukh, T.T. Krishnamachari and Morarji Desai—but the response had not been encouraging. But my officers remained eager to give it another try. It was then that I discussed the issue with the Finance Minister who had always been a valuable guide to me. He suggested that I talk to a cross-section of people without giving an indication of what the government was contemplating.

Having done that, I also talked to the Prime Minister, who advised me to prepare a note indicating the pros and cons of the scheme. After all these exercises were done, and having gained broad support from my senior colleagues, I submitted a cabinet note. And then the Voluntary Disclosure Scheme was approved by the cabinet and put into operation through an Ordinance on 8 October 1975. The essential feature of the scheme was that the rate of income tax to be payable under the scheme was 50 per cent (against the normal rate of 60 per cent) and the name and identity of the declarer would be kept confidential. Two-and-a-half per cent of the disclosed income and wealth was to be invested in specified government securities. There would be no penalty and prosecution for the income and wealth so disclosed under the scheme. However, the immunity would not be extended if, on subsequent information, any undeclared concealed income and/or wealth was unearthed. People detained under COFEPOSA were not eligible to avail of the scheme.

An all-out attempt was made to make this effort successful.

The then Chairman of the Central Board of Direct Taxes (CBDT), S.R. Mehta, made a valuable contribution to its success. A two-pronged strategy was adopted: raids and searches were intensified in almost all major cities. I toured many cities, as did S.R. Mehta and other CBDT board members. We addressed professional organizations, chambers of commerce, tax consultants, lawyers, chartered accountants, clubs and societies, throughout urging people to buy peace by taking the opportunity offered by the scheme. At such meetings, I used to say: 'I would invite every tax dodger to be our guest by 31 December 1975 and if they do not accept my offer, I shall be an unwelcome guest at their houses after 31 December.' This statement became very popular. We also launched a massive information campaign throughout the country: hoardings, posters and media advertising started appearing.

From October to December that year, I addressed twenty-seven meetings across the country. In the initial stages, the response from taxpayers was not very encouraging. A few people responded to the scheme but the amount received was disappointing. There was then a suggestion to extend the date. I refused to accept the suggestion, and the Finance Minister as well as the Chairman of CBDT supported my view. Any extension would only expose the government as weak. I spoke to the Prime Minister who, too, agreed with my view, but said that all efforts should be made to ensure that the scheme did not flop. I assured her that it would not.

From the second week of December, the drive gathered momentum. It was made clear that there would be no extension of the date and people started availing of the scheme. In the last few days of the month, the tempo reached its peak. During this period, a couple of big business houses were raided, creating some panic among tax evaders. Some thought that these raids were organized deliberately to inject fear among the people. But it was not so. Those who were acquainted with the system knew that such raids were the culmination of two to three months of information gathering and due diligence. And, in the case of big corporates, extra care was taken. Consequently, for raids executed in November–December 1975, preparatory groundwork needed to have been done months ahead.

When the results of the Voluntary Disclosure Scheme started coming in, I was in Chandigarh attending the 75th session of the Indian National Congress. I received the figures over the telephone, and was specifically asked by the Prime Minister to quote the figures and explain the economic policies in detail in my speech to the economic session.[36] The delegates broke into loud applause as I read out the figures of the concealed income and wealth disclosed through the scheme: close to Rs 1,500 crore! I told the session that this gain to the national exchequer was the Prime Minister's new year's gift to the nation.

Many had doubted the success of this scheme. 'This young man will burn his fingers one day,' some senior ministers had jokingly commented. One exception was Babu Jagjivan Ram. 'Pranab is clever enough and surely he will be successful,' Jagjivan Ram had quipped. When I informed him of the result, he hugged me warmly. 'Well done!' he said.

I came back to Delhi and met C. Subramaniam, who was still recovering from his illness. He agreed to pay one month's salary as 'bonus' to all staff associated with the scheme, for which we later faced some criticism from our colleagues who contended that government officials should not be rewarded for doing their routine duty. Technically correct as they were, they had failed

---

[36]Illness had prevented Finance Minister C. Subramaniam from attending the Congress session that year. Consequently, I took his place.

to appreciate the facts fully. While it was the routine job of the income tax department, the scheme would not have succeeded without the total commitment of the people executing it. I thought I was more than justified in strongly defending the decision to pay the bonus.

On 2 January 1976, I addressed the nation on All India Radio, detailing the scheme and its results, besides outlining our future programme. This national broadcast was relayed by every radio station (see Appendix 7 for extracts from the broadcast).

The *Times of India* (Delhi, 2 January 1976), in its editorial, observed:

> The Union Minister of State for Revenue and Banking, Mr Mukherjee (Pranab), is fully justified in taking credit for the success of the Voluntary Disclosure Scheme. Whether only 10 percent of the total amount of black money with the public has surfaced as a result or twice as much, the fact remains that Rs 1,500 crores of concealed income and wealth has now come into the tax net and the government's own revenue has swollen because of the windfall gain of Rs 250 crores. By contrast, the aggregate sums disclosed in all the three previous schemes floated till 1965 was a mere Rs 265 crores and the tax yield no more than Rs 62 crores. The two reasons advanced by the Wanchoo Commission in 1971 for opposing the idea of reintroducing any such scheme were that it would shake the confidence of honest tax payers in the capacity of the government to deal with the law breakers, and undermine the morale of the tax administration. But, in this event, its fears on either score have proved groundless. For the latter had launched a vigorous drive against tax evaders fairly early in the day and managed to keep the pressure on them even when the scheme was in

force. In consequence, the yield from direct taxes this year before the new scheme came into force went up by nearly 30 percent despite a cut in the rates of personal taxation. What is more, the amount of disclosure has exceeded even the most optimistic expectation of officialdom. That apart, the velocity of circulation of black money, which exerts an inflationary pressure on prices, has been indisputably slowed down. One can, however, deny that the concealed income or wealth that still plagues the economy is many times more than what has been revealed to the authorities. But that only highlights the importance of not only stepping up the momentum of the current drive against the tax dodgers but also rationalizing the whole structure of taxation, as Mr Mukherjee (Pranab) has indeed promised to do. Plainly, action in a number of areas is urgently called for if the tax system is to sub-serve the wider objectives of promoting growth, savings, individual efforts, and social equity...

Many other newspapers wrote articles and editorial comments that were appreciative of the success of the scheme.

In an editorial, *The Indian Express* (Delhi, 2 January 1976) made the following observation:

The Minister for Revenue Pranab Mukherjee has hinted at further rationalization of the structure of direct taxation. Exercises in this connection are going on in the Finance Ministry. Their outcome will be known when [the] Finance Minister presents his Budget for the next financial year a few weeks hence. Rationalization, as it has been advocated by and on behalf of different interest groups, is merely a euphemism for reduction in the marginal rates of direct tax liability. The case for it has been greatly strengthened by buoyance in revenue collections after sizable reduction in their rates for top income brackets in response to the recommendation of the Wanchoo Committee Report. The success of the Voluntary Disclosure Scheme is also attributed to the generous concessions, immunities and incentives offered to those willing to take advantage of it to declare their unaccounted incomes and wealth. The problem of tax reforms has, however, wider dimensions than a general reduction in tax rate. There is obviously a limit to tax concessions which the government can grant if it is not to erode its ability to raise adequate resources to fulfil its responsibilities and obligations in the sphere of administration, defence and development. It is also to be considered whether the role of fiscal policy in regulating the production and consumption pattern and the distribution of income and wealth on which so much stress was laid in the past, should be totally extinguished. The implications of any 'rationalization' of the tax structure are thus of far-reaching nature and will impinge on many a proclaimed objective of socio-economic change.

The Statesman in its editorial (Delhi, 2 January 1976) observed:

The need for rationalization of direct taxes received more than the usual emphasis in the Parliamentary debate on the Bill to replace the Ordinance on Voluntary Disclosure Scheme. The Minister for Revenue and Banking Pranab Mukherjee almost conceded it is principle. Even those who dismissed the Wanchoo Committee's suggestion for reduction in the maximum rates of income tax to check tax evasion as wishful thinking appear to have had second thoughts after the success of the Voluntary Disclosure Scheme, based on much lower rates of taxes than those payable if there had been no evasion. There is now cautious optimism about the possibility of a realistic attitude being adopted in the next Budget to some of the issues relating to taxation. There is a long list of suggestions from the tax executives and Chambers of Commerce which include several reasonable and practicable proposals. The loss of revenue if any from accepting them will be more than made up through better collections and larger yields arising from economic growth.

Tax reforms were not confined merely to reducing the rate of taxes but were supplemented by institutional arrangements, too, such as the setting up of a settlement commission, recommended by a number of expert groups. A large portion of revenue was held up every year due to litigation, and it was thought advisable to have an agency like the commission whose verdict would be acceptable both to the department and the assessees. Such was the environment created that even tax dodgers and evaders were prepared to cooperate through this institutional arrangement.

Another tribunal was set up to identify and take necessary action with regard to undisclosed properties of smugglers (particularly in Mumbai, where real estate has always been a business with huge cash flows) and foreign exchange manipulators. The law was passed and this tribunal was to implement the provisions of this Act.

The attempt at reforming tax laws was not confined to direct taxes; indirect tax also came into the ambit, particularly as huge amounts were collected through central excise and customs. In fact, during the 1970s, the share of indirect tax to total tax revenue had already reached a staggering 75 per cent. Not surprisingly, there was a need to initiate reforms in this area, too. During this time, I made a minor attempt at some reforms in customs duty when we switched to BTN

(Brussels Tariff Nomenclature) through legislation.[37] An expert committee[38] was appointed to consider reforms in central excise (Finance Minister C. Subramaniam announced this in his budget speech of 1976-77) under the chairmanship of L.K. Jha, the then Governor of Jammu and Kashmir. The committee submitted its interim report in 1977.

While valuable recommendations were made, some of which remain relevant even today, we could not put this report into action. By the time the committee submitted the report, we were out of office. With an attitude of 'whatever the Congress did was bad', the Janata government did not examine the report's recommendations, let alone implement them. When the Congress returned to power in 1980 and R. Venkataraman was entrusted with the Ministry of Finance, he did not show much interest in the report either. Rather, he preferred some of the recommendations of L.K. Jha, who was then working in a different capacity as a one-man Economic Administration Reforms Commission. By the time I took over as Finance Minister in 1982, many of the recommendations had lost their relevance. However, I accepted those which were still relevant and implemented them in my taxation policy.[39]

---

[37]This is a standardized system for the classification of imported goods for statistical and duty determination purposes.

[38]Its members were M.V. Arunachalam; Raja Chelliah; J. Sengupta; G.B. Nawalkar; K. Narasimhan; and Manmohan Singh, then the Chief Economic Advisor. Manmohan Singh resigned from the committee on his appointment as Secretary to Government of India and S.S. Marathe was appointed in his stead.

[39]One interesting development took place with regard to taxation under the newly introduced tariff item No. 68. When it was introduced for the first time in the budget of 1976, we did not take any credit in our revenue calculation of this item. The position we maintained in Parliament was that this proposal was not a revenue yielding measure, but we wanted to have it for statistical purposes. The then Finance Secretary, H.N. Ray, made a nice remark before the Finance Minister. 'Sir, to you this may appear as an innocuous non-revenue item, meant only for statistical purpose, but your successors may not look at this item with

■

During 1975-77, a number of reforms were initiated in the Ministry of Finance, and not least among those was banking reform. When the new socio-economic programmes were adopted, it was observed that banks were to play a crucial role in implementing them. As many as twelve points in the 20-point programme were directly or indirectly related to the banking system.

The first major initiative in this area was the establishment of Regional Rural Banks (RRBs) to cater to rural credit. The abolition of unauthorized moneylending mentioned in the 20-point programme was not possible without providing adequate facilities for institutional credit. A committee (under the chairmanship of K. Narasimhan, the then Additional Secretary for Economic Affairs) was appointed to make recommendations for providing institutional credit to rural areas. According to an RBI study (1974-75), the total requirement of rural credit amounted to Rs 3,000 crore per year. All institutional arrangements available at that time (including cooperative societies, land development banks, rural branches of commercial banks, etcetera) could not provide more than Rs 800 crore a year. In other words, not even 30 per cent of the total requirement of rural credit was available from institutional arrangements. For the remaining 70 per cent, the rural population had to depend on moneylenders whose lending rates ranged from 30 per cent to 50 per cent. Therefore, it was

---

the same approach. You are showing them a green pasture for higher revenue yield.' And that is exactly what happened. Within a couple of years, the rate of taxation under this item increased from 1 per cent to 8-10 per cent and was considered an important revenue earning measure. Later, however, V.P. Singh abolished this item by restructuring the excise tariff. The idea of MODVAT (Modified Value Added Tax) introduced by him in his budget proposals for the year 1986-87 also came from this report.

felt that an institution was necessary to provide rural credit and save the rural population from the clutches of moneylenders—and thus the Narasimhan Committee recommended the establishment of RRBs.

The model was to be that of a low cost banking institution which would combine the efficiency of commercial banks with the flexibility of cooperative societies. RRBs were to be grown as local institutions steeped in the area's cultural ethos and manned by people possessing intimate knowledge of the local economy and culture. The objective of these banks was to cater to the needs of the weakest of the weak—small and marginal farmers, agricultural labourers, rural artisans and sharecroppers.

The Ordinance was passed on 26 September 1975 and the formal inauguration was scheduled for 2 October, the birth anniversary of Mahatma Gandhi. On that day, five RRBs were inaugurated: two in Uttar Pradesh (Moradabad and Gorakhpur), one in Rajasthan (Lawan), one in Haryana (Bhiwani) and one in West Bengal (Malda). Finance Minister C. Subramaniam inaugurated the first RRB in Moradabad and I, along with Siddhartha Shankar Ray, the then Chief Minister of West Bengal, inaugurated the Gour Gramin Bank in Malda. Each RRB was to be sponsored by a nationalized bank, with an authorized share capital of Rs 1 crore and paid-up capital of Rs 25 lakh. The Union government, sponsoring banks and the state governments were to be shareholders to the tune of 50 per cent, 35 per cent and 15 per cent, respectively. Of the nine directors, four were to be nominated by the Union government, three by the sponsoring bank and two by the state government.

At the Malda function, I announced that by the end of the financial year 1975-76, fifteen banks were to be opened and, by the end of 1976-77, the number of such banks was expected to reach fifty. I emphasized the need for stepping up agricultural credit and the role assigned to RRBs in that sphere. In fact, after December 1975, when the department of banking was entrusted to me, I stepped up the activities of RRBs considerably. As many as forty-eight banks were established by March 1977. In West Bengal alone, apart from the Gour Gramin Bank, three more were established: Mayurakshi Gramin Bank at Birbhum, Mallabhum Gramin Bank at Bankura, covering three districts (Midnapur, Bankura, Purulia) and North Bengal Kshetriya Gramin Bank at Cooch Behar (Cooch Behar, Jalpaiguri and Darjeeling).

With the defeat of the Congress government it seemed that the fate of RRBs was sealed, as the Janata Party government stated that these were set up to serve the partisan interests of the Congress. Fortunately, good sense prevailed at the end of the day and an expert committee under the chairmanship of Professor Dantwala, an eminent economist, was set up to look into the issue. The Dantwala Committee, in its report, highlighted the relevance of RRBs in tackling problems of rural credit, and also made some recommendations. However, in spite of this validation, the expansion of RRBs did not garner the desired momentum. We had to wait till the Congress returned to power in 1980, when it set a target of 170 RRBs during the Sixth Five-Year Plan. The target was achieved by 31 March 1985.

In January 1976, the Ordinance establishing RRBs was replaced by an Act. While piloting the Bill in the Lok Sabha, I pointed out that each state would have its share of RRBs but priority would be given to unbanked states. The credit requirement in rural areas was estimated at Rs 3,000 crore by the end of 1978-79 and, out of this amount, a sum of Rs 1,700 crore was expected to be provided by the rural branches of commercial banks, cooperative societies and other such institutions. The balance Rs 1,300 crore was to be provided by RRBs if the entire credit requirement of the rural areas was to be met through institutional arrangements. I further assured the members that the rules governing RRBs would be simpler than those of commercial banks. I disagreed with two suggestions made by some members: (*a*) to have elected representatives of Kisan Sabhas and other such entities on the board of directors and (*b*) to make RRB pay scales at par with those of commercial banks. My logic for opposing the former suggestion was that the nomination route was better given that professionals and experts were needed on the board. Experts in agriculture or allied areas could be nominated by any of the three authorities (Union government, state government and sponsoring bank). My argument against parity in pay scales was simple: if these banks were to be operated at reduced costs, we could not afford the higher pay scales of commercial banks. Moreover, I pointed to an earlier formulation that pay scales of the employees in rural banks should be at par with those of state government employees at a similar level.

Keeping in view a variety of factors—the nationalization of fourteen scheduled commercial banks a while ago, the rapid growth in deposit mobilization and the felt need for social banking—in December 1975, a separate Department of Revenue and Banking was carved out of the Ministry of Finance and placed under my responsibility. I was appointed Minister of State in charge.

I decided to have my first meeting with the chief executives of nationalized banks,[40] identifying the important areas for discussion: advances to the priority sector, branch expansion,

---

[40]The meeting was attended by all chief executives of nationalized banks, the Governor and the Deputy Governors of the RBI, the Secretary to the Government of India in the Department of Banking, the Chief Economic Advisor and other senior officers. The meeting was held at the conference room of North Block on 24 February 1976.

deposit mobilization, and a focus on sick industries and bad investments by banks. I focused on the twelve points in the 20-point programme which were related to banks, and emphasized that banks had an important role to play in eliminating rural indebtedness. I stressed the need for creating rural banks for this specific task: 'I am hoping that the attitude of each one of the rural banks would be something in the nature of operation credit flood.' The need for the flow of credit to the handloom sector was emphasized. This sector of the Indian economy was very important from the point of view of both employment and foreign exchange earning. To this end, there was need for banks to undertake 'a critical assessment of their lending experiences and the problem of overdues in respect of recoveries.' I explained the action plan for the handloom sector: as many as thirteen intensive development projects and twenty export production projects were to be established. The government agreed to fund them fully by providing 75 per cent loans and 25 per cent grants-in-aid. The resources to fund a major part of these projects would have to come from government financing. I advised them to liaise with state governments so as to be able to provide the necessary assistance to this sector.

The question of loans to sick industries was also discussed. I pointed out that huge amounts of bank money were locked up in sick private industries. Some amount of the bank's credit got frozen when an industrial unit was taken over by the government under the IDR Act.[41] Normally, a moratorium was declared on all pre-takeover liabilities of these units and bank advances were also subject to such moratorium. As a result, bank profitability reduced as 'bad debts' increased every year. I pointed out that the banks

---

[41]The Industries (Development and Regulation) Act, 1951, which provided for the development and regulation of certain industries.

should be able to spot the first signs of trouble by monitoring the unit's cash flow. If this was done carefully, remedial steps could be taken at an early stage. I observed, 'What is, therefore, necessary is for the banks to devise a suitable information system to detect cases of incipient sickness so that corrective action can be taken well in time.'

# CHAPTER FIVE

# THE STUNNING DEFEAT AND ITS AFTERMATH

D ramatic as always in her decision-making, Indira Gandhi announced elections on 18 January 1977, despite the fact that she had the option, under the Emergency, to defer them for another year. Many were convinced that her call for elections was due to her confidence that she would return to power. This, her critics said, came from the fact that a significant number of opposition leaders were in prison, trade union activity was practically non-existent, and there was hardly any open political activity. However, Indira Gandhi's decision was prompted by her concern that the continuance of the Emergency would harm Indian democracy, a concern that was in turn prompted by disquieting reports of the misuse of power at various levels.

Hence, despite knowing full well that the Congress (and she) would be swimming against the tide, she announced elections. A section of Congressmen had been against the Emergency and people like Jagjivan Ram and Hemvati Nandan Bahuguna abandoned ship, feeling that the Congress was losing ground.

After its stunning defeat in the March 1977 Lok Sabha elections, the Congress took time to recover. The Union

Cabinet under Indira Gandhi resigned on 22 March, and the Janata Party government under Morarji Desai was in office on 24 March.

And then started the propaganda holding Indira Gandhi and her younger son, Sanjay Gandhi, responsible for the party's electoral debacle. A group of Congressmen chose to avoid any responsibility, attributing the debacle to the excesses committed by the so-called 'extra-constitutional centres of power', thus laying the blame solely and entirely on Indira Gandhi.

Siddhartha babu's antagonism was not surprising. His bad days had started after the Allahabad High Court verdict. Sanjay Gandhi felt that the case had been improperly handled (Siddhartha babu had been Indira Gandhi's legal advisor). In 1976, when Sanjay Gandhi began coming into political prominence, a small group in West Bengal started asserting themselves against Siddhartha babu; core among them were A.B.A. Ghani Khan Choudhury, Sato Ghosh and Somen Mitra, with D.P. Chattopadhyaya, too, getting into the act. Though I was not in favour of disturbing Siddhartha Shankar Ray, my name too came to be identified with this group as well. In addition, the growing infighting within the West Bengal unit of the Congress damaged Siddhartha babu's image as a party manager, and his ad hoc and inept handling of state matters did not project him as a good administrator. His anxiousness to show his proximity to the Prime Minister was disliked by many who termed it as exhibitionism. One senior central leader once sarcastically remarked: 'When Siddhartha was central minister [Education, 1971], his job was to look after West Bengal, but when he became Chief Minister of West Bengal, he took upon himself the responsibility to look after India.' It was meant to be a joke but Siddhartha babu's frequent visits to Delhi earned him the reputation of being a 'Delhi-based' Chief Minister.

Some Congressmen started a signature campaign demanding the resignation of Congress President Dev Kanta Barooah, following up with a demand for the resignation of the entire CWC. Faiz Mohammad Khan, a Rajya Sabha member of the party from Karnataka, went on hunger strike demanding Barooah's resignation, along with the resignation of all other office bearers (some CWC members like Bansi Lal had already resigned).

At the first meeting of the Congress Parliamentary Party (CPP) after the general elections, Y.B. Chavan was elected leader, with the crucial support of Barooah. Within a few days of the defeat the old alignment had changed, and party members switched loyalties swiftly. Congressmen like Barooah, Chavan, Swaran Singh, Siddhartha Shankar Ray, Chandrajit Yadav, Priya Ranjan Dasmunsi, Purabi Mukherjee and Rajni Patel came together and formed the anti-Indira group while others like Om Mehta, Bansi Lal and V.C. Shukla withdrew, demoralized. Those like A.R. Antulay, A.P. Sharma, Vasant Sathe and I remained loyal to Indira Gandhi, and Sanjay Gandhi, too, retained some of his old group. The scenario in the states also changed considerably after the elections.

I was asked by Nurul Islam of West Bengal to meet Indira Gandhi. I had met her earlier on this matter but she had chosen not to say anything then. This time I asked her whether it was time for us to act. 'Why not?' she said, and suggested that I meet leaders like A.P. Sharma, C.M. Stephen, B.P. Maurya and A.R. Antulay. Accordingly, I did.

The CWC met in Delhi on 12-15 April 1977 to discuss the election debacle and to review the post-election situation. Apart from members of the CWC, permanent invitees, state Congress Presidents, leaders of the state legislature parties and a few former central ministers also attended the meeting. So did the AICC observers in the states.[42] A day before the meeting, Indira Gandhi was nominated to the CWC by the Congress President, filling the vacancy caused by Chavan. This had become necessary as the moment she ceased to be an MP and leader of the CPP, her membership of the CWC also ceased. She was not among the ten members elected to the CWC in 1977; she was an ex-officio member.

As the meeting started, a few members, including Sitaram Kesri, Shankar Dayal Singh and Syed Mir Qasim, asked about Indira Gandhi's absence and wanted Barooah to persuade her to participate. Barooah, accompanied by Y.B. Chavan and Kamalapati Tripathi, left for Indira Gandhi's residence and persuaded her to attend the meeting. As a result, the meeting started forty-five

---

[42]The following were present at the meeting, with the Congress President D.K. Barooah in the Chair: *Members*: Indira Gandhi, Swaran Singh, Y.B. Chavan, Siddhartha Shankar Ray, Kamalapati Tripathi, N.D. Tiwari, C. Subramaniam, V.P. Naik, Syed Mir Qasim, P.C. Sethi, Chandrajit Yadav, Vayalar Ravi, Giani Zail Singh, Muhammad Ali, M. Chandrasekar, Purabi Mukherjee, A.R. Antulay, V.B. Raju. *Permanent Invitees*: Shankar Dayal Sharma, K.D. Malaviya, B.C. Bhagwati, Kartik Oraon, Om Mehta, Rajni Patel, K. Raghuramaiah, Henry Austin, Nawal Kishore Sharma, Tarun Gogoi, Devaraj Urs, S.B. Chavan, Hari Krishan Shastri, P.R. Dasmunsi [he was appointed as President, Indian Youth Congress, immediately after the debacle, replacing Ambika Soni], and Margaret Alva. *Special invitees*: (a) Leaders of the Congress Legislature Party in the states: J. Vengal Rao, Sarat Chandra Sinha, Madhav Singh Solanki, Jagannath Mishra, Banarsi Das Gupta, K. Karunakaran, Shyam Charan Shukla, Williamson A. Sangma, Binayak Acharya, Harideo Joshi, Radha Raman, A.N. Naik. (b) PCC Presidents: Lalit Kumar Doley, Sitaram Kesari, M.R. Vyas, Amarnath Chawla, Kantilal Ghiya, Rao Nihar Singh, Sat Prakash Mahajan, Mufti Mohammad Sayeed, S.B. Nagaral, A.K. Antony, N.K. Sharma, M.N. Tidke, H. Nilmoni Singh, Hokishe Sema, Chintamani Jena, Mohinder Singh Gill, Girdhari Lal Vyas, G.K. Moopanar, Mohsina Kidwai, A.K. Maitra, Gara Partin, Bhupal Singh, Sulochana Katkar. (c) AICC observers: R.D. Nimbalkar, Mathuradas Mathur, Jagdish Joshi, Shankar Ghosh, Sudhakar Pandey, Harcharan Singh Josh, H.M. Trivedi, Mangat Ram Sharma, Girdhari Lal Dogra, Mange Ram, Sawai Singh Sisodia, M.R. Krishna, Dawaipen Sen, Ranbir Singh, Maimoona Sultan, Lalit Sen, Ushi Khan, Kumud Ben Joshi, Savita Behan. (d) CEC members: K. Brahmananda Reddy, Shankar Dayal Singh, Mallappa Kollur. (e) Others: Shah Nawaz Khan, Chaudhury Ram Sewak, V.P. Singh, K.C. Pant, B.P. Maurya, B.R. Bhagat, G.S. Dhillon, Darbara Singh, Raj Bahadur, Nitiraj Singh, V.C. Shukla, J.B. Patnaik, V.N. Gadgil and Ambika Soni.

minutes late. After Barooah made brief introductory remarks, Indira Gandhi spoke. She observed that she had initially wanted to keep away from the meeting so that a free and frank discussion on the party's election reversal could take place. She said that as she was the leader of the government which had lost the election, she could not escape taking responsibility for the party's poll debacle. However, she told Congressmen not to lose heart at this defeat. She emphasized that the party had a great future and appealed for organizational unity so that the party could play its new role while at the same time revitalizing itself. In fact, before the meeting of the CWC, she had sent a letter to the Congress President in which she observed, 'as one who led the government, I unreservedly own full responsibility for this defeat', and this letter was circulated among the members of the committee.

The debate on the causes for the defeat continued for three days and, after a comprehensive review of each state, the CWC approved and put out a statement on the reasons for the party's debacle (see Appendix 8 for extracts from the statement).

During these three days, many direct and indirect references were made to Indira Gandhi, Sanjay Gandhi, Bansi Lal, Om Mehta, V.C. Shukla and a few others. Terms such as 'extra-constitutional authority', 'caucus' and 'gang of four' were liberally bandied about as Siddhartha babu, Priya Ranjan Dasmunsi, Chandrajit Yadav and D.K. Barooah, among others, continued their attack. I, too, was not spared. While the others were the main targets at the national level, I was targeted by the Assam and Bengal group, and criticized for intensifying the drive against economic offenders. The detention of Gayatri Devi, the Rajmata of Jaipur, was described as an act of high-handedness. Dasmunsi was particularly critical of me. Though the official statement did not reflect the significant discord, the tone and tenor of the speeches made by some participants made it abundantly clear that they were not going to allow Indira Gandhi to remain in peace.

The CWC accepted the resignation of D.K. Barooah as Congress President, but the resignations of other members of the committee, which had been tendered earlier, were not accepted. The inner struggle which began after the defeat took its toll. Bansi Lal was expelled from the party's primary membership for a period of six years.

> After considering the view of the Haryana Chief Minister, P.C.C. President and other important Congressmen, the Working Committee is of the view that the undemocratic, autocratic and undignified actions of Bansi Lal have damaged the image of the party and he is guilty of deliberately acting in a way calculated to lower the prestige of the Congress. The Working Committee resolves that Bansi Lal be expelled forthwith from the Party, from all its committees and from the primary membership of the party for a period of six years.[43]

Immediately after the defeat of the party, Barooah had demanded that Bansi Lal resign, and he did. Sanjay Gandhi also resigned from the Congress. Barooah met Indira Gandhi on 9 April, after which he told the press that neither Sanjay Gandhi nor Bansi Lal were discussed. He also told the press that both he and Indira Gandhi had agreed not to launch a witch-hunt or sling mud at each other. He specifically mentioned that since Bansi Lal had resigned from the CWC, the question of his attending committee meetings did not arise. Nor was there any question of taking action against Sanjay Gandhi, who had also resigned from

---

[43]The resolution was adopted at the meeting of the committee held at 5 p.m. on 15 April 1977. This meeting was attended only by the core members of the committee; Indira Gandhi was absent.

the Congress. Barooah further stated that Bansi Lal's misdeeds were unparalleled, and that Sanjay Gandhi's acts of omission or commission were no match for them.

The action against Bansi Lal, who had become one of the main 'villains' of the Emergency, was predetermined. He was not given any chance to defend himself. The *Economic Times* (15 April 1977) observed:

> The issue of taking disciplinary action, it was now revealed by the Party General Secretary Purabi Mukherjee, was raised yesterday (13.4.77) by the Chief Minister of West Bengal, Siddhartha Sankar Ray. It was stated that even yesterday, a formal decision was taken on the nature of disciplinary action to be taken. Today (14.4.77) it was formalized through a proper resolution.

Bansi Lal was expelled and V.C. Shukla was to be reprimanded. The form of reprimand was to be decided by the Congress President.

It is, therefore, quite clear that the decision regarding Bansi Lal had already been taken and the endorsement of the CWC was a mere formality. In their desperation to hang the culprit, the judges did not care to listen to him or to give him an opportunity to speak in his defence. This act of the CWC encouraged the Janata Party government in Haryana to take vindictive action against Bansi Lal by publicly parading him in handcuffs in Bhiwani only a couple of months later. One may argue that the Janata Party might have done the same thing even without the Congress action, but that does not absolve Congress leaders of the malice and vindictiveness with which they acted. There were many prophets of sanity and sobriety after the defeat but where were they earlier? The seeds of the split were sown by this very attitude.

I made up my mind to remain with Indira Gandhi, come what may. I knew that I had no skeletons in my closet and though mud was slung at me by the media, the baseless allegations did not bother me too much. Some newspapers reported that my passport had been impounded—a curious assertion, given that till then I did not even have a regular permanent passport. (All my travels abroad had been on official work, on an official passport, which was given back to the ministry on my return.)

*Blitz,* a news magazine run by R.K. Karanjia, a close confidante of Indira Gandhi at one time, claimed that my wife was in Copenhagen, supposedly at the expense of the State Bank of India (SBI)—another curious assertion, given that she had not visited Europe before 1978. The same magazine alleged that the then Chairman of the SBI, T.R.Varadachary, had personally carried Rs 9 crore in 'tin boxes' to my constituency (Malda) and to Sanjay Gandhi's constituency (Amethi).

> It is alleged, for example, that Varadachary personally carried Rs 9 crores in tin boxes to Malda from where former Banking Minister Pranab Mukherjee was contesting the Lok Sabha elections as well as Rae Bareli and Amethi, Indira and Sanjay Gandhi's constituencies and supervised the cash handouts to voters. Evidence of this outrage is reportedly available from Marxists' quarters. They quietly put signs on the boxes containing the money and witnessed Varadachary personally carrying them to the constituencies for distribution.[44]

It had occurred to no one to try and locate the 'tin boxes', thus 'signed', and frame charges against the culprits. Nobody spared a thought about the number of tin boxes one would require to

---

[44]*Blitz,* Bombay, April 1977.

carry Rs 9 crore, presuming that all currency notes would be of 100-rupee denomination. Higher denomination notes of 1,000 rupees could not be used for normal transactions in those days. Could any individual, let alone the Chairman of SBI, handle so many boxes? There had to be at least ninety such tin boxes, if one is to make a rough calculation. The same story stated that, 'Apart from this it is reported that Pranab Mukherjee's unjustified visit to Copenhagen where a number of other top bank officials had also been holidaying, was paid for by the State Bank for reasons which can be fathomed only by a proper enquiry.'

This was the level of propaganda some of us faced. And this wasn't the last time I had to face the brunt of unfounded allegations.

I do not quote from media reports with any sense of malice or anger. I quote the reports only to highlight the atmosphere that prevailed in those days. Mere allegations were sufficient to write people off. Anger and venom had replaced cold logic and the need for proof. The general mood of the people was frenzied. They had not approved of the Emergency and thought that everything, and every individual, associated with it should be discarded ruthlessly. Sanity and rationality were replaced by strong emotional resentment.

■

With Barooah's resignation as Congress President, Swaran Singh took over as the interim President. It was decided that an AICC meeting should be convened to elect the new Congress President and the ten members of the CWC. In its meeting on 22 April 1977, the CWC advanced the date of the AICC meeting from 13-15 May to 4-5 May, and the venue was shifted from Bangalore to Delhi. The following agenda was set: (a) Election of the

Congress President; (*b*) Election of ten members of the CWC; and (*c*) Election of seven members of the Central Election Committee (CEC).

The hardcore anti-Indira group notwithstanding, there were others too who were unfavourably disposed, though they had not overtly adopted a hard line against her. It was in this context that the question of choosing the new Congress President came up. Various names were suggested and discussed: Swaran Singh, Siddhartha babu, Karan Singh, Y.B. Chavan, Mir Qasim, P.V. Narasimha Rao and C. Subramaniam. I was then working with A.P. Sharma, C.M. Stephen, R. Gundu Rao and Vasant Sathe, and we took an active role against Barooah. We usually moved in a group and took direction from Kamalapati Tripathi and Indira Gandhi herself.

Indira Gandhi mooted the name of K. Brahmananda Reddy for President. Chavan, Tripathi, Mir Qasim, Subramaniam and other senior leaders supported her choice. Reddy was a senior Congress leader with vast experience at the centre as well as the state level. In addition to this, he hailed from South India, where the Congress had fared well in the Lok Sabha elections. In fact, out of the 154 Congress members in the Lok Sabha, about 100 were from South India.

Suddenly, the neo-radical group led by people like D.K. Barooah and Chandrajit Yadav put up Siddhartha babu as a candidate.

Finally, there were four candidates in the field: K. Brahmananda Reddy, Siddhartha Shankar Ray, Dr Karan Singh and Neki Ram Sharma.[45] A slew of people, including myself, contested for the ten CWC seats and the seven CEC seats. Though Indira Gandhi,

---

[45]Devaraj Urs, who had also filed his nomination papers, withdrew from the contest at a later stage.

Y.B. Chavan and other senior leaders agreed on a common candidate for the office of the President, they refrained from interfering with candidate selection for the CWC and CEC. We had discussed this issue with Kamalapati Tripathi but even he would not give us any direction. Therefore, the elections to the CWC and the CEC were a free-for-all.

The result of the presidential election came first. K. Brahmananda Reddy was elected by an overwhelming majority, getting 317 votes. Siddhartha Shankar Ray got 160 votes while Karan Singh and Neki Ram Sharma got 16 and 3 votes respectively.

The results of the elections to the CWC and CEC could not be announced till the following morning as counting took longer. While the polling for the Congress President was decisively in favour of Indira Gandhi's nominee, the results of the CWC and CEC elections were mixed. Later, she admitted to me that we should have conducted the CWC election in a more organized manner instead of allowing it to be a free-for-all.

From our side, Zail Singh and I were miserably defeated. A distinguished loser in the other camp was Purabi Mukherjee. Those elected to the CWC were: Dr Shankar Dayal Sharma, V.P. Nayak, K.C. Pant, P.V. Narasimha Rao, M. Chandrasekar, Priya Ranjan Dasmunsi, Chandrajit Yadav, A.P. Sharma, C.M. Stephen and Muhammed Ali. The Congress President nominated the following to the CWC: Indira Gandhi, Y.B. Chavan, Kamalapati Tripathi, C. Subramaniam, Swaran Singh, Virendra Verma, P.V. Raju, Buta Singh, Dr Ram Subhag Singh and Mir Qasim.

Only three of the ten elected CWC members were with us when the split occurred: P.V. Narasimha Rao, A.P. Sharma and M. Chandrasekar. However, among the nominated members, we had Mir Qasim, Kamalapati Tripathi and Buta Singh, apart from Indira Gandhi. Hence, out of the twenty members of the CWC, our group constituted seven. After the elections in Andhra Pradesh, Karnataka and Maharashtra in March 1978, three elected members of the CWC came to our side—Dr Shankar Dayal Sharma, C.M. Stephen and Virendra Verma—taking our number to ten.

■

The future of state governments, largely controlled by the Congress, became uncertain. A few chief ministers, such as Siddhartha Shankar Ray, congratulated the newly elected Prime Minister, Morarji Desai, and assured him of their fullest cooperation. Some, like Kazi Lhendup Dorjee of Sikkim and P.K. Thungan of Arunachal Pradesh, joined the Janata Party and converted the state unit of the Congress into the state unit of the Janata Party. Siddhartha babu's telegram (of 24 March) and letter to Prime Minister Morarji Desai created a great deal of confusion. Some newspapers reported Ray as having said that he wanted to wash his hands off the Emergency and the measures taken during it. This was debated in the West Bengal assembly on 6 April. Ray gave a spirited reponse and denied the newspaper report. He read out the telegram he had sent to Morarji Desai:

> On behalf of the people of West Bengal and the West Bengal government and also on my personal behalf I send you best wishes. I can assure you that our government will fully cooperate with the centre on all constructive work and I have no doubt that the cooperation that existed between this government and the former central government will continue.

On the face of it, there seemed nothing objectionable in the telegram and, under normal circumstances, one would have accepted it as a matter of common courtesy. But some people, including a section of the press, refused to accept it at face value. They tried to read between the lines. Ray's own shifting attitude and statements only added to the confusion. While he accepted his association with the Emergency on the floor of the assembly, he backtracked in the months to come.

On 6 April he had observed:

> It had been suggested I do not accept any responsibility for the Emergency. How could this be? Was I not the Chief Minister when Emergency was promulgated? Congressmen will have to accept this responsibility. We worked according to the Emergency. This is no cheap politics. Whether we stay or not will be decided by the people but we will never tell the people untruths.[46]

The Congress focused on the possibility of their state assemblies being dissolved. Immediately after assuming office, the Janata Party demanded the dissolution of Congress-led state assemblies on the grounds that the ruling parties in the states had lost the people's mandate, reflected in the decisive defeat of the Congress in the Lok Sabha elections. Charan Singh, the then Home Minister, wrote a letter to the chief ministers of the nine states where Congress had lost the Lok Sabha elections miserably: Uttar Pradesh, Bihar, Madhya Pradesh, Rajasthan, Haryana, Punjab, Himachal Pradesh, Orissa and Gujarat. He suggested that they recommend dissolution of their respective assemblies to their governors. The communication also suggested that if the chief ministers followed this advice they could continue as chief ministers of the caretaker ministry until fresh elections were

---

[46] *Times of India*, New Delhi, 7 April 1977.

held. It was a clever ploy, and Charan Singh thought that many would fall into his trap and recommend dissolution. But the Congress stood firm on this issue (see Appendix 9 for the CWC resolution on Congress' stand on the dissolution of Congress-led state assemblies).

The CWC had a series of formal and informal meetings, and Congress chief ministers were directed to ignore the Home Minister's appeal. The central government, however, dissolved the assemblies in these nine states nonetheless. The *Hindustan Times* (New Delhi, 23 April 1977) reported that West Bengal Chief Minister Siddhartha Shankar Ray had written to the Union Home Minister Chaudhary Charan Singh suggesting that the opinion of the Supreme Court might be sought before taking any action in the proposed direction. Obviously, this suggestion was ignored. The proclamation dissolving these assemblies was initially not signed by the Vice President, B.D. Jatti, then the acting President. He sought some clarifications from the central government. But when the Janata Party threatened to gherao him if he withheld his signature to the proclamation, he gave in. The CWC met on 1 May and approved a critical statement to be issued by the AICC on the subject of the dissolution (see Appendix 10 for this statement).

Some state governments, including that of West Bengal, went to the Supreme Court challenging the decision. The Congress supported this move. However, the judgement of the Supreme Court went in favour of the central government, as it accepted the 'mandate theory' and justified the proclamation dissolving the state assemblies.

So now the Congress geared up to face state elections. During this time, the process of 'de-Indiraization' began. She had already expressed her disinclination to campaign, and the party made no effort to persuade her. She wasn't even asked to campaign for the Nagaland assembly elections, which took place that year. Some senior Congress leaders started saying that she was unable to collect even a dozen people to listen to her.

Although Brahmananda Reddy was elected Congress President with her blessing and support, some of the elected members of the CWC were totally opposed to her. Even in speeches felicitating the newly elected Congress President, the venom against Indira Gandhi and her followers was clearly, and ominously, evident. Chavan observed, 'You have won the election and we have won democracy.' Ray said that the new Congress President faced the onerous task of taking firm action against those who had misled the party and used party power to amass huge fortunes. 'The nation will judge us by what we do and if we fail to project a proper image before the people, we will not be forgiven by posterity...'[47]

Hearing such comments, one wonders what these paragons of propriety were doing during the past few months. Chavan was part of the Congress high command since the mid-1960s and Ray stepped into Indira Gandhi's charmed circle after the split of 1969. So how could things deteriorate so fast under the very noses of these gentlemen? No answer to this question was forthcoming from them. We found our own answers: these 'big leaders' were little more than 'paper tigers'. They had not dared to utter a word against Indira Gandhi when she was in power, and were the first to abuse her the moment she was out of office. Not only did this undermine their public image, but it also prevented the possibility of building a collective leadership and sharing responsibility within the Congress. When there was no leader, the question of collective leadership didn't arise. Congressmen realized that their 'tin god' leaders were

---

[47] *The Encyclopaedia of the Indian National Congress*, vol. 24, p. 221.

incapable of leading a historic organization like the Indian National Congress.

The attitude of 'passing the buck to the fallen leader' dampened the spirit of Congressmen and, conversely, inspired the Janata Party government to be at their vindictive best when it came to Indira Gandhi and her followers. Instead of opposing the malicious witch-hunt in the name of enquiry commissions, the AICC started supporting the Janata government's decision to set them up. The political resolution passed by the AICC observed:

> The AICC does not wish to justify any misuse of power by individuals or groups during the Emergency. A number of enquiry commissions have been set up by the government and, if conducted fairly, these should bring about quite clearly how much truth there is in the various allegations and insinuations that had been made and continue to be made. It has never been the policy of the Congress to try and hide its mistakes and if unfortunately any Congressmen are found to be guilty of misuse of power, they will certainly have to face the consequences of their actions.[48]

The results of the assembly elections in the nine states were not great either, but there were some improvements compared to the Lok Sabha elections. The Congress bettered its performance in all nine states except West Bengal.

After the assembly elections, I was invited to a meeting of the extended CWC, held over 23-24 June. There, I had a confrontation with Ram Subhag Singh over the detention of Gayatri Devi. He was critical of the detention, and though I explained the logic of the action, he was determined not to listen to reason. A few other members and invitees were also

---

[48]AICC resolution passed at the meeting held in New Delhi on 5 May 1977.

hostile towards me. Those who had once praised Sanjay Gandhi suddenly started finding every sort of vice in him.

A number of peculiar allegations were made during the June session of Parliament, which met after the state assembly elections to pass the budget. Jyoti Basu claimed that we had fudged the amount collected through the Voluntary Disclosure Scheme as well as the number of declarers. He was particularly virulent about my 'high-handedness' and 'vendetta' against Maharani Gayatri Devi who had been arrested during the Emergency. I was further accused of multiple misdemeanours—from being the author of the 'raid raj' during the Emergency, to being responsible for removing the SBI Chairman, R.K. Talwar, because of his alleged refusal to give Sanjay Gandhi a loan, to even conducting a raid on Baroda Rayon merely to recover some incriminating documents. Raised by private members, these allegations were allowed to go on record, undenied, as the ministers who were in possession of the facts (as custodians of government files and papers) did not bother to provide the correct and full information. It became clear that some of us would not get any protection either from the government or from our own party. I did occasionally try to defend myself through my interventions in the Rajya Sabha or through the media, but was not always successful.

In the House and lobby, I was avoided by almost everybody, apart from two CPI Rajya Sabha members, Bhupesh Gupta and Kalyan Roy, both good friends, and Congress leaders A.R. Antulay, Saroj Khaparde and Pratibha Singh. I became a common sight in the lobby as I whiled away time alone, smoking my pipe. To each his own share of woes.

CHAPTER SIX

# BATTLE LINES DRAWN IN
# THE CONGRESS

It became amply clear, particularly after the assembly elections, that Indira Gandhi was to be relegated to an insignificant position. While Brahmananda Reddy seemed cordial towards her, accommodating some people close to her as members/invitees of the CWC, her views were brushed aside while selecting candidates for the assembly elections. Indira Gandhi sent me to K.C. Pant, the then General Secretary in charge of West Bengal, for help with candidate selection from the state. Pant was extremely cordial when I met him, but perhaps he was rendered powerless in face of Priya Ranjan Dasmunsi and his group.

Indira Gandhi suggested that I meet Y.B. Chavan. Barkat (A.B.A. Ghani Khan Choudhury) and I met Chavan at his Race Course residence. He, too, was cordial and receptive but when we talked about the dominance of the group led by Dasmunsi, he made it clear that we would have to accept his guidance. He told me bluntly that I should not forget that Dasmunsi had been elected to the CWC while I had been defeated in that election. I emphasized that we were not questioning Dasmunsi's leadership but wanted Chavan to be aware of Dasmunsi's starkly partisan behaviour. Chavan, however, could not be convinced. Many Congressmen believed that Dasmunsi had been wronged during the Emergency. His overwhelming success in the election to the CWC and CEC was also based on this perception.

I worked hard for the West Bengal assembly elections. I was on both the campaign committee and election manifesto committee. Siddhartha babu and his supporters were against me but the PCC President, Arun Maitra, had been cordial. I conducted a low-key campaign mainly in Malda, from where I had contested unsuccessfully in the previous Lok Sabha elections, and also in Birbhum and Burdwan.

Siddhartha babu did not contest the election. Most of the ministers and leaders who contested the election were defeated. Out of 294 seats, the Congress got only twenty. Almost all ministers (except Barkat, who won by a margin of 43,569 votes), including Abdus Sattar, Jainal Abedin, Bholanath Sen, Suniti Chattaraj and Atish Sinha were defeated. The percentage of votes polled by the Congress also came down sharply (from 34 per cent in the Lok Sabha elections to 23 per cent in the assembly elections). 'Mr Dasmunsi said anti-CPI(M) votes in West Bengal were divided between the Janata Party and the Congress. Had there been an alliance between Janata and CPI(M), the Congress could have fared better.'[49]

The first part of Dasmunsi's observation was correct because the Janata Party and the Congress together polled about 56 per cent of the votes and the Left about 44 per cent. But if the Janata and the Left had combined, the chances of the Congress would have been further diminished, as was evident in the Lok Sabha elections. The votes polled by the Janata Party were not anti-Left but anti-Congress because the Leftists came to power

---

[49] *The Encyclopaedia of the Indian National Congress*, vol. 24, pp. 293.

only after the election.

The Congress lost as it had no courage or conviction to fight, and was a divided house. Even before the battle began, the Congress had lost the war because its general (the Chief Minister) had run away from the battlefield. Siddhartha babu's supporters had assiduously floated and popularized the view that the Congress's Lok Sabha loss in West Bengal was because a section of Congressmen (with the help of Sanjay Gandhi) had worked at destabilizing the 'most popular' Chief Minister West Bengal had ever had. The truth was that the people's verdict in the Lok Sabha election was a reaction to the factional fight within the Congress over the previous four-five years, misdeeds of some ministers, the policy of alienating the traditional Congress base and the overall reaction against the Emergency. Else, why would such a 'popular' Chief Minister refuse to contest the assembly election from the safest constituency in West Bengal, Chowringhee—a seat which had remained vacant since Sankar Ghosh's election to the Rajya Sabha in 1976?

■

At the national level, the early signs of the split started showing in the Youth Congress. Immediately after the Lok Sabha elections, D.K. Barooah replaced Ambika Soni with Priya Ranjan Dasmunsi as the President of the Youth Congress. History witnessed a complete twist—tragic or comic, I cannot tell. It was the same Barooah who, on a cold November evening at my 11 Ashoka Road house, asked Dasmunsi to tender his resignation as the President of the Youth Congress in the presence of D.P. Chattopadhyaya (considered a member of the Dasmunsi camp), and me. This was done only to satisfy Sanjay Gandhi, who wanted to control the Youth Congress and who didn't consider

Dasmunsi an able Youth Congress President. Now, with Sanjay Gandhi's fall, the same Congress President who had removed him now reinstated Dasmunsi with the only difference being that the venue was not my residence.

The Youth Congress got a bad name. A section of Congressmen believed that the party was routed in the Lok Sabha elections because of the misdeeds of the Youth Congress. At the CWC review (between 12-15 April) of the party's performance in the Lok Sabha election, a large number of state representatives accused the Youth Congress of being responsible for the defeat of the Congress. So charged was the atmosphere then that it was completely devoid of logic or rationality. It's no surprise, therefore, that the party decided to do away with the Youth Congress. It was decided that organizational elections to the Youth Congress committees at various levels were to be held after one year.

It is interesting to note that Sanjay Gandhi's 5-point programme, directed at correcting ecological imbalance and population control, was completely forgotten, losing its relevance and importance with the fall of its author. Sanjay Gandhi became anathema, as did all his programmes.

During these days, I spent a lot of time with Indira Gandhi and Sanjay Gandhi. Indira Gandhi had shifted to 12 Willingdon Crescent, and Maneka was helping Sanjay Gandhi, who was involved in managing a series of inquiries by multiple investigating agencies, civil and criminal, while running her newsmagazine, *Surya*.

My discussions with Indira Gandhi revolved around our future course of action. After the assembly elections, we started contacting people: B.P. Maurya, Khurshed Alam Khan, A.R. Antulay, Bhagwat Jha Azad, Saroj Khaparde, Margaret Alva, Pratibha Singh, Venkat Swamy and B. Shankaranand. Sanjay Gandhi suggested that I form a group of younger members and, with that in mind I got in touch with Lalit Maken and a few other boys from Delhi. Vasant Sathe had already taken up the cause of Indira Gandhi in the Lok Sabha and Kalpnath Rai did the same in the Rajya Sabha.

We obviously did not wait for the decision of the CWC because we knew that the Youth Congress would be buried deep, without any chance of revival. We, therefore, worked out our own course of action and began reorganizing the youth under another umbrella. After a few discussions with Sanjay and Indira Gandhi, we set up a youth forum, on a very low key. A meeting was convened at the Vithalbhai Patel House in New Delhi, with those present including Ram Chandra Rath, Ghulam Nabi Azad, Tariq Anwar and Lalit Maken. A total of seventeen youth activists attended the meeting. I presided over it, and we formally launched the youth forum with Ram Chandra Rath as convener. It was resolved that state units of the forum would be established and contact would be made with activists in different parts of the country. Erstwhile Youth Congress activists joined the forum in their thousands and long before the formal split of 1978, we were able to install units of the forum in almost all states. In West Bengal, Somen Mitra was given charge, and he continued to head the youth organization in West Bengal till 1986. In no time we were able to garner the support of a large number of the youth. In the years to come, all leaders of the forum were to play important roles in Congress politics.

■

A couple of months after this, Indira Gandhi came out of her self-imposed confinement and started touring the country. She met Vinoba Bhave at Paunar and JP at Patna. Her visits to Uttar Pradesh, Bihar (Belchi) and Andhra Pradesh drew huge crowds and it was clear that the crowd-puller in her remained as active as ever. The Janata Party, aided by a section of Congressmen, continued with their relentless slander campaign, with the media (government and otherwise) supporting them. The Shah Commission drama, which started at the end of September, took this slander campaign to its peak. It was then that the surge of popular enthusiasm for Indira Gandhi reassured us that the party could overcome all crises under her leadership. We started the groundwork for restoring her authority within the party.

The first signs of the impending split in the party became visible immediately after the party's debacle in the general elections in March 1977. Through a signature campaign, some AICC members demanded a meeting to remove Barooah from the office of Congress President. A signatory myself, I helped collect a number of other signatures, making it clear that I considered Indira Gandhi's leadership indispensable for the party, and that I would stay with her. Everybody knew of my affiliation, and I did not give them reason to believe otherwise till the day she died.

The 153 signatures collected were placed before the CWC at its meeting on 13 April 1977. However, this was a wasted exercise as, at the meeting that day, Barooah, owning responsibility for the party's debacle at the polls, conveyed his decision to resign from the office of the President of the party.

However, the situation did not improve much after the election of the new Congress President and the formation of the new team. The planned process of denigrating Indira Gandhi and isolating her followers continued unabated. She was not even considered a part of the collective leadership. While she toured the country, her programmes were avoided by local party organizations with the tacit support of the party's national leadership.

The election to the Congress Parliamentary Party was held during the budget session of Parliament (June-July). Backed by the high command, most of those elected were those who had dissociated themselves from Indira Gandhi and, except for Kalpnath Rai and Vasant Sathe, almost all the others were hostile towards her. MPs issued statements at regular intervals denouncing Indira Gandhi and her so-called caucus, with the party leadership taking no steps to restrain them.

A pressure group—the 'Thursday Club'—suddenly surfaced and tried to dominate the Congress Parliamentary Party. Comprising, among others, Bipin Pal Das (Assam), Amjad Ali (West Bengal), Vitthal Gadgil (Maharashtra), Devendra Dwivedi (UP) and Dr V.A. Seyid Mohammed (Kerala), their initial target was the 'mafia gang' of Sanjay Gandhi. But they soon trained their guns on Indira Gandhi, too. This group had done fairly well in the elections to the CPP, and Sardar Amjad Ali was elected Secretary and Bipin Pal Das was appointed Chief Whip.[50] Y.B. Chavan utilized this group fully till the split in the party, though after the March 1978 elections in Andhra Pradesh, Karnataka and Maharashtra, this group collapsed like a pack of cards.

■

Battle lines were being drawn in West Bengal too, particularly after the debacle in the assembly elections. During the assembly elections, I tried my best to bring about a compromise, and worked hard to prepare the manifesto and raise funds. I tried to speak to all stakeholders to expand the area of agreement, and had several rounds of talks with D.P. Chattopadhyaya, Arun Maitra, Dr Gopal Das Nag, Priya Ranjan Dasmunsi, Prafulla Kanti

---

[50]Vasant Sathe originally belonged to this group but because of his strong pro-Indira stance, the group discarded him.

Ghosh and Siddhartha Shankar Ray. That said, I was rebuffed by almost everyone except Dr Nag and Arun Maitra.

It was time for the election of the Pradesh (state) Congress Committee (PCC) President as Arun Maitra had resigned, owning responsibility for the party's debacle in the assembly elections. Maitra, however, could not be held responsible as he had to contend with infighting by Dasmunsi and others. I was not very close to Maitra back then but had great respect for him. A perfect gentleman, with a strong sense of duty, he became a victim of group politics. After Maitra resigned, Abdur Rauf Ansari took over as interim President. *The Statesman* (Calcutta, 7 July 1977) reported:

> Elections are soon to be held to elect a President of the West Bengal Pradesh Congress Committee to replace Mr Arun Maitra who has resigned. The central leadership of the Congress party has agreed to hold an election rather than nominate or impose him from above, Priya Ranjan Dasmunsi said here today. Dasmunsi said he had talks in this connection with the Congress President K. Brahmananda Reddy, the General Secretary K.C. Pant, and the Leader of the Opposition Y.B. Chavan. They all agreed that there should be an election and that no ad hoc committee should be appointed.
>
> Our Siliguri staff correspondent writes: Arun Maitra told reporters here today that he, too, would like to see his successor elected rather than be chosen through a 'staged' consensus. Only if there was an election the unit would be able to defeat a move by 'Pro-Sanjay Gandhi elements' to capture the State party apparatus, he said.
>
> Maitra said that the word 'unanimity' had lost meaning because of infighting. He felt that the State Congress would

not be acceptable to the people of West Bengal unless it was purged of 'Pro-Sanjay elements'.

Maitra said that the Congress had suffered reverses in the Assembly elections because of the 'forcible inclusion' of several Pro-Sanjay stalwarts in the party's list of candidates. It is learned that Sanjay Gandhi's supporters want Abdus Sattar, MLA, as President of the State unit. Their opponents prefer Purabi Mukherjee, a General Secretary (former) of the AICC. The new PCC President will be elected by the end of this month.

Barkat and I took the lead in consolidating pro-Indira elements. As I have already mentioned, the grouping was along the old lines of 'pro-changers' and 'no-changers', with the difference being that the pro-change group had been reduced in strength. I had the support of Nurul Islam, Ananda Mohan Biswas, Gobinda Naskar, Somen Mitra, Debaprasad Roy (Mithu) and Birendra Mohanty, besides Barkat. In fact, this was the nucleus which formed the Congress (I) in the days to come.

We took up the challenge with all seriousness and, on 8 July, met to work out a strategy to ensure that Abdus Sattar got the support of the majority of PCC members. I knew there was no way out except to resort to a show of strength. We decided to travel to the districts and contact PCC members personally. Each person in our group was allocated specific districts, and it was decided that Barkat, Sattar and I should visit as many districts as possible. There was no other way to deal with the opposing group which was determined to eliminate us politically.

The election was fixed for 12 August 1977, at Laha House in central Calcutta, with K.C. Pant, AICC General Secretary, as the observer. Somen Mitra had put up a huge banner on Amherst Street ('No Indira, No Congress') and garnered media attention. However, our efforts did not yield the desired result. Abdus Sattar was defeated by Purabi Mukherjee by a margin of 60 votes.

I was dejected. Some of the district leaders we had counted heavily on had let us down. All the heavyweights of the West Bengal Congress—Siddhartha Shankar Ray, D.P. Chattopadhyaya, Dasmunsi, Subrata Mukherjee—had worked hard for Purabi Mukherjee. And Subrata Mukherjee's switchover to the Purabi Mukherjee camp tilted the balance in her favour. Barkat and the others came to my room at Nizam Palace that night, entirely downcast. I told them that we needed to prepare ourselves for the worst in the coming months. I knew that a long and tortuous winter was awaiting us with hardly any ray of light in the all-encompassing darkness.

The general body of the West Bengal Congress met the following day, and I put in a brief appearance to formally congratulate Purabi Mukherjee. I left Calcutta for Delhi the same day, en route attending two Independence day celebrations at Asansol organized by some trade unions. The evening radio bulletin broadcast the news of the arrest of R.K. Dhawan, Yashpal Kapoor and others. I smiled. The famous words of Mr Micawber from Dickens's *David Copperfield* echoed in my mind: 'The die is cast—all is over.' No occasion for tears or trepidation; I needed all my strength to fight back.

■

On 3 October 1977, the CBI arrested Indira Gandhi from her residence at 12 Willingdon Crescent. I was at home when I got the news from a United News of India correspondent that Indira Gandhi, along with K.D. Malaviya, H.R. Gokhale, P.C. Sethi and D.P. Chattopadhyaya, had been arrested. The correspondent told me that I, too, was likely to be arrested. I requested a friend (who was visiting) to go fetch my wife, Geeta, who had gone out to watch a movie. And then I waited on the lawn with my pipe, tobacco, matchbox and a small suitcase. I decided I would not apply for bail, and prepared myself for an indefinite stay in jail. Geeta came back and together, we waited for the police, but nobody came. After about 11 p.m., I told Geeta that instead of waiting for the police, we could go to Indira Gandhi's residence and find out what was happening there. We left a note with our servant in case the police came looking for us—that we would be at 12 Willingdon Crescent.

At Indira Gandhi's residence, we found several people, but not Sanjay and Rajiv Gandhi. Sanjay Gandhi came in later, and was surprised to see me. He had been told that the police had already picked me up. I heard from him the details of Indira Gandhi's arrest, and then we talked about making arrangements for the next day. I returned home at 2 a.m., only to go back to 12 Willingdon Crescent a few hours later. The area had now been cordoned off, and it required a fair amount of coaxing for me to be allowed in. Having met the others inside, Vasant Sathe and I left for Police Lines, where we were told that Indira Gandhi had been taken to court. We headed there, making our way past numerous groups of pro- and anti-Indira demonstrators. The anti-Indira rallies were mostly Janata Party demonstrations against her. 'Hang her!' they shouted. Some of their slogans were in very bad taste. The pro-Indira demonstrators, on the other hand, were shouting slogans against the high-handedness of the Janata government and the politically motivated arrest of Indira Gandhi.

The courtroom was crowded and we would not have made it inside without police help. Indira Gandhi stood in the dock, a Shantiniketan bag hanging from her shoulder. She saw me and asked, 'How come you are here?' I told her what had happened.

A few minutes later, the judge, R. Dayal, delivered his judgement and she was honourably acquitted. We returned to her residence, which was now surrounded by Seva Dal volunteers distributing sweets. Inside, too, there was a crowd: Kamalapati Tripathi and Brahmananda Reddy were among the senior Congress leaders present; foreign and Indian correspondents waited to chat with Indira Gandhi. After spending some time with them, she climbed up a ladder to the terrace, where a microphone had been fixed for her to address the rapidly increasing crowd outside. The crowd chased away author and journalist Uma Vasudev (who had written *Two Faces of Indira Gandhi* just after the Emergency). Purabi Mukherjee came but nobody paid much attention to her.

Officially, the Congress organization reacted strongly to Indira Gandhi's arrest. When the news broke, Brahmananda Reddy hastened to her residence and waited there till she was taken away by the police. Y.B. Chavan, who was out of town, rushed back to Delhi to strongly condemn the Janata Party's action as vindictive. The same night, an urgent meeting of the CWC was convened and a resolution (see Appendix 11) was passed condemning her arrest and that of four other Congress leaders.

The following day (4 October) the CWC met again. At the outset, K.C. Pant, General Secretary, reported the spontaneous but peaceful demonstrations being held throughout the country, despite the unprovoked and ruthless attacks by the police and hirelings of the Janata Party, and the subsequent arrest of scores of Congress workers. Another resolution was passed condemning these arrests, urging Congressmen to build up a resistance movement peacefully throughout the nation (see Appendix 12). The reaction of common Congress workers was spontaneous and angry, but determined.

Notably, however, a section of the leadership kept absolutely quiet regarding the arrest. The media and most opposition parties gave full support to the Janata government's decision, the only exception being S.A. Dange, a veteran leader of India's communist movement, who spoke against the Janata Party's vindictive attitude towards Indira Gandhi and reminded the people of her anti-imperialist role in the past.

■

The arrest was full of drama. The police came at 3 p.m., without a proper warrant. They produced one only when this was pointed out to them. In the meantime, uniformed as well as plainclothes policemen surrounded the house. Maneka Gandhi contacted as many people as she could (her phone had been spared from being disconnected), and a large number of Congressmen and leaders assembled at 12 Willingdon Crescent. The lawyers—who had a previously scheduled appointment with Indira Gandhi for 3 p.m. that day—got into an argument with the CBI's N.K. Singh. The drama notwithstanding, Indira Gandhi was taken away late that evening, but not before she made a brief statement to the press that the arrest was politically motivated. While Sanjay Gandhi did not react, Rajiv Gandhi's reaction was sharp. He pointed out that the Janata Party government was unlikely to have anything against Indira Gandhi, aside from some flimsy charges of 'illegal connivance' to secure some jeeps for the party.

Indira Gandhi was followed by her lawyers, a group of loyalists and family members—Rajiv, Sonia, Sanjay and Maneka Gandhi. It was decided that Nirmala Deshpande would accompany her into custody. The police wanted to take her to the Badkhal Lake guest house in Haryana. When the convoy stopped at a level crossing near Faridabad, Sector II, Indira Gandhi stepped out and sat on a culvert. Her lawyers argued with the police personnel that taking the 'prisoner' outside the city's territorial jurisdiction was not legally tenable. The police had to concede to this legal obligation, and took her back to Police Lines in Old Delhi.

The wayside drama was reported by some newspapers in Delhi the following day. A correspondent of *The Patriot* who followed her convoy got to interview Indira Gandhi as she sat on the culvert. On 4 October 1977, *The Patriot* reported:

> On her way to detention Indira Gandhi forecast the imminent fall of the present government. 'The government which fears [political opponents] cannot govern the country,' Mrs Gandhi added. Asked what she thought could be the immediate provocation for the Janata government to arrest her, Mrs Gandhi said, 'I think my visits to Agra and Kanpur...'
>
> Q. How did the CBI officials come to you and why? What were you doing then?
> Mrs Gandhi: It was about 3 p.m. I had an appointment with some lawyers... But I asked them to wait for a few moments.
>
> Q. What sort of harassment did you undergo during the past few months?
> Mrs Gandhi: You know they have been preventing people from meeting me. I did not get my mail... During the last few days they did all that they could [to] wreck my nerves. But I can tell you they could not succeed. My nerves are as strong as they had always been.
>
> Q. How are you feeling now?
> Mrs Gandhi: I am feeling perfectly all right.
>
> Q. What are the charges levelled against you?
> Mrs Gandhi (with an air of disgust): Some corruption charges in connection with jeeps, I think.

Newspaper reports indicated that the Janata Party had a difference of opinion regarding the arrest of Indira Gandhi. On the same day, that is, 4 October, *The Patriot* published a report headlined 'Janata Rift Over Arrest', and it read:

> The decision to arrest Mrs Gandhi was taken late on Sunday night by top leaders of the Janata Party. The faction led by Prime Minister Morarji Desai, Home Minister Charan Singh and members of the erstwhile Jana Sangh were able to prevail over the others on this issue.
>
> Discussion on whether or not to arrest Mrs Gandhi had been on ever since 25 September when a letter written by Mr Jayaprakash Narayan was received by party chief Chandra Shekhar. Mr Narayan had reportedly painted an alarming picture of the situation developing in the country—the growing unrest among the people and the fact that Mrs Gandhi was out to take advantage of the situation. The letter prompted Chandra Shekhar to invite Home Minister Charan Singh to his house for dinner. The very next day, discussions continued for four hours, according to reliable sources. This was followed by a Cabinet meeting, but still no final decision could be taken.
>
> A dominant section in the Janata Party is reported to have sought Mrs Gandhi's arrest by 28 September. But the issue was put off again till Sunday night when the final go-ahead was issued to the CBI.
>
> According to sources, some top Janata Party leaders were unaware of the decision till Monday afternoon when the plainclothes men were posted and the CBI officials were prepared to go to Mrs Gandhi's residence. While CBI officials were haggling with Mrs Gandhi's supporters and legal advisors, a large number of Congressmen arrived at her residence.

I do not know the extent to which the report is correct, but when the 'arrest' ended in a fiasco, there was utter confusion within the Janata Party. Many of them blamed Charan Singh and held him responsible. This action had serious repercussions within the Janata Party, and its government lost face, crucially with the masses. It not only reflected the vindictiveness of the Janata Party government but also proved its utter inefficiency and casual attitude towards administration. A joke doing the rounds in those days was: 'Look at the competence of this government. A woman who had put a few hundred leaders in jail for nineteen months could not be put behind bars by them even for nineteen hours.'

It was also rumoured in Delhi that Justice Shah expressed annoyance over the arrest and wanted to tender his resignation but was prevailed upon by the Prime Minister not to do so. But on our part, we needed to focus on the difficult task at hand. Indira Gandhi was to face significant challenges in the months ahead, within her party and outside, and we prepared ourselves to deal with them.

The initial reaction of the CWC, as I have stated before, was correct, but when they saw the sympathetic and spontaneous reaction within the rank and file of the Congress against Indira Gandhi's arrest, they started dragging their feet. Rather than strengthening her position, the then Congress leadership was more interested in ensuring that she disappeared into oblivion. The mass euphoria, wherever she went, not only unnerved the Janata Party leaders but also had a similar effect on those within the Congress. Congress President Brahmananda Reddy, though a good soul and personally loyal to Indira Gandhi, could not muster sufficient courage to overcome the influence of anti-Indira elements in the party. They took the usual stand that she had not dissociated herself from the 'caucus' and she was guided by them.

The AICC session subsequently called to condemn the repression by the Janata Party government instead turned into a forum for condemning Indira Gandhi. Even a senior leader like Swaran Singh joined her critics in the open session. K.P. Unnikrishnan called her a 'Bourbon' monarch who refused to learn lessons from history. A host of speakers were handpicked by the President to attack Indira Gandhi and the so-called Emergency excesses, as allegedly revealed by the findings of the Shah Commission.[51] Many of us were denied a chance to speak at the AICC meeting. While I was unsuccessful all the three times I tried, Sathe did get the chance, and spoke forcefully and effectively to expose the 'sycophants of yesterday turned rebels of today'. But he was alone. Outnumbered.

However, it is not as if Indira Gandhi was bereft of supporters. When C. Subramaniam rose to speak, a large number of AICC members protested against him for his evidence before the Shah Commission. While deposing before the Commission on 1 October, Subramaniam had blamed Indira Gandhi and had said that he had made some appointments to the RBI and other banks on her instructions. Subramaniam could not complete his speech, as slogans and counter-slogans were raised for and against Indira Gandhi. The tone of the meeting was totally against the spirit of the formal resolution. It seemed to me that perhaps the speakers did not read the resolution or deliberately utilized the forum to propagate their anti-Indira stance. Indira Gandhi came to the meeting in the evening and spoke dispassionately, ignoring all insinuations and insults. She reminded the Congress members of their future tasks.

---

[51]The Commission had started its inquiry from the last week of September and, as discussed earlier in this book, about half a dozen former ministers passed the buck on to Indira Gandhi, pleading their innocence while deposing before the Commission.

We were utterly disappointed with the outcome. I had sincerely hoped that the leadership would rise to the occasion and take this opportunity to bury the hatchet. The surge of emotion building up around Indira Gandhi and her humiliating arrest was played down by the leadership which thought it best to let her fight her own battles. Not a word was uttered against the ministers who shamelessly shirked their responsibilities before the Shah Commission, and no decision was taken on how to deal with such politically motivated commissions.

A.R. Antulay, Bhagwat Jha Azad, Vasant Sathe, B.P. Maurya, A.P. Sharma, Buta Singh, Kalpnath Rai, a few others and I started meeting frequently at Antulay's residence. We were working on a strategy to overcome the impasse, and discussed these with Indira Gandhi and Kamalapati Tripathi regularly. It was decided that we should contact grass-root Congress workers so as to ascertain their views. Indira Gandhi had re-established her hold over the masses substantially and we had to see to what extent the Congress rank and file could be mobilized. We had detailed talks with state-level leaders, getting the support of most from North India, particularly those from Uttar Pradesh, Bihar, Madhya Pradesh and Rajasthan.[52]

It was our conviction that the Congress organization could

---

[52]Prominent among them were N.D. Tiwari, Mohsina Kidwai, Rajendra Kumari Bajpai, Virendra Verma, Shyamlal Yadav (UP); Kedar Pandey, Jagannath Mishra, Pratibha Singh (Bihar); J.B. Patnaik and Ramchandra Rath (Orissa); Jagannath Pahadia, Nawal Kishore Sharma, G.L. Vyas (Rajasthan); H.K.L. Bhagat, Radha Raman (Delhi); Sultan Singh, Dalbir Singh (Haryana); Zail Singh, Darbara Singh (Punjab); Ram Lal (Himachal Pradesh); Krishan Pal Singh (Madhya Pradesh); Saroj Khaparde (Maharashtra); Chandrasekar, G.K. Moopanar, Nedumaran, Ramamurthi (Tamil Nadu); the entire leadership of Karnataka (except the group of K.H. Patil); P.V. Narasimha Rao, G. Venkat Swamy, Janardhana Reddy (Andhra Pradesh); Anwara Taimur, Bishnu Prasad (Assam); Ashok Bhattacharya (Tripura); Madhav Singh Solanki, Yogendra Makwana, Ratubhai Adani, Jinabhai Darji, Sanat Mehta (Gujarat); and Barkat, Sattar, Somen, Narul, Ananda and Gobinda (West Bengal).

not be made dynamic without a change in leadership. After the AICC session of October 1977, the leadership had made it abundantly clear to us (through a series of measures adopted by it) that it was more interested in distancing itself from the past. It was thus decided that we should try to organize a show of strength by sending a notice of requisition for an AICC meeting. Arrangements were made to collect signatures from AICC members. We also decided that we should speak out and express our views about what was going on in the organization.

I addressed the media in Calcutta where I disclosed that seventeen signatures had been secured for the requisition notice and that it was more than what we had expected. In order to avoid any 'hide and seek' which some people were prone to do, I disclosed the names of the signatories: A.B.A. Ghani Khan Choudhury, Abdus Sattar, Kazi Abdul Gafoor, Ajit Kumar Panja, K. Sheikh Daulat Ali, Shanti Mohan Roy, Ananda Mohan Biswas, Gobinda Naskar, Sunil Mandal, Suhas Dutta Roy, Raj Kumar Mishra, Ajit Banerjee, Tuhin Samanta, A.K.M. Ishaque, Fazle Haque, Gautam Chakravarty and Pranab Mukherjee.

The *Amrita Bazar Patrika* (Calcutta, 25 October) reported:

Pranab Mukherjee, leader of the pro-Indira group in West Bengal claimed in Calcutta on Monday that he had received signatures from 18 [sic] out of the 51 AICC members demanding for a requisitioned meeting of the All India Congress Committee to install Mrs Indira Gandhi as its President in place of Brahmananda Reddy. Mr Mukherjee said the pro-requisitionists are in a majority in AICC but in West Bengal, of course, they were in a minority. However, he was talking to various leaders in the State and he hoped that some who were yet to make up their mind might join them at the last moment.

The former Union Minister, Mr Mukherjee who is said to be very close to Mrs Gandhi was very frank in expressing this opinion. He said, 'Mrs Gandhi is indispensable for the Congress organization. Those Congress leaders who are publicly humiliating Mrs Gandhi [and] issuing statements against her are directly responsible for the split in the Congress Party. We do not want a split. We want unity under the effective leadership of Mrs Gandhi who had given a remarkable leadership during the last twelve years. We need her very much, particularly at this moment when the party is in deep crisis.'

Mr Mukherjee is leaving for a meeting of requisitionists to be held at the residence of Kamalapati Tripathi in Delhi. The number of signatures received in favour of the requisitioned meeting will be known at that meeting and it will be decided when they are going to present the list demanding for the meeting....

Asked whether they had approached Mr Siddhartha Shankar Ray, Mr Mukherjee said he did not want him to join their group. Another leader of the pro-Indira group in West Bengal, Nurul Islam, said that, 'Even if he wants to join our camp we will not welcome him because he is a doubtful character in Indian politics.' Mr Mukherjee said that he also contacted Mr Debi Prasad Chattopadhyay, a former Union Minister, but the latter refused to give his signature in favour of their move. Subrata Mukherjee also refused to be associated with them.

The anti-requisitionists were also active. A day after my media interaction, Subrata Mukherjee made a statement that he would go to Burdwan to prevail upon Tuhin Samanta to withdraw his signature. In fact, some of the signatories like Tuhin Samanta,

Ajit Banerjee and Sunil Mandal did ultimately back out.

Madhu Limaye, the General Secretary of the Janata Party, wrote a letter to Brahmananda Reddy, warning him about the 'designs' of Indira Gandhi and her 'caucus' to oust him as Party President and capture the organization. He also suggested that the Congress might gain credibility if the leadership could come out of the clutches of Indira Gandhi and her coterie. This letter caused a lot of embarrassment for the Congress leadership. Grass-roots Congressmen were stunned at the audacity that prompted an outsider to interfere with the internal affairs of a party. To save face, some Congress leaders openly criticized Madhu Limaye's letter. Purabi Mukherjee, the then President of the West Bengal Pradesh Congress Committee, observed that the letter was uncalled for. She said, 'Our fight is our internal affair. Janata Party is a separate political organization. Why should we take advice from another political party? We do not want it. He has no business to write a letter about our internal affairs.'[53] Her reaction was not supported by the attitude of the senior leaders of the party.

■

Since October, the crisis in Karnataka had deepened with K.H. Patil (state Party President) on one side and Devaraj Urs on another. The official group was prepared to support Devaraj Urs provided he ditched Indira Gandhi. Devaraj Urs suspected that with the help of K.H. Patil, who later caused defections in the legislature party, the Janata Party government at the centre would dismiss his ministry. He knew that once he was out of office, the central leaders would ditch him. The central government had

---

[53]As quoted in *Amrita Bazar Patrika*, 25 October.

already appointed a commission under Justice Grover to look into allegations against him and his government. It is in this context that he understood that Indira Gandhi was his key to success in the elections, as she alone could draw people's support to the Congress. Being a shrewd politician, he realized that her influence over the people in his state, particularly among the women and the weaker sections, was tremendous. In the ensuing elections, Indira Gandhi would be the star attraction and without her help, electoral success was impossible. Consequently, he went about organizing Indira Gandhi's visits in Karnataka. These rallies pulled huge crowds, though they were almost invariably disturbed by a small group of demonstrators generally organized by the Janata Party. The differences between Patil and Urs resulted in a tussle for chief ministership. Gundu Rao, F.M. Khan and a couple of other strong supporters of Indira Gandhi sided with Urs.

The CWC wanted to solve the problem and worked out a 5-point formula at its meeting held on 6 December 1977. Y.B. Chavan and Kamalapati Tripathi, two members of the CWC, were entrusted with the task of talking to both Patil and Urs, and getting them to accept the following formula:

1.  K.H. Patil will continue as President of the Karnataka Pradesh Congress Committee.
2.  Devaraj Urs will be made a Permanent Invitee of the Congress Working Committee and the Central Election Committee, even if the Ministry is dismissed or the assembly is dissolved and he does not remain Chief Minister.
3.  A Pradesh Election Committee will be appointed by the AICC, giving weightage to Devaraj Urs by giving him [a] majority of one.
4.  The Congress Working Committee will appoint a representative to attend the Pradesh Election Committee meeting for

coordinating and smooth functioning of the committee.

5. All disciplinary action taken and disciplinary proceedings initiated by the PCC President K.H. Patil, including suspension of [the] committee, will be reviewed by the AICC to create a better atmosphere of understanding in the State so that the party can present a united image to confidently face the electorate in the coming assembly elections.

This formula did not work, however. On 10 December, Y.B. Chavan and Kamalapati Tripathi, entrusted with the job of negotiating with Patil and Urs, reported to the CWC that they had failed to work out a rapprochement between the two warring camps in the Karnataka Congress. Chavan reported that Devaraj Urs did not even meet him. The CWC left the matter at that.

Meanwhile, K.H. Patil engineered a defection in the legislature party and urged the Governor to dismiss the Urs government on the grounds of losing majority. Asked by the Governor to show his majority, Urs convened the assembly session. However, two days before the session, the ministry was dismissed and the assembly dissolved.

The Karnataka debacle was one of many issues which ultimately led to the split in the Congress. This is not to forget that long before this event, seeds of the split were sown by systematic campaigns against Indira Gandhi.

# CHAPTER SEVEN

# TOWARDS THE SECOND SPLIT

We know that Brahmananda Reddy, elected Congress President with Indira Gandhi's blessings, had turned against her. Soon after his election as the Party President, the anti-Indira brigade started working on Reddy and succeeded in weaning him away from her.[54] It was made amply clear that she was 'unwanted' in all Congress campaigns before the assembly elections. While Kamalapati Tripathi announced that she would campaign for the Congress, General Secretary K.C. Pant had declared that she would not. 'She will not campaign,' he told reporters categorically. Asked whether she would issue an appeal to the electorate, Pant brushed the question aside with an indifferent 'I don't know'. At a press conference, Brahmananda Reddy declared that the party manifesto had not been cleared by Indira Gandhi; in fact, she hadn't even been shown the text, he said.

She was not consulted about the presidential candidate either. The Janata Party had recommended the name of N. Sanjiva Reddy, and Y.B. Chavan and Brahmananda Reddy had approved

---

[54]Janardan Thakur, *Indira Gandhi and Her Power Game* (New Delhi, 1979), p. 26.

it on behalf of the Congress. We were all taken by surprise but there was nothing we could do. The Janata Party continued to abuse Indira Gandhi, her family and her supporters.

On 28 May, a notification appointing a commission of inquiry to look into the Emergency excesses was issued. Home Minister Charan Singh declared that Indira Gandhi's 'crimes' deserved a trial of the nature of Nuremberg. On 13 July, he told the Lok Sabha that there was a covert intention (vichar) on the part of the previous government to shoot political leaders in detention. Such reckless statements were made every day without any evidence or substantiation. Vasant Sathe protested sharply against such irresponsible statements. Indira Gandhi refuted them. But the Congress, with 154 members in the Lok Sabha, and more than two-third members in the Rajya Sabha, remained largely noncommittal in response to such statements.

Indira Gandhi decided to come out in the open. All of us (Maurya, Sathe, Antulay, Tripathi and myself) requested her to meet people. Indira Gandhi had an excellent sense of timing and place. She started her tour from Vinoba Bhave's ashram in Paunar in July 1977, and was received by enthusiastic crowds on the way from Nagpur to Paunar. Vinobaji blessed her with the cryptic remark, 'Chalte raho.' This immediately became the war cry of Congressmen: 'Indira Gandhi aage badho, hum tumhare saath hain (Indira Gandhi march ahead, we are with you).'

As I have mentioned earlier, the people's response scared her detractors and they sharpened their attack against her. The CPP became a forum to vilify her. Even her attendance at small social gatherings drew adverse remarks from a section of Congress leaders and the press. A simple dinner for MPs, organized by Devaraj Urs at Karnataka Bhawan and attended by Indira Gandhi, came to be termed as Indira Gandhi's 'dinner diplomacy'. Journalist Nikhil Chakravartty observed, 'The cat was on the prowl—out to gobble up as much of the Congress as possible.'[55] About a hundred MPs who were assembled at the residence of Dr V.A. Seyid Muhammad (Minister of State for Law, Justice and Company Affairs during the Emergency) deplored the 'pernicious trend of inner get-togethers in the cause of Smt. Gandhi'[56] and declared that 'collective leadership does not mean a collection of three or four… It meant revitalization of all the committees from village level to parliamentary board.'[57] Most of these leaders who ranted against Indira Gandhi and her so-called 'caucus' belonged to a group of MPs known as the 'Thursday Club', of which mention has been made before. All of them were backbenchers at that time, but they served as useful instruments for senior leaders to hit out at Indira Gandhi. Most of them did a volte-face when she came back to power and some of them were even rewarded with offices—junior ministerships, diplomatic assignments and nominations to the Rajya Sabha.

By this time, the news of the Belchi massacre had come in. Eleven harijans had been burnt to death by kurmis (or rich farmers) in Belchi, a small village in Bihar's Nalanda district. The chilling incident had hit national headlines, but it failed to perturb the Congress high command. There was an announcement that the leader of the opposition, Y.B. Chavan, would visit the district. But the Congress failed to attack the government effectively on this issue.

The question came from Indira Gandhi: 'How is it that with the Janata Party coming to power, atrocities on harijans and minorities have increased?' The place was inaccessible but she was undaunted. Accompanied by Pratibha Singh, Saroj Khaparde, Jagannath Mishra, Kedar Pandey and a few others, she reached

---

[55] *Mainstream*, 30 July 1977.
[56] *The Statesman*, 5 August 1977.
[57] Ibid.

the site. Janardan Thakur, author and a bitter critic, described her journey to Belchi, though not without a pinch of sarcasm in his book:

'No lunch, let us leave,' said Smt. Gandhi firmly. 'The route is very bad,' mumbled Kedar Pandey. 'No cars can reach Belchi.' Not to be deterred, Smt. Gandhi said, 'We shall go walking, we shall go there even if it takes us all night.'

The motorcade moved through the lanes of Bihar Sharif, and when it stopped everybody was scampering out after her. It was the Bari Dargah which has a tomb of Hazrat Sheikh Sharfuddin Yahya Maneri. She had been told that if one prays at this dargah one gets whatever one asks for. She prayed, her eyes closed.

Some miles out of the town, the road petered out into a muddy track. The road to Belchi had begun. Smt. Gandhi's jeep got stuck in the mud and a tractor was brought to pull it out.

Even the tractor got stuck. 'There ends the trip to Belchi', quipped a TV cameraman. [The author made a mistake by attributing this quote to a TV cameraman. Indira Gandhi had already been blacked out by TV and radio.] But Smt. Gandhi was out of the jeep, walking through the mud, followed by her cheerleaders. 'She can't go very far like that,' said a Congress leader, frightened by the prospect of walking all the way to Belchi. 'They say you have to wade through waist-deep water,' he said and sunk back to be in the comfort of his car.

Smt. Gandhi was still marching on, her saree raised above her ankle. 'Of course, I can wade though water,' she was telling her frightened companion, Pratibha Singh. It was getting tougher every minute, but a thoughtful Babu Saheb of the area had sent his elephant to carry the lady to Belchi.

'But how will you climb the elephant?' Kedar Pandey and others asked anxiously. 'Of course, I will,' she told them impatiently. 'This is not the first time I have ridden an elephant.' Next moment she was sitting pretty atop the animal. But Pratibha was all nervous as she climbed, virtually clinging to Smt. Gandhi from behind as the tusker heaved up. A delighted cameraman burst into 'Long live Indira Gandhi.' And Indira Gandhi smiled back at him.

From where she got off the jeep, it was three and a half hours to Belchi. But she made it purely by her grit and determination and was hailed as saviour of the harijans. Who could imagine a Y.B. Chavan or a Brahmananda Reddy or any of those leaders doing what she had done. Around midnight on her way back from Belchi, Smt. Gandhi was delivering a speech at a roadside college.[58]

The next morning, she met JP at his Kadam Kuan residence. She looked relaxed and rested and everyone who knew what she had been through the previous night was surprised. They spoke for about an hour and JP came out to see her off. His good wishes to her for 'a bright future, brighter than the bright past she had had' created a furore. The event triggered a deluge of interpretations. A section of the press and political leaders doubted the authenticity of this remark and contended that it was a story manufactured by her to brighten her image. Some Janata Party leaders suo motu denied that any such remark had been made. Only Indira Gandhi and JP remained unruffled. In their vehement anti-Indira obsession, her detractors forgot that despite bitterness and differences, JP was a great family friend of the Nehrus and that Indira Gandhi had profound respect for him.

In Patna, Indira Gandhi addressed a big gathering at

---

[58] Janardan Thakur, *Indira Gandhi and Her Power Game* (New Delhi, 1979), pp. 33-34.

*Indira Gandhi with Rajiv Gandhi, Sanjay Gandhi and*
*Sonia Gandhi, in February 1968.*

*Sheikh Mujibur Rahman talking to local and foreign journalists at his residence, in January 1972.*

*Minister of Industrial Development C. Subramaniam addressing a meeting of the Paper and Pulp Industry in New Delhi on 18 September 1973. Pranab Mukherjee, then Deputy Minister of Shipping and Transport, is also seen.*

*Swearing-in ceremony, 1973.*

*Swearing-in ceremony, 1974.*

*Pranab Mukherjee and Y.B. Chavan
with the UN Secretary General Kurt Waldheim.*

*Pranab Mukherjee, then Minister of State for Finance, inaugurating the Regional Provident Fund Commissioner's Conference in New Delhi on 26 May 1975.*

*Contraband goods worth Rs 10 lakh seized in Calcutta on 27 August 1975. The photograph shows packages of ganja and other contraband goods stacked in the Calcutta Customs' godown.*

*Indira Gandhi seen with Sanjay Gandhi,*
*Defence Minister Bansi Lal and others.*

*Pranab Mukherjee, the then Minister of State for Finance, addressing the conference of income tax commissioners in New Delhi on 9 May 1976.*

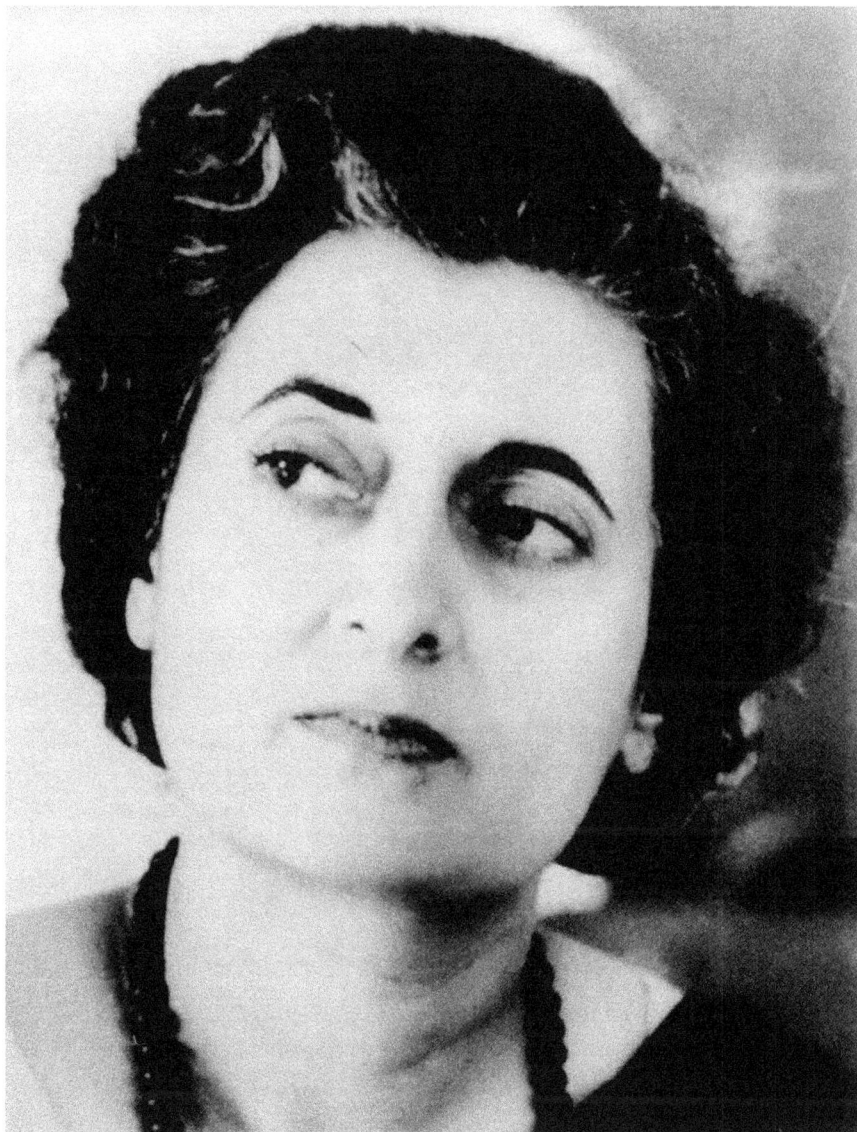

*Indira  Gandhi*

*Pranab Mukherjee, the then Minister of State (in charge) of the Department of Revenue and Banking, addressing a meeting of bank executives in New Delhi on 21 January 1977.*

*President Neelam Sanjiva Reddy and Pranab Mukherjee as Steel Minister.*

*Swearing-in ceremony, 14 January 1980.*

*Swearing-in ceremony, 14 January 1980.*

*Kamalapati Tripathi, P.V. Narasimha Rao, Pranab Mukherjee,*
*J.B. Patnaik and B. Shankaranand at the swearing-in ceremony.*

*Pranab Mukherjee, Union Minister of Commerce, and Metod Rotear, Foreign Trade Minister of Yugoslavia, signing the economic agreement in the presence of Prime Minister Indira Gandhi and H.E. Veselin Djuranovic, President of the Federal Executive Council of the Socialist Federal Republic of Yugoslavia, in New Delhi on 26 September 1980.*

*Pranab Mukherjee, then Union Minister of Commerce, inaugurating a workshop on Export Promotion in New Delhi on 9 October 1980.*

*Pranab Mukherjee with Neelam Sanjiva Reddy and Indira Gandhi.*

Sadaquat Ashram, the state Congress headquarters. Chavan and Brahmananda Reddy had addressed a gathering there a few days earlier. That had been big, but no match for the crowd that had gathered to listen to Indira Gandhi.

Thereafter she went to Haridwar. Here she was accompanied by B.P. Maurya, Vasant Sathe and a few others. At every important place en route she received a warm welcome from big crowds. There were organized demonstrations against her in some pockets, particularly where Jat leader Charan Singh was powerful, but the warmth and enthusiasm outweighed all acrimony. She addressed big gatherings at Modi Nagar, Meerut and Muzaffarnagar. Later she told me that the response of the crowd was not only cordial and friendly but also very warm. Sanjay Gandhi, too, was received warmly everywhere and people were more than eager to see him. The adverse media publicity and abuse by Janata Party leaders had earned him sympathy which became apparent during this tour. He and his mother came to be regarded as victims of the conqueror. It also became clear that his boys would never leave him and, in times to come, Sanjay Gandhi's boys became the cornerstone of our new movement.

However, the plan to isolate Indira Gandhi continued: her close supporters were still branded as the 'caucus' and condemned. Though Sanjay Gandhi was helping us, he was behind the scenes and had declared publicly that he had resigned from the Congress. Despite her many clarifications, Indira Gandhi's detractors never missed an opportunity to allege that she was encircled by this 'caucus' and that everything she did was at its prompting. The contention did not contain a grain of truth. None of the leaders who were active during the Emergency were ready to launch such a movement. Except for me, none of the organizers were even summoned by the commission set up to enquire into the Emergency. Prominent leaders of this group like Vasant Sathe, A.R. Antulay, Bhagwant Jha Azad, B.P. Maurya, P.V. Narasimha Rao, Buta Singh, A.P. Sharma, Darbara Singh and M. Chandrasekar were not mentioned in any inquiry commission. And although Zail Singh, Dr Jagannath Mishra, Devaraj Urs and I continued to be summoned by various commissions, prominent leaders and activists during the Emergency, like Om Mehta, Bansi Lal, V.C. Shukla and Rukhsana Sultana, were nowhere near this group. 'Give a dog a bad name and hang it', goes the proverb.

Our campaign gathered momentum. Indira Gandhi met Brahmananda Reddy late one night and tried to work out a settlement. She pointed out that the Congress must not lie low and should not accept humiliation at the hands of the new rulers. From every corner of the country, news of torture and harassment of Congressmen was pouring in. Left to himself, Brahmananda Reddy was prepared to go by her advice. But more often than not, he lacked the strength to ward off pressure from the anti-Indira faction. He told the media that he was prepared to step down from Congress presidentship in favour of Indira Gandhi, a statement that was more than welcomed by Congress workers. A group of important Congressmen, including a large number of party MPs assembled at Karnataka Bhawan, passed a resolution urging the AICC to elect Indira Gandhi as the Congress President. The resolution also thanked Brahmananda Reddy for having 'agreed to step down in her favour'. But Reddy later clarified his position to *India Today* (15–31 January 1978): 'I was only being respectful and considerate to her feelings and I said I am prepared to consider stepping down if she asks me. But she never asks for anything herself. Never. She wants others to do everything for her.'

This resolution was bitterly thwarted by leaders opposed to Indira Gandhi. They started asserting that she was working for the second split in order to turn the party into an outfit for enthralled minions serving her personal interests. Most of the senior leaders, including Kamalapati Tripathi, Syed Mir Qasim and Azad were against a split. Kamalapati Tripathi clearly said that he would not leave Indira Gandhi's company and he would not break the party ('Main Congress nahin todunga, Indira Gandhi ka saath nahin chhodunga'). Vasant Sathe argued she was the star attraction as far as the people were concerned and she must be one of the important players, if not the captain. Azad told us sharply that we had no business destroying the party. Restoring Indira Gandhi to her proper place in the organization was important but not at the cost of a split. Antulay and I were all for the split. We were sure that the Congress could not be revived without a split. Devaraj Urs strongly backed us, though he had his own reasons, as we've seen earlier in the book.

Dr M. Chenna Reddy resigned as Governor of Uttar Pradesh and was prepared to support Indira Gandhi. But most chief ministers of the Congress were opposed to Indira Gandhi: A.K. Antony of Kerala, S.C. Sinha of Assam, Captain William Sangma of Meghalaya, Vengal Rao of Andhra Pradesh, and Vasantrao Patil of Maharashtra. They were opposed to any change in the office of the AICC President, or the idea of splitting the party for that matter. Senior leaders from our side were also eager to avoid any showdown.

We retreated, and Kamalapati Tripathi continued to work hard for unity. It was on his advice that Indira Gandhi met Brahmananda Reddy at his residence at midnight on 17-18 November 1977. On the evening of 18 November, there was another meeting at 12 Willingdon Crescent. Vasantrao Patil, Rajni Patel, Kamalapati Tripathi and a few others (including Antulay and I) were present. The meeting went on well beyond midnight. Just when the clock struck twelve, Rajni Patel picked a flower out of a flower arrangement on an adjacent table and handed it to Indira Gandhi, wishing her 'many happy returns'. It was 19 November, Indira Gandhi's birthday.

We had already worked out a 9-point charter as the compromise formula. Some of these points were: (*a*) Indira Gandhi should be consulted on all major issues; (*b*) the CWC and the Central Parliamentary Board should be reconstituted in consultation with Indira Gandhi; (*c*) disciplinary actions taken against members indiscriminately after the Lok Sabha elections should be suspended; (*d*) the party must effectively oppose the anti-people policies and actions of the ruling Janata Party, and so on.

At the late-night meeting of 18-19 November, Vasantrao Patil and Rajni Patel requested Indira Gandhi to exercise her good offices to overcome the impasse. They suggested that she should prevail upon the requisitionists to withdraw the requisition notice. We pointed out that we had accepted the collective leadership concept evolved at the AICC session held in May 1977 and we had expected that in this collective leadership Indira Gandhi would have a 'rightful' place. Collective leadership, for us, did not mean a combination of a handful few to exclude and isolate a 'leader' who commanded the largest following among the masses. We further pointed out that we were not focused on splitting the party. It was to avoid a split and find areas of agreement that Indira Gandhi visited the Congress President at his residence. We requested Vasantrao Patil and Rajni Patel to prevail upon the leadership to follow the correct path, but they did not give us any assurances. The issue of appearing before the Shah Commission and other commissions also came up for discussion. We pointed out that the party had failed to take any decision on this issue. It was imperative to fight the politically motivated commissions set up to malign the Congress and its leaders. Most of the ministers deposed against the decisions taken by their own government and passed the buck on to the former Prime Minister. The leadership failed to realize the looming danger of instability and the erosion of credibility of a government run by the oldest party in the country. Nothing moved them. We had no choice but to raise these issues at our meetings with Patil and Patel.

Our emissaries promised to take up these issues with the leadership but ultimately nothing happened. Two appeals were issued—one by Brahmananda Reddy and another by Indira Gandhi—for unity. We dropped the demand for requisition. At Kamalapati Tripathi's request, Antulay handed over all papers to him. But no initiative was taken by the leadership to settle the issues raised by us.

The CWC met on 5 December. This meeting was attended by Indira Gandhi. A few members, including A.P. Sharma, insisted that the Committee should take a view on the issue of appearance before the Shah Commission. This led the committee to pass the following resolution:

> The question of Congressmen appearing before the Shah Commission was discussed in all its aspects, including the legality of the appointment of the Commission and the procedures adopted by it. In the course of the discussions, members expressed the view that the legal aspects should be examined. If necessary, it should be raised in Parliament also.

We also wanted the CWC to take a uniform decision with regard to requests of the Shah Commission to Congressmen to appear before it. After the discussion, the committee took the following decision:

> The Congress Working Committee advises members of the Congress to appear before the Shah Commission only at the appropriate stage and in case summons are issued.

This delayed decision lacked political punch and most Congressmen appeared before the Shah Commission merely on 'request' rather than waiting for 'summons' to be issued. I was called twice by the Shah Commission to give evidence, first on 1 October 1977. On that day, I queried my being called without proper legal summons. This was based on the fact that I was a central minister, and all ministers are bound by the oath of secrecy not to divulge any information or matter which they arrived at in their capacity as ministers. I, too, had taken this oath when I had been sworn in as Minister of State for Finance. My question to the Shah Commission thus was that by giving evidence before them, was I not violating the oath of office as a minister? I then asked the Shah Commission to give its ruling in writing so that in case it deemed it appropriate for me to give evidence disregarding my oath as a minister, I could challenge it in the court of law. However, they refused to provide anything in writing, and Justice Shah simply said, 'You are not violating oath of office by disclosing facts before the Commission.' Hence, as I was not given anything in writing, I could not take recourse to the law.

On 19 November 1977, I was again called by the Shah Commission, now in connection with the detention of Maharani Gayatri Devi under the COFEPOSA Act. I raised my question again, and also asked why we could not get the assistance of legal counsel. In response, Justice Shah said, 'At this stage of the inquiry, when I am trying to find out your involvement in certain transactions, you are not prima facie guilty and in case found guilty, you will all get legal protection prescribed by the law at that stage. As of now, you have been asked to cooperate with me.' I then asked Justice Shah if such 'cooperation' was compulsory or optional, to which Justice Shah responded, 'You are free to cooperate or not. You are free to come and go.'

As a result, I chose not to cooperate.

This was the background for my refusal to provide evidence before the Shah Commission. It is for this refusal that Justice Shah prosecuted me under IPC 178-179.

Something similar occurred when Indira Gandhi was asked to appear before the Shah Commission on 22 November. Rather than go to the witness box, she made a full-fledged statement pointing to the lacunae in the functioning of the Shah Commission, and accused the government of setting it up as a tool of political persecution. She, too, was prosecuted under IPC 178-179, with a criminal case being filed in the magistrate's court.

A section of anti-Indira Congressmen criticized my action. However, my stand was vindicated when, in a subsequent case, Justice Chawla of the Delhi High Court upheld my contention and, till date, that judgement continues to prevail.

∎

We met again and reviewed the situation. It was decided that we should launch an offensive as the other side was simply not prepared to accommodate reason. Indira Gandhi had been directly insulted by Y.B. Chavan. When she said that her followers were persecuted in the party, Chavan retorted caustically that she herself had been running the party in Uttar Pradesh 'as a royal preserve'. In our informal group meetings attended by P.V. Narasimha Rao, Antulay, Kamalapati Tripathi, B.P. Maurya, Buta Singh, M. Chandrasekar, Bhagwat Jha Azad, Vasant Sathe and myself, Devaraj Urs argued very strongly in favour of a split. Most amongst us were not prepared for this because of a genuine apprehension that a split could destroy the party. The ideal case scenario would have been to try and take control of the party, but the success of such an effort was unlikely as it became increasingly clear that most of those once close to Indira Gandhi had actually deserted her. Out of the twenty-one (including invitees) members of the CWC, Indira Gandhi had the support of only five: Kamalapati Tripathi, P.V. Narasimha Rao, M. Chandrasekar, Buta Singh and A.P. Sharma.

The requisition move was dropped and it could not be revived again. Indira Gandhi resigned from the CWC and the Congress Parliamentary Board on 18 December. The reaction to this move was far from conciliatory; in fact it was rather hostile. A senior Congress member said (*The Statesman*, New Delhi, 20 December 1977): 'To say the least, we have mortgaged our souls to her for eleven years—many of us who are much senior to her in the organization.' Later, Brahmananda Reddy was reported to have stated in Hyderabad, 'She wanted us to fight, take to the streets and go to jail. We are not afraid of going to jail. We have been in jail for years while she has been to jail only for nine months... But have we to involve ourselves in a scuffle with Janata leaders? Or should we agitate to support Sanjay Gandhi, Bansi Lal or Yashpal Kapoor?' According to a report in *The Statesman* (New Delhi, 18 January 1978), Reddy observed that the organization had been 'brought down with the tipping of a twenty-seven-year-old lad as the future Prime Minister. *Vinash kale, vipreet buddhi* [At the hour of destruction, one loses the sense of judgement].' No one had to guess too hard to know the attitude of the Congress leadership towards Indira Gandhi in those days.

On 18 December, we formally met at Antulay's residence at 2 Janpath, New Delhi, and constituted a steering committee to hold a National Convention.

The committee constituted a total of seventy-two members, and while some people like F.M. Khan and Chaudhary Randhir Singh were unhappy about not being included, I was determined to avoid controversial names to the extent possible. We met almost every day. Buta Singh, H.K.L. Bhagat, Lalit Maken and Jagdish Tytler were responsible for arranging accommodation, pandals and food. Antulay, a few others and I were in charge overall. I drafted all resolutions in consultation with P.V. Narasimha Rao, Bhagwat Jha Azad, Maurya and Bihar's D.P. Singh. I was also entrusted with collecting funds. Devaraj Urs and a couple of others helped us. Everything was running smoothly. It was decided that invitation letters would be issued in the names of P.V. Narasimha Rao, Buta Singh, A.P. Sharma and M. Chandrasekar, all members of the CWC. Kamalapati Tripathi would preside, while Mir Qasim would inaugurate and Indira Gandhi would address the convention. The steering committee issued an appeal to all Congressmen across the country. It cited the reasons for such a convention.

CHAPTER EIGHT

# THE BIRTH OF CONGRESS (I)

The National Convention of Congressmen was held on the lawns of Vithalbhai Patel House in New Delhi on 1-2 January 1978. Driving to the venue with Indira Gandhi on the second day of the convention, our car was held up at Janpath due to a traffic block for the visiting US President, whose entourage was passing through. Indira Gandhi poignantly remarked that this was probably the first time she was not going to be present to felicitate a distinguished foreign visitor to India. While as the Prime Minister she had been at the forefront, she had also been Jawaharlal Nehru's official hostess during his tenure as Prime Minister.

More than five thousand delegates from across the country attended the convention and elected Indira Gandhi as the Congress President. The opening speech by Syed Mir Qasim, Indira Gandhi's introductory remarks and the political resolution adopted at the convention explained the reasons for the split as well as those for holding the convention.

Referring to the dismissal of the Karnataka government and the collusion at the behest of Congress President K. Brahmananda Reddy's faction of the Congress, Mir Qasim asked, 'Was this expected of Congressmen and was it democratic?' Criticizing the Janata Party government, he said:

> They talked of secularism but communal riots were happening. There was a feeling of insecurity among the minorities. Harijans had been deprived of their lands. There was general erosion of law and order. Regional and fissiparous tendencies were raising their heads. The Congress leadership was unresponsive to these burning issues. The reaction of the Congress Party in Parliament was not up to the expectations of the Congressmen in particular and the people in general. Even the Congress Working Committee was not allowed to play its effective role.

In her introductory remarks, Indira Gandhi dealt with the policies and programmes of the Janata Party government, pointing out how those policies were anti-people and retrograde. She said that the foremost impression one got was that of a 'drift'. No one knew in which direction the government was steering the nation. She emphasized that a meeting of the AICC should have been convened to discuss the problems facing the country, which had not been done. She also called for unity—that all of us were essentially Congressmen and should stay together in the Congress, which is why everyone had been invited to the convention (including Brahmananda Reddy). She said she was ready for action with the cooperation of those who had faith and conviction in the ideals of the Congress. She emphasized the need to rejuvenate the Congress organization so that it lived up to the expectations of Congressmen in particular and the people of India in general. The Congress, she felt, had to launch a peaceful movement to protect the Harijans and minorities who were being harassed and deprived of the benefits that had accrued to them during the previous Congress rule.

On the alleged mistakes committed by some individuals during the Emergency, Indira Gandhi said that she did not know what these mistakes were but they had no right to participate in Congress politics if they had incurred the wrath of the common masses. She also said it was necessary for those who believed in the well-settled left-of-centre policy to unite.

She strongly condemned Brahmananda Reddy for his action of suspending Devaraj Urs's Congress membership, as also for his role in effecting the dismissal of the Congress ministry in Karnataka, particularly when it was known that Urs's ouster would harm the Congress and help the Janata Party in that state.

On 2 January 1978, Indira Gandhi was elected President of the party, though she did not preside over the session on this occasion. It was a short resolution, handwritten by me, and which we had kept a close secret. The intention was to let the demand come spontaneously from the delegates themselves, instead of us moving a formal resolution for their approval. Our strategy worked rather well. A large number of delegates demanded that Indira Gandhi should take over the party leadership, and the resolution was welcomed with a deafening applause:

> The convention representing the Indian National Congress, in which a majority of the members of AICC are also present, in view of its being the truly representative convention of Indian National Congress and in order to provide effective leadership to meet the challenges before the nation and the Congress, unanimously elects Indira Gandhi as Congress President.

By the same resolution, she was authorized to take appropriate steps to organize the party at all levels.

It is possible for critics to doubt the authority of the convention to replace the Congress President, since, according

to the party constitution, only the delegates to the open session
or AICC members can elect a Congress President. In fact, the
Election Commission did take this stand and did not allow our
party to adopt the name of Indian National Congress and its
reserved election symbol, the 'calf and cow'. We had to choose
a new symbol, and add '(I)' to the name of Indian National
Congress. 'I' obviously stood for 'Indira'. However, after the
Lok Sabha polls in 1980, both the Election Commission and
the Supreme Court, in their judgement on cases pending since
1978, ruled in favour of our party. The National Convention
was later recognized as the 76th session of the Indian National
Congress. We were allowed to use the original name of the Indian
National Congress and its reserved symbol. Later, at a meeting
of the CWC, we decided to bring back the original name, but
retained the symbol of a 'hand', which had become very popular
by then. That was how Congress (I) became Indian National
Congress though, in common parlance, the name Congress (I),
suffix included, continued.

The resolution adopted at the convention inspired the
Congress rank and file tremendously. Their sagging morale
received a shot in the arm and they found new vigour and spirit
to fight and assert the party's identity as the premier party of
the country. The resolution can be categorized into three parts.
In the first part, the anti-people policies of the ruling Janata
Party were highlighted as well as the inherent contradictions,
both ideological and functional, of the combination of parties
which constituted this coalition government. In the second part,
the deficiencies of the Congress leadership were brought out,
particularly their failure to guide and inject confidence into
the rank and file. The third part of the resolution provided an
action plan, both short term and long term. In fact, after the
10-point programme of the Bangalore Congress and the 20-point

programme of 1975, Congress members received a new set of programmes and their enthusiasm knew no bounds, despite the fact that they were going to work in a hostile environment. Charged with new confidence, they returned home.

The Congress leadership at the centre and state levels had become apologetic and seemingly guilt-ridden, failing to realize that the electoral success of the Janata Party and the Congress' debacle was a part and parcel of a parliamentary democracy. They allowed themselves to be carried away by the propaganda of the times, which said the 'Emergency excesses' were the sole reason for the Congress' defeat. If they had looked beyond their noses, they would have realized that it was the non-Congress vote in the Hindi heartland, coupled with strong organizational backing of support groups, that had ensured the success of the Janata Party. The Congress never ruled by securing the majority of votes in any election; it ruled by securing the majority of the seats. In all general elections when the Congress won a majority of the seats, it did not get more than 43-48 per cent of the total votes polled. The remaining votes were shared by other political parties. Such an outcome is inevitable in a multi-party democracy.

The way in which the Congress could secure a majority of seats was by bagging the single largest chunk of minority votes which, however, accounted for less than 51 per cent. But that chunk of votes helped the Congress get more votes than any of its opponents. The Congress leadership should have realized that it was only a matter of time before the Congress vote bank, which had diminished in the Lok Sabha elections, grew back in size again. They should have taken note of the improvement in the percentage of votes manifest in the assembly elections only a couple of months after the Lok Sabha polls. But what could you expect from a leadership that was suffering from a crisis of confidence? How could they instil confidence in the minds of the grass-roots Congress worker? Laudable as their theory of constructive cooperation with the Janata Party government appeared to some, it was nothing short of a spectacular surrender to a ruling party determined to destroy the Congress organization in its entirety. In their heart of hearts, they wanted to come out of the shadow of the past and completely delink themselves from Indira Gandhi's leadership, without having the courage or conviction to act on their own. These leaders became hesitant, weak and faltering, to the disgust of the members at the grass-roots. The latter found in Indira Gandhi the promise of undaunted struggle, clear focus and iron will. After the first couple of months following the crisis, it took her little time to re-assert her leadership.

That the fighting spirit of the Congress was revived under the leadership of Indira Gandhi was evident from the action programme recommended by the CWC and approved by the AICC at its meeting in January 1978. It included 'Organizing Dissent and Resistance'. The programme outlined by the resolution touched the most sensitive and the weakest sections of the community. Little wonder, therefore, that when the other Congress outfit concentrated only on the so-called 'Emergency excesses' perpetrated by Indira Gandhi and her alleged caucus, a vast number of common Congressmen plunged into resistance movements and identified themselves with the suffering millions. The base of Congress (I) had thus been firmly established among the masses. Political programmes in different forms stretched across 1978 and 1979 and by the time the Janata Party crisis occurred, in mid-1979, the Congress (I) under Indira Gandhi had become the only viable alternative to the Janata Party government.

Y.B. Chavan made a sarcastic remark to the media when Indira Gandhi was elected as the Congress President after the split. 'Thank God,' he retorted, 'they have not declared her the Prime Minister of the country.' He went on to ask: 'Who are they to elect her as the Congress President? They are nobody in Congress.' This was followed by C. Subramaniam, senior Congress leader and former Finance Minister in Indira Gandhi's Cabinet, contending that the ideological roots of the Congress split lay in 'Emergency excesses'. Indira Gandhi reacted to this in a meeting of the CWC on 21 January: 'It is true, as has been stated by Shri Subramaniam, that ideological differences are at the root of the present Congress change.' But she dismissed the charge that such ideology had anything to do with the alleged 'excesses' during the Emergency. She reiterated that the Emergency was a stringent measure taken to meet the demands of a particular situation prevailing at that time. The very proclamation of Emergency was to preserve and protect the Congress ideology of upholding the integrity of the nation and introducing discipline which was threatened by the breach of law and order throughout the country. This was due to the defective implementation of certain programmes taken up at various stages by the administrative set-up.

Indira Gandhi said:

A campaign of vilification engineered by the reactionary and communal forces throughout the length and breadth of the country resulted in the defeat of the Congress party in the general election. Even then, on many occasions, regrets had been expressed for the hardship and other difficulties suffered by the people. The real ideological conflict involved in the present change, as also in the earlier, emanates from the implementation of progressive Congress policies of emancipating the poor masses from their economic and social miseries. No doubt, the policies of the Congress have always been there and will remain there but as and when the implementation is taken up in earnestness, only then the spokesmen of the vested interests in the country feel uneasy and resort to confrontation with those who are determined to move forward and implement the radical programmes and policies of the Congress with vigour. As in 1969, in the present also, the basis remains the same.

We wanted the Congress to be strong, vigilant and a positive opposition party. But, to the utter surprise of Congressmen, our so-called collective leaders started adopting an apologetic and defeatist attitude in every forum, under the guise of constructive cooperation to the Janata Party government.

This had a demoralizing and disheartening effect on some of our members' pride but that the rank and file of Congressmen throughout the country remained confident and determined to face the onslaught of the Janata Party government and to resist the growing repression and harassment of the Congressmen as well as the poor, the minorities and the weaker sections. An impression had been created that there was a possibility of the Janata Party government being able to edge out the right reactionaries. On the contrary, the actual power is increasingly getting concentrated in the hands of Jan Sangh and its militant wing, the RSS, and the BLD which is promoting casteism in a big way. It is in this context that the Congress party feels called upon to play its historic role as champion of the downtrodden, the oppressed and the depressed, kisans and peasants and working classes. After the Janata party government came to power at the centre, we became obsessive with the happenings in court. The important question is whether the Congress is merely to exist and that too with an understanding with the Janata Party or are we to move firmly on our chosen path of democracy, socialism and secularism? The Congress can survive only through its dynamic programmes and policies by complete identification with the masses.

We are fighting not only for the survival of the Congress but for the cause of India's great mass.[59]

This observation by Indira Gandhi clearly highlights the philosophy behind the grand split in 1978. She correctly assessed the mood of the masses supporting the Congress and the undaunted spirit of a large number of Congress workers. They were ready to fight and face any eventuality. They just needed leadership, which was lacking. When Indira Gandhi came forward with her indomitable grit, they flocked around her.

The Congress leadership was not the only one that failed to realize the significance of the split; the fourth estate also ridiculed the move. Indira Gandhi's act, they maintained, was merely an attempt to turn the party into her fiefdom. Media reports and editorials stated that Congress workers would not respond to her call and that her party was bound to be a big flop show. Like most senior Congress leaders, the media, too, was obsessed with the Emergency 'excesses'. They firmly believed that this aberration would 'write off' Indira Gandhi from Indian politics. It took them just two months to realize how wrong they were.

I am reminded here of an interesting anecdote. As mentioned earlier, both Indira Gandhi and I were prosecuted by the Shah Commission for refusing to take oath to give evidence before it under sections 178-179 of the IPC. We were required to appear in person before a magistrate of Delhi's Tis Hazari court. On the appointed day, both of us appeared before the magistrate,

[59] *The Encyclopaedia of the Indian National Congress*, 1978-83, vol. 25, pp. 61-63.

pleaded not guilty and were granted bail on PR (personal recognizance) bonds. Our counsels, the late Frank Anthony and Madan Bhatia, requested the magistrate to fix a date sometime in March for the subsequent hearing, given that both of us would be busy campaigning for Congress (I) candidates for the imminent assembly elections. The Shah Commission counsel could not help but pass a sarcastic comment: 'Is there a party known as Congress (I)?' Anthony shot back: 'You will soon know.' We had forgotten the incident. But when, in the first week of March, we appeared before the magistrate, Congress (I) had already emerged victorious in Andhra Pradesh and Karnataka. Now it was Frank Anthony's turn to return the favour to the Shah Commission counsel. He looked at Karl Khandelwal, the counsel for the Commission, and quipped, 'Now perhaps my learned friend has come to know that there is a party known as Congress (I) which has formed the government in three states.' Khandelwal was left speechless.

Before January end, Indira Gandhi had constituted the CWC and appointed office-bearers of the AICC. The CWC consisted of the elected and nominated members of the committee who had joined us. She nominated Kamalapati Tripathi, Virendra Verma, Syed Mir Qasim, Buta Singh, Devaraj Urs, Chenna Reddy, Zail Singh, Madhav Singh Solanki, A.R. Antulay and me. It was decided that the three elected committee members who joined us—P.V. Narasimha Rao, M. Chandrasekar and A.P. Sharma—would continue as members and the remaining seven seats would not be filled up. Later, C.M. Stephen and Dr Shankar Dayal Sharma also joined our party. The Central Parliamentary Board consisted of Kamalapati Tripathi, P.V. Narasimha Rao, A.P. Sharma and M. Chandrasekar. Buta Singh and A.R. Antulay were appointed general secretaries and Chandrasekar was appointed treasurer of the party. A little later, I was appointed treasurer of the AICC and continued to hold this office until 1980, when I joined the Union Cabinet.

At the initial stage, we did not have many MPs. However, the situation changed dramatically after the assembly elections in Andhra Pradesh, Karnataka, Maharashtra and Assam. A large number of Congress MPs joined our party, and Congress (I) became the largest opposition party in both the Lok Sabha and the Rajya Sabha. C.M. Stephen, who had joined us by this time, was appointed the leader of the opposition in the Lok Sabha and Kamalapati Tripathi got back his position as the leader of the opposition in the Rajya Sabha. I became treasurer of the Congress (I) in Parliament, too.

The task before us was to contest the assembly elections and to constitute the state units. We decided to hold state level conferences, attended by Indira Gandhi and other important leaders.

I, too, attended a few conferences, tasked as I was with oversight of the Northeastern states, including Assam, where we were to fight the elections. I spent about fifteen days in West Bengal and addressed district-level conferences in North 24-Parganas, Hooghly, Birbhum, Burdwan, Midnapore, Nadia, Murshidabad and South 24-Parganas, before constituting the PCC. A.B.A. Ghani Khan Choudhury was appointed PCC President. Ananda Mohan Biswas, Abdur Rauf Ansari, Nityananda Dey and Santi Roy were appointed Vice Presidents; Nurul Islam, Gobinda Chandra Naskar and Subrata Mukherjee were appointed general secretaries; and Deoki Nandan Poddar became treasurer.

The Congress had only twenty members in the West Bengal legislative assembly in those days. Of these, nine members joined us, all MLAs of the minority community. Haji Lutfal Haque, who had been a member of the West Bengal assembly from 1951 to

1962 and again from 1977 till his death in 1987,[60] was chosen as the leader of the party in the assembly. Abdus Sattar became the President of the Murshidabad District Congress Committee. By the end of February, we had constituted all District Congress Committees.

However, by mid-January, I had to leave for Assam. Asoke Bhattacharya came to my aid by taking responsibility for Tripura. Off to Assam I went, and with Guwahati as my operational base, I toured Nagaland, Manipur, Meghalaya, Arunachal Pradesh and Mizoram. At first, we did not get any outstanding leader from any of the Northeastern states. Captain William Sangma of Meghalaya, Hokishe Sema of Nagaland and R.K. Dorendra Singh of Manipur were with the erstwhile Congress till the end of 1978. All Congress members from Sikkim and Arunachal Pradesh had defected to the Janata Party, along with their chief ministers. The situation was no better in Tripura. (A large number of Congress leaders in Tripura, including ex-ministers, had joined Congress for Democracy [CFD] and the Janata Party.) Despite the poor response, I established state units in all but Arunachal Pradesh, and appointed the following to head the state units: Edward P. Gayen (Meghalaya), Lal Thanhawla (Mizoram), Chiten Jamir (Nagaland) and Professor N.Tombi Singh/Rishang Keishing (Manipur). I decided to concentrate on Assam as the election was imminent. Other areas could wait till this was over.

I toured all districts of Assam, along with state leaders. Of the important state leaders who joined us were Tilak Gogoi (Rajya Sabha MP), Harendra Nath Talukdar (former minister), Bishnu Prasad (former minister), Anwara Taimur,[61] Dharnidhar

---

[60]He was in the Lok Sabha for fifteen years, between 1962 and 1977.

[61]She was a Minister of State when she joined the National Convention and declared her resignation from the government along with N.K. Tirpude of Maharashtra.

Basumatari (former MP), and Dhruba Barua, the Secretary of the PCC. These few known names were all we had. A large number of students and youth remained with Hiteswar Saikia, who was Barooah's blue-eyed boy. None of the elected members of the Lok Sabha were with us (the Congress won 10 seats out of 14 in 1977) and there was only one Rajya Sabha member.

Despite all odds we decided to contest the election. I suggested that we should be modest while doing so and not field more than fifty candidates. But there was no stopping the local leaders. Election fever had caught on and eventually we had to select 115 candidates (for 126 seats). Mobilizing resources was a Herculean task; most thought we had huge resources, which we did not. But who would believe that? After much effort, I was able to raise some funds from Calcutta and Assam, and the central office also helped with some contribution. But what all that added up to was far from adequate.

The lack of resources eventually became one of the main reasons for our failure. Indira Gandhi toured Assam for four days and addressed about fifty-seven meetings. Her day started at 6 a.m. and usually ended at 3 a.m. the next morning. Meetings were well attended, but beset by demonstrations, disturbances and heckling: at Bongaigaon, we could not even hold a meeting; at the Silchar meeting I was hit by a stone. There were violent demonstrations at Guwahati, Nagaon, Sibsagar and Jorhat. We carried on undaunted, with leaders and workers from West Bengal, Bihar and Tripura helping us. Mohsina Kidwai, A.P. Sharma, Ram Dulari Singh, A.B.A. Ghani Khan Choudhury and Asoke Bhattacharya campaigned for party candidates. Indira Gandhi's meetings had a good impact but, in the absence of local organizations, we could not cash in on the response. She spent a day in Meghalaya where we had fielded about fifteen candidates, but the show was poor.

The Janata Party benefitted from the split of Congress votes between the two Congresses. It emerged as the single largest party, with no party achieving absolute majority. Congress (I) got 8 seats and the other Congress—Congress(O)—got 26. Of all our important leaders, only Syeda Anwara Taimur was elected from the Dalgaon constituency. The rest, including Bishnu Prasad and Harendra Nath Talukdar, were defeated. From Cachar, we won only 2 seats, and the number was the same from the tea gardens, too. The remaining 4 seats were from the migrant Muslim-dominated areas like Barpeta and Dhubri.

However, the results in the Andhra Pradesh and Karnataka elections were spectacular. Congress (I) secured about two-thirds of the total seats in both states and witnessed the routing of the other Congress. The Janata Party came a distant second. And though we could not defeat the other Congress or Janata Party in western Maharashtra and the Konkan regions, we did capture Vidarbha. In Maharashtra as a whole, the other Congress emerged as the single largest party, followed by Congress (I) as a close second, and the Janata Party was pushed to the third position. The performance of the Janata Party in Maharashtra came as a shock to many: only a year ago, in the Lok Sabha elections, it had mopped up a little less than 50 per cent of the total seats in the state—i.e., 21 out of 48 seats. Much to their dismay, they could not take advantage of the split in Congress votes in Maharashtra.

The results of the assembly elections came as a jolt to the other Congress—Congress (O)—led by Y.B. Chavan and Brahmanada Reddy. Both of them were routed in their own citadels by Indira Gandhi. To the Janata Party, the re-emergence of Indira Gandhi, whom they had written off from the Indian political scenario, was a rude shock.

The media, too, was puzzled. Many media professionals who had trailed Indira Gandhi on her election tours had privately, but admiringly, conceded that there was simply no match for her tenacity and spirit. They stared awestruck at the public euphoria she was able to generate, particularly from amongst the downtrodden and weaker sections of the Indian electorate. There were constituencies where people would wait for five to six hours simply to catch a glimpse of her or to hear her speak. Wayside meetings and receptions pulled unprecedented crowds. This was reason enough for a section of the media to feel frustrated; their sustained propaganda had all come to nought. Indira Gandhi had re-emerged, to the anguish of her detractors still desperate to deny her any credit, least of all for this success. Willy nilly, they attributed the success to the popularity of Devaraj Urs and Chenna Reddy as also to the (non-existent) power of money. So overwhelmed were they with this perverse thinking that after her victory from Chikmagalur later that year, even a senior national leader like late J.B. Kripalani commented that Devaraj Urs could even get 'schoolgirls' elected from Karnataka.

A crucial question stared the other Congress in the face: whose support would they seek to form the government in Maharashtra? If they went with the Janata Party, they would be thoroughly exposed before their own partymen. But if they wanted to form a coalition with Congress (I), they would actually have to condescend to start a dialogue with a leader who they had 'expelled' and abused as 'authoritarian'. They condescended.

The rank and file of the Congress (I) were against going with the other Congress. But the importance of ensuring Congress rule in Maharashtra overruled other considerations. A coalition government was formed in Maharashtra with Vasantdada Patil (of the Congress [O]) as Chief Minister and N.K. Tirpude of Congress (I) as the Deputy Chief Minister. However, the coalition did not last long and, in 1979, there was mass defection from Congress (O) under the leadership of Sharad Pawar, who now formed the government with the help of the Janata Party.

It will not be out of place to mention that S.B. Chavan, a former Chief Minister of Maharashtra, joined the Pawar ministry as Finance Minister. In 1977, he had quit the Congress but by the end of 1979 he had joined Congress (I) like many others—and was elected to the Lok Sabha. In November that year, Brahmananda Reddy also joined Congress (I). However, after the 1978 election Devaraj Urs was chosen by the party as the Chief Minister in Karnataka and Chenna Reddy in Andhra Pradesh.

In March 1978, biennial elections to the Rajya Sabha took place. While in the previous year, the Janata Party was a hopeless minority in the Upper House, in 1978 it improved its numbers by securing a large number of seats from Uttar Pradesh, Bihar, Madhya Pradesh, Rajasthan, Punjab, Haryana and Orissa at the cost of the Congress. In West Bengal, neither the Janata Party nor the two Congresses got any seats—all went to the Left Front. We had a little problem in Uttar Pradesh: The strength of our MLAs in the state assembly allowed us only one seat. Kamalapati Tripathi was on the verge of retirement, and he was our natural choice for the Rajya Sabha from this state. However, B.P. Maurya had staked his claim to this seat. It was not easy to persuade him to sacrifice his interest in favour of Kamalapati Tripathi. However, it was finally done, and Maurya was accommodated from Andhra Pradesh where Congress (I) had four seats. Apart from this, A.P. Sharma from Bihar, N.K.P. Salve and Sushila Adivarekar from Maharashtra, and Bhimraj from Rajasthan were elected to the Rajya Sabha.

Congress (I) started playing an effective role in the Rajya Sabha, with the days of appeasement now a thing of the past. The level of debate was outstanding, in tune with the tone set by Nehru in the early years. We took up issues and confronted the ruling party. Kalpnath Rai, N.K.P. Salve, Saroj Khaparde and Margaret Alva played a prominent role while I spoke on all major economic issues and became the party's spokesperson on such matters.

# CHAPTER NINE

# CRISIS IN THE JANATA PARTY

The inherent contradictions of the 'conglomeration' known as the Janata Party had surfaced soon after it assumed office. Individual ambitions, mutual distrust (almost to the point of hatred) ideological differences, lack of commitment to any programme and the absence of effective leadership made the coalition crumble long before expected. Janardan Thakur described the characteristics of the triumvirate of the Janata Party—Morarji Desai, Charan Singh and Jagjivan Ram—in the following manner:

> Each one of the gerontocrats thought and behaved as though he himself had brought about the victory. Desai was acting 'Sarvochch' again. After all, it was under his chairmanship that the Janata Party had won the victory and this was the time to pick up the thread where it had lost years ago, when he had been denied his succession to the throne. He had always thought of himself as Nehru's logical heir but he had been 'cheated' by the machinations of 'small men' in politics. He had repeatedly staked his claim to the Prime Ministership, but each time he had been thwarted by

a 'chit of a girl' who was 'not suitable' for the office and whom he had considered his 'duty' to oppose. Even more than him, Charan Singh considered himself the 'architect' of not only the Janata Party but even more of its victory at the polls. The clean sweep from Amritsar to Patna, as he was to claim later, was entirely due to him. If anybody deserved the crown it was him. So also thought Jagijvan Ram, who had nursed as great an ambition to become the Prime Minister as Desai or Charan Singh. He had no doubt that the victory was entirely due to him. If he had not exploded his 'bomb', Ram was convinced, Mrs Gandhi would have come back to power. Why had he left her if he could not become the Prime Minister even now? What was the point in all the fight against 'dictatorship' if he were to remain content with ministership? Even Mrs Gandhi would have given him that, and perhaps, if he had bargained hard enough she might even have made him the Deputy Prime Minister. His sly aide, H.N. Bahuguna, felt even more frustrated, for he had hoped to rule the country from behind Babuji's [Jagjivan Ram] chair.[62]

No wonder, therefore, that the Janata Party leaders started working at cross purposes from the very beginning. The erstwhile Jana Sangh faction was the single largest group among the party's MPs. It had an organized cadre in the RSS and wanted to take advantage of the factionalism and ambitions of the three 'ex-Congressmen'. They played their cards cleverly. Two of their leaders holding Cabinet rank, A.B. Vajpayee and L.K. Advani, did well for themselves both as ministers and leaders. As a Minister of Information and Broadcasting, Advani had launched an all-out campaign against Indira Gandhi and her party, with both the

---

[62]Janardan Thakur, *Indira Gandhi and Her Power Game* (New Delhi, 1979), p. 112.

government and the private media aiding this purpose. In all other ministries and departments the influence of the RSS and Jana Sangh elements was quite evident. It was quite natural, therefore, that they exploited the individual rivalry of these leaders. At the centre they supported Morarji Desai but at the state level they made adjustments with the Charan Singh faction.

The Janata Party came to exist formally after the election of 1977 but they fought the election as one party with one symbol. However, friction reigned supreme from the very inception. Charan Singh wanted to head the party but Morarji Desai was chosen as the Chairman. Thereafter, Charan Singh was nullified by being given charge of the northern states. After the election, he could not become the Prime Minster as the mantle fell on Morarji Desai again. Charan Singh wanted to have Karpoori Thakur as the first President of the Janata Party but, again, he was frustrated as Chandra Shekhar was chosen by JP as the first President of the Janata Party. From the very outset, Charan Singh became a disgruntled element and considered himself 'cheated'. Hence it was no wonder that his camp followers started building up an anti-Desai campaign inside the party and outside.

In June 1978, the simmering difference came out in the open. Raj Narain, who described himself as the 'Hanuman' to Charan Singh, called a press conference and launched an attack against the party President Chandra Shekhar, as also against the party's national executive and parliamentary board. All these were ad hoc committees and must be scrapped, he said. Every other day he attacked Chandra Shekhar and brought new allegations against him. Describing him as an 'illegal' President, accusing him of hobnobbing with those forces who were propagating the idea of the 'third force' as an alternative to Congress (I) and the Janata Party. Even Industry Minister George Fernandes, in a note to the National Executive Committee, admitted that there was a gradual erosion of the party and the government and 'all of us are guilty of thinking and acting as members of the merging parties rather than as members of one political party'.[63] Referring indirectly to the working triumvirate at the top (Desai, Charan Singh and Jagjivan Ram), he urged them to exercise their political and moral authority to keep the party in shape. 'This they owe to the country, to the party and to posterity. If they fail, the consequence will be tragic for everyone,' he added.[64]

This was a tall order for the leaders, quarrelling continuously for their pounds of flesh and caring two hoots for the country or the people. 'Desai was never tired of privately condemning Jagjivan Ram for private immorality and corruption,' wrote Madhu Limaye in the annual issue of *Mainstream* (1979): 'Desai's hypocrisy knows no limits. While publicly supporting Ram's claim for forming a government, privately he has been denouncing Ramji in strong words saying, "I shall never allow that man who lacks private morality and public integrity to become the Prime Minister."'[65]

Such was the relationship of the three top leaders of the ruling party within a year of their coming to power. Therefore, when Raj Narain started a concerted attack against his Party President, there was little doubt that it was an early component in the master plan to remove first the Party President and then the Prime Minister. The Bharatiya Lok Dal (BLD) faction of the Janata Party worked out its strategy on the basis of the support it expected from the Jana Sangh group of the party which had the largest number of MPs. In 1977, the two had arrived at a deal for the northern states. As a result, the chief ministership of Uttar Pradesh and Bihar went to the BLD faction while that of Madhya Pradesh and Rajasthan went to the Jana Sangh group.

---

[63]Janardan Thakur, *Indira Gandhi and Her Power Game* (New Delhi, 1979), p. 118.
[64]Ibid.
[65]Ibid.

This plan was upset by a statement of Sunder Singh Bhandari, an important Jana Sangh leader. Bhandari pointed out that there was no in-built provision for the continuity of this arrangement and that 'none of us can take each other for granted' in our respective designs. He did not agree with Raj Narain's contention that the National Executive Committee was illegal and he made it clear that the Jana Sangh group would not support any no-confidence motion against Prime Minister Morarji Desai. This was enough to shelve the scheme for the time being.

Raj Narain was publicly reprimanded by Morarji Desai at the Delhi airport when the former put 'attar' on him on his return from a trip abroad. Desai alleged that Raj Narain had been playing foul during his trip abroad. On 22 June, Raj Narain was accused by the National Executive Committee for going public with intra-party differences, thereby violating the directive of the National Executive of the party. When Raj Narain was cornered in the party, his mentor Charan Singh came to his rescue. From a health resort in Surajkund, where he was recuperating from an illness, Charan Singh issued a statement at midnight on 28 June 1978, accusing, in strong words, a government of which he was a part. But the subject of his statement was his favourite theme: 'Indira baiting'. He said the government could not govern the country as it was a 'pack of impotent people'. 'Perhaps, those who differ from me, do not realize sufficiently the intensity of feelings among the people of our country on the government's failure to put the former Prime Minister behind the bars by now.' He said that a section of the people wanted Indira Gandhi to be detained under the Maintenance of Internal Security Act (MISA). If the government did this, he said, 'hundreds of mothers of Emergency victims would celebrate the occasion like Diwali...'

This was the proverbial last straw that broke the camel's back.

Morarji Desai asked his Home Minister, Charan Singh, to resign from the cabinet for violating the principle of joint responsibility of the cabinet. Raj Narain was also asked to resign from the cabinet for his behaviour in Shimla, where, as a Minister, he violated the prohibitory order issued under Section 144 of the Code of Criminal Procedure.

Madhu Limaye, a parliamentarian and a socialist, was one of the General Secretaries of the Janata Party. He could not stand the RSS and resisted its growing influence in the Janata Party. The occasion of enrolment for party membership gave him an opportunity. He knew that in the membership drive the organized RSS cadre would outnumber the rest and capture the party as and when organizational elections took place. Limaye convinced Raj Narain that once the Jana Sangh was isolated, Morarji Desai would be helpless and Charan Singh would emerge as the most powerful entity in the party.

The Jana Sangh faction did not remain idle during this period either. It knew its strengths and weaknesses, and was fully aware of the chances of a split in the party and the collapse of the government. Given that it was the biggest beneficiary of the power-sharing arrangement at the centre it, understandably, tried to bring Charan Singh and Morarji Desai together. It emphasized the need for unity between these two leaders for the smooth running of the party and government. Some other leaders like Biju Patnaik and Chandra Shekhar, too, worked hard to bring Charan Singh back into the government.

In such a situation, Charan Singh returned to the government as Deputy Prime Minister (and as Finance Minister). Morarji Desai agreed to the arrangement but remained true to his game by making Jagjivan Ram Deputy Prime Minister (also Defence Minister) as well. Desai scored another point over Charan Singh by refusing to accommodate Raj Narain. Wiser in humiliation,

Charan Singh accepted the offer and rejoined the government in January 1978. But even this arrangement could not save the government from its inevitable downfall. It was just checked for a short while. Since Raj Narain was left high and dry, he spared no effort in pulling the Desai government down.

Developments in the Congress (I) also influenced the Janata Party. The leaders of the Janata Party had always been obsessed with Indira Gandhi, and during the nearly three years that it was in office, the Janata Party could not come out of her shadow. With the expulsion of Devaraj Urs they thought she had been cornered and that her chances of returning to power were slender. They were proved wrong.

The first symptoms of the Janata Party's disintegration started showing at the state level. As has been mentioned before, the BLD and Jana Sangh factions had an understanding on sharing chief ministership across a few northern states: BLD nominees in UP, Haryana and Bihar and Sangh nominees in Madhya Pradesh, Rajasthan and Himachal Pradesh. The toppling game began shortly after, and Ram Naresh Yadav (UP), Karpoori Thakur (Bihar) and Devi Lal (Haryana) were replaced by Banarsi Das (Uttar Pradesh), Ram Sundar Das (Bihar) and Bhajan Lal (Haryana) as chief ministers. Factionalism became so rampant that, on 13 June, the Janata Party central leadership had to issue a show cause notice to the Chief Minister and Janata Party Chief of Haryana for sabotaging his own party nominee in a by-election to an assembly seat from Narnaul.

A day before, Raj Narain was removed from the National Executive Committee of the Janata Party for a year for publicly speaking against his party colleagues and the government's policies. Charan Singh, who was holidaying in Shimla (in fact, for the most part of his ministerial tenure, Charan Singh had to be lodged in a hospital or a health resort, and was jokingly called 'Minister for

Rest') replied with 'no comment' to all questions asked on this issue.

Apart from the Raj Narain group, others, too, got busy. Madhu Limaye organized a meeting on 17 May to explore the possibility of Left unity in the country.[66] George Fernandes was not far behind. He convened a conference of the erstwhile socialists in July 1979. At this conference, he strongly advocated the unity of the Janata Party, the failure of which would pave the way for the 'dictator' to return.

Charan Singh's camp was divided between the hawks and the doves. The hawks wanted Charan Singh to quit the Janata Party and revive his BLD, while the doves, including his wife, advised him that there was no point returning to political wilderness. After all, there was no denying that he was now Deputy Prime Minister of the country with a Finance portfolio. Even Charan Singh was reported to have told Mani Ram Bagri, an MP, 'You people are breaking the party. It is against the interest of the party and the nation. You should not do it.' In the meantime, Raj Narain resigned from the Janata Party.

There was also some activity in the Congress (Urs)[67] camp and H.N. Bahuguna suggested that Congress (Urs) leaders move a motion of no-confidence against the government after the resignation of Raj Narain from the Janata Party. Congress (Urs) leaders knew that there would be no serious outcome of the no-confidence motion, but their leader Y.B. Chavan tabled it if only to prove that he could fight too and that Indira Gandhi

---

[66]Prominent among those who attended were Bhupesh Gupta, C. Rajeswara Rao, P. Ramamurthy, Harkishan Singh Surjeet, Basavapunnaiah, and the representatives of the RSP, PWP and FB. Others included Chandrajit Yadav, Raghunatha Reddy, K.D. Malaviya, Karpoori Thakur, Shyam Nandan Mishra and Chaudhury Brahm Prakash. Some of those present at this meeting later provided a strong support base for Charan Singh to form his own government.

[67]See Chapter Ten for a detailed description of how Devaraj Urs split from Congress (I) to form his own faction.

was not the singular crusader against the Janata Party, as the whole country was learning with time.

The position of the Congress (I) was clear. Any move against the government had to be supported because it was no less than another opportunity to expose the misdeeds of the ruling party on the floor of the House. We were certain that though the government might survive, Raj Narain would play havoc and the government would face an embarrassing situation. Sanjay Gandhi and some of his colleagues were working very secretly on the Raj Narain faction.

By the evening of 8 July, five MPs had decided to quit the Janata Party and join Raj Narain in the House itself. At this point, Devi Lal sprang into action and persuaded another five MPs to quit the party on the first day of the Parliament session. The next day, the second round of defections took place from the Janata Party: as many as nine defectors from Bihar alone. As defectors grew in number, even the doves in Charan Singh's camp were thrown off balance. Devi Lal, Karpoori Thakur, Raj Narain and others managed to bring hundreds of socialist and BLD workers from Bihar and Haryana to Delhi to psychologically pressurize fence-sitters to quit the Janata Party. By 10 July, the Janata Party's majority margin was reduced to three. Charan Singh, who all the while was watching everything silently, pulled the plug only when Congress (I) decided to support the no-confidence motion. Asked to oppose the no-confidence motion, he was reported to have told Morarji Desai, 'I shall be guided by my followers and do whatever they want me to.'[68]

Jagjivan Ram invited Janata Party MPs for tea at his residence on 11 July. The press was told that 135 members attended. The apparent reason for convening such a gathering was to

---

[68] *The Statesman*, 11 July 1979.

promote unity within the party, but the underlying message was clear: Jagjivan Ram's strength in the party. The same evening, the Congress for Democracy (CFD) group met and some of Bahuguna's supporters suggested that the group should quit the Janata Party. Jagjivan Ram opposed this and said it would mean resorting to 'Machiavellian tactics' to cross the floor at that point. He had his own plans. He wanted to project himself as the alternative leader of the Janata Party, the strength of which had already come down to 260 by then.

On 12 July, both Bahuguna and Biju Patnaik met Morarji Desai but the meeting did not go well. Morarji Desai was furious with Bahuguna and could barely hide it. The same night, Bahuguna, Biju Patnaik and Madhu Limaye met Party President Chandra Shekhar. They suggested that the only way to save the situation was to throw out the Jana Sangh group from the party. But Chandra Shekhar refused to buy it. He said, 'You want me to throw out the people who are sitting quietly and to placate those who are defecting. What sort of logic is this?' Who better than Chandra Shekhar to know that the party could hardly afford to throw out the single largest group of MPs?

At the Janata Party Parliamentary Board meeting on 14 July, George Fernandes proposed that Morarji Desai should step down. Jagjivan Ram nodded in support but Chandra Shekhar did not agree. Morarji Desai refused to budge: 'Only 47…[have] so far left the party and the government could survive even up to 70 defections'. On hearing that, Bahuguna left the party.

On the night of 14 July, Jagjivan Ram wrote a letter to Morarji Desai which was a virtual indictment of his government. He sent copies of this letter to Bahuguna and Chandra Shekhar. However, the matter was thrashed out when Jagjivan Ram met Morarji Desai and it was agreed that the issues raised in the letter would be taken up after the censure motion was over.

Jagjivan Ram spoke in defence of the government in the House. So did George Fernandes. He strongly defended the government and spoke against his permanent target—Indira Gandhi. But then, having made a powerful speech, he resigned from the government.

By the afternoon of 15 July, Morarji Desai assessed the situation carefully and came to the conclusion that he was going to be defeated. He tried his best to get the support of the All India Anna Dravida Munnetra Kazhagam (AIADMK), CPI and CPI(M). Had he managed to get this support against the motion, perhaps the government could have survived. But Bahuguna managed to ensure that CPI and CPI(M) did not support the Desai government. Desai tendered his resignation to President Neelam Sanjiva Reddy, drawing the curtain over the Janata Party rule.

After Morarji Desai's resignation, the President called Y.B. Chavan, as the leader of the opposition, to try and form the government. Chavan tried for a few days and then informed the President that he was not in a position to do so (he had sought the support of Charan Singh's followers but that proved futile. Charan Singh himself was itching to become Prime Minister). Chavan's failure was predictable. Without the support of the Congress (I) or the Jana Sangh group of the Janata Party, it was impossible to have a working majority in the House. The Jana Sangh was a part of the Janata Party and the Congress (I) could not think of supporting Y.B. Chavan, the leader of Congress (Urs), a party which we had never ever recognized as the true Congress.

There was, however, the possibility of a coalition between Charan Singh and Chavan under the leadership of the former. This was indicated in the letter written by Chavan to the President of India, while expressing his inability to form the government: 'As a result of our efforts, there has emerged a combination of parties and groups which to my mind would be able to provide a viable and stable government. I trust you will consider this new situation and deal with it as you in your wisdom deem proper.'

After Chavan's failure, the President invited both Morarji Desai and Charan Singh to furnish evidence of their claimed majority within forty-eight hours. He called Morarji Desai as he continued to be the leader of the Janata Party; he had refused to resign from the leadership of the Janata Party when he resigned from the office of the Prime Minister. His logic was that he was elected the leader of the Janata Party's parliamentary wing for five years and that he could be removed from that position only by a two-third majority of the House.

Congress (I) suddenly found itself in a key position to strike a political balance. Without our support, nobody could form the government. To support Morarji Desai was out of question as we were party to the motion of no-confidence. We were clear in our mind about every faction of the Janata Party. We knew that the Janata Party was bound to get crushed under its own weight. We wanted to ensure that it broke from within. Consequently, we decided to support the Charan Singh faction against Morarji Desai. As mentioned earlier, Sanjay Gandhi was in touch with Raj Narain and, through him, Charan Singh was informed of our decision. When he staked his claim to form the majority, C.M. Stephen and Kamalapati Tripathi, leaders of Congress (I) in the Lok Sabha and the Rajya Sabha respectively, informed the President of our support to Charan Singh.

∎

While the crises was brewing, so was the volatility in the relationship between Charan Singh and Morarji Desai. On his return from a tour abroad, in mid-1978, Prime Minister Morarji Desai had demanded the resignations of Home Minister Charan Singh and Health Minister Raj Narain. The media was agog with stories about the differences between Charan Singh and Morarji Desai. Newspapers published the correspondence exchanged between Singh and Desai. In an interview to *Sunday* (2 July 1978), Charan Singh commented that he was relieved to be out of a government infested with corrupt people. Raj Narain went to the extent of publishing practically the entire correspondence between himself and the Prime Minister.

The Parliament's monsoon session started on 17 July, and we decided to use the parliamentary forum to the fullest extent possible to expose the Janata Party government. It was the time to go on the offensive. We met regularly to work out our strategy. Indira Gandhi addressed the Congress Parliamentary Party (CPP) and guided us. Meanwhile, we amended the party constitution and elected Indira Gandhi as the Chairperson of the CPP. The party constitution was amended to provide that anyone who had occupied the office of the leader of the House (both in the Lok Sabha and the Rajya Sabha) and continued to be the member of the party would be an ex-officio member of the parliamentary party. The amendment was made to ensure that Indira Gandhi could participate in all deliberations of the CPP. This apart, she attended most meetings of the Congress (I) party in Parliament as the Party President.

The strategy for the monsoon session was that we should attack the government in both the Houses but concentrate on the Rajya Sabha where the ruling party was numerically weaker. Accordingly, Pandit Kamalapati Tripathi, as the leader of the opposition in the Rajya Sabha, raised the issue of corruption as a special mention. He observed:

Sir, I wish to draw the attention of the House to an extremely serious issue of importance for India. Chaudhary Charan Singh has made serious allegations of corruption against the Prime Minister's son, against many other ministers named and un-named and generally against the government in which he was the Home Minister for the past fifteen months. He has gone on record to say that while in government he was surrounded by many corrupt persons, that he had committed two serious mistakes, one of which was to make Morarji Desai the Prime Minister, that as Home Minister he had been trying to root out corruption from all high places, but his efforts were brought to nought because such more powerful forces were protecting corruption and that his ouster from the Cabinet was because he had suggested an enquiry against the Prime Minister's son and some other ministers and their relations and wives. It has been reported that several letters were exchanged between the then Home Minister, Charan Singh, and the Prime Minister on the subject of corruption of the latter's son. Extracts of some letters have appeared in a widely read section of the press. The press reports in their fragmentary form are highly scandalous and extremely damaging to the image of the government of this great country. On the other hand, after all this happened, a last minute pitiful and pathetic effort has been made to sweep the entire public scandal under the carpet and draw the curtain over the whole sordid story. The leaders of the government have sought to treat all these public issues as their private affairs and the whole government as their private property. Sir, I say that the nation has a right to know the truth.[69]

---

[69] *Rajya Sabha Debates*, vol. CVI, no. 1, 17 July 1978, pp. 189-194.

Kamalapati Tripathi demanded that a commission of inquiry be set up to bring the guilty to book before 'the bar of public opinion'.

After this observation, Kalpnath Rai of Congress (I) and some other members went on to demand a response from the government. But nobody from the treasury benches responded to the demand. The disturbances continued. The House was adjourned for lunch at 1.22 p.m. During the recess, Kalpnath Rai, Shyamlal Yadav and Ramanand Yadav, along with the leader of opposition and a few others, including me, went to the Chairman's chamber. The leader of the House and other party leaders were also present. We could not reach any agreement. When the House reassembled at 2.33 p.m. the scene was repeated. Kalpnath Rai went on speaking. The Deputy Chairman, Ram Niwas Mirdha, tried to stop him and passed the order not to record Rai's speech but could not prevent him from speaking. Even the other opposition parties got into the act, adding to the confusion. No government issue or any other business could be taken up. At last, the Deputy Chairman adjourned the House for the day at 2.41 p.m.[70]

On 18 July 1978, at a meeting in the chamber of the Chairman, and in the presence of leaders of all major parties, it was decided that the matter would be discussed through a 'Call Attention Motion' on the following day. On 19 July 1978, the motion was moved by A.P. Sharma, and Prime Minister Desai made a brief statement:

Mr Deputy Chairman, Sir, the notice given by A.P. Sharma and nine other honourable members seeks to call my attention to the reported exchange of correspondence between me and Charan Singh when he was the Home

[70] *Rajya Sabha Debates*, vol. CVI, no. 1, 17 July 1978, pp. 189-194.

Minister and the allegation reportedly made by him that he was surrounded by corrupt persons. The latter part appears to be based on a press report of an interview of Charan Singh by a Calcutta weekly on the 1st of July. In that interview, Charan Singh is said to have made the following observations in reply to a question, after he resigned from the government: 'I feel relieved. In the government, I was surrounded by many corrupt persons.'

I presume that Charan Singh was referring to his assessment of corruption in general. There can be no difference of opinion about the need to root out corruption. Throughout my career, both in the government and outside, I have been an unrelenting advocate of strong and effective measures to deal with this evil and have dealt strictly with any prima facie case brought to my notice.

As regards the first part of the question, it is well recognized that communications between ministers are privileged communications. The reasons behind this principle is that the effective functioning of the government requires that there should be full and frank exchange of views between ministers which would be hampered if ministers could be compelled to disclose the contents of such communication. This has been recognized in May's Parliamentary Practice also. Charan Singh has marked his correspondence 'Secret' and my replies are marked likewise. I, therefore, propose to adhere to that inviolable principle in the transactions of government business and I seek the indulgence of the House in enabling me to do so.[71]

Morarji Desai's curt reply: 'Sir, I have not asked any question and I do not have to reply to anything. I do not want to add

---

[71] *Rajya Sabha Debates,* Vol. CVI, No. 3, 19 July 1978, pp. 240-241.

to what I have said in my statement,' stunned the whole House with its arrogance. I did not want to miss the opportunity and allow the situation to slip from our grip. From what Morarji Desai had to say, I figured out that the government would not yield. A.P. Sharma, the mover of the motion, made a lengthy speech lasting nearly thirty minutes but the ruling party did not respond on any issue.

I rose on a point of order and was permitted to make a brief observation. I argued that since the contents of some of these letters had already appeared in the media and had been owned by one of the authors (that is, Charan Singh), the Prime Minister could not claim 'privilege'. These had to now be placed on the table of the House and the country had to know who was lying. The Prime Minister was not really convinced by this argument but it gave a handle to others to mount an attack on the government. Bhupesh Gupta, Devendra Nath Dwivedi, Dinesh Goswami and Vishwanath Menon pressed the government to disclose the correspondence. Pandemonium reigned. The Prime Minister left the House in a huff, presuming that the matter was over, and this added fuel to the fire. The House was adjourned at 4.26 p.m. and no other business could be transacted.

The next day, on 20 July, the issue of corruption came up again. Kamalapati Tripathi made a statement demanding that the whole issue be reopened and the correspondence between the Prime Minister and the Home Minister be tabled. He pointed out that the question of 'secrecy' was no longer tenable and that another Cabinet Minister, Raj Narain, had gone to the media with the entire correspondence between him and the Prime Minister. He further observed that people in the country as well as outside were debating this issue, but MPs, who represented the nation, were denied authoritative information from the government. He held the government responsible for the impasse created in the House and strongly criticized the behaviour of the Prime Minister who had left the House before the discussion on the subject had concluded.

After Kamalapati Tripathi, L.K. Advani, leader of the House, spoke. He referred to the stalemate created in the House and gave the views of the government. He justified the action of the Prime Minister in leaving the House and sought cooperation from the leader of the opposition in ensuring the smooth functioning of the House.

Kamalapati Tripathi, in his turn, observed that it was not the sole responsibility of the opposition to run the House, and that the reply of the leader of the House was far from convincing. With the permission of the House, I rose to my feet and made the following observation:

> Sir, the Hon. leader of the House has mentioned in reply to the observations of the Hon. leader of the opposition that the matter has been settled. What was our demand? We know that the Home Minister of the country was asked to resign by the Prime Minister along with another Cabinet Minister, who was in charge of Health and Family Welfare. It is normal parliamentary practice that when a minister resigns, he comes before the House to which he belongs, makes a statement and explains the reasons of his resignation. In this case, the two persons who resigned—not voluntarily but were asked by the Prime Minister [to] tender their resignations—chose not to make any statement before the House to which they belonged. The Prime Minister also did not make any statement on what prompted him to ask these two ministers to resign. So, many things have come in the press, but the members of parliament, to whom the ministers are collectively and individually responsible and

accountable, did not have an opportunity to know what happened between the two persons who occupied high offices in the government and the circumstances under which the Prime Minister directed his Home Minister and Health Minister to resign from the government. The leader of the House is coming forward and preaching the sermon that the whole matter has been settled. How has it been settled? Can any member belonging to his party tell [us] what are the reasons for their resignations? What is the authoritative version of their resignations? Are the members of parliament not entitled to know? If these gentlemen would have come forward and made a statement suo motu on the floor of the House on the situation in which he was compelled to direct these two gentlemen to resign from his Cabinet, one could have understood that the matter had been settled.

The plea taken by the Prime Minister yesterday was that these were secret documents, which is also not acceptable and [is] untenable. There are hundreds of instances. When Mohan Dharia was directed by the then Prime Minister to resign from the Council of Ministers, in his statement on the floor of the House, he revealed the entire contents of his letter to the then Prime Minister and those of the then Prime Minister's letter to him.[72]

After my observation, the issue continued to be debated. However, as the House could not be brought to order, it was adjourned at 2.47 p.m. till the next day. Again, no official business could be transacted. The issue was taken up again on 24 July 1978, and Shanti Bhushan responded to the points raised by various members. He repeated the arguments of the Prime Minister

---

[72] *Rajya Sabha Debates*, 20 July 1978, pp. 248-250.

that the correspondence between cabinet ministers should be considered confidential for the effective functioning of the government. In the course of the debate, he also said that 'the government would be willing to abide by the advice of the Chairman...that you as Chairman should evolve some method by which the anxieties can be allayed and yet a bad precedent may not be laid down on such an important principle...'[73]

Shanti Bhushan put the ball in the court of the Chairman, and the Chairman fell into the trap, and subsequently told the House that 'I have advised the government that it would be better if the government places this correspondence in the Chairman's chamber for perusal by the leader of the opposition and the leaders and some members of the other parties and groups in the House, who attended our meetings...' The opposition had scored a point with the government agreeing to disclose the contents of the letters to some members, if not to the whole House.

∎

N.K.P. Salve of the Congress (I) tabled a motion asking for two separate commissions of inquiry to look into allegations of corruption against members of the families of the then Prime Minister, Morarji Desai, and the former Home Minister, Charan Singh.

Not all opposition parties, which accounted for about two-thirds of the total strength of the House, supported us on the issue of setting up the commission of inquiry. With their support, the motion was sure to have been carried, but that was not to be; the fear of the re-emergence of Indira Gandhi caused many opposition parties to support the ruling Janata Party. The ruling

---

[73]*Rajya Sabha Debates*, vol. CVI, no. 6, 24 July 1978, pp. 187-188.

party also successfully divided the opposition with the help of the Congress led by Y.B. Chavan. The latter did not take too kindly to the aggressive role the Congress (I) had been playing ever since the split. They had not succeeded in coming out of the 'spell' of 'constructive cooperation' yet. The role of the other opposition parties was hardly significant. In fact, ever since the 1978 split, the role of the other non-ruling parties had become rather insignificant, with the Congress (I) taking centre stage as the key opposition. The others argued that since the recommendation of the Rajya Sabha for appointing the inquiry commission would not have any 'legal binding' (as the Act provided authority to appoint such commissions only on the Lok Sabha and state assemblies), the motion could not recommend such an appointment. We were insistent, particularly given the precedent set by the Janata Party government of appointing commissions against Congress leaders at random. A compromise formula was evolved: Bhupesh Gupta suggested to me that we should recommend a commission in our motion; other opposition groups would recommend an amendment to the motion, suggesting the appointment of a committee of the House to guide the government in matters such as these. We agreed to the compromise in order to defeat the government on the floor of the House on this issue. Indira Gandhi also agreed to this formula.

N.K.P. Salve made a brilliant speech on this occasion, and his attack was devastating. He levelled as many as twenty-nine specific charges of irregularities against the family members of the Prime Minister. His debating skill sparkled as he went on to quote some of the adverse remarks made against Morarji Desai by Chandra Shekhar, A.B. Vajpayee and George Fernandes in a debate held in August 1968. He told the House that all three, who had then levelled charges of corruption against Morarji Desai, were now the first to rush to his defence. This irony, he told the House, was compounded by another: that some speakers defending the government had to fall back on the certificate once given to Morarji Desai by the then Prime Minister Indira Gandhi.

The House enjoyed the repartee gleefully, but Morarji Desai's reply was dignified and bold. His main contention was that there was no prima facie case and since there was no specific charge against any of his family members, there was no need to appoint an inquiry committee. Drawing instances from the past when similar charges had been made against his son, he pointed out that investigation into these cases by various agencies, including the Central Bureau of Investigation (CBI), had revealed nothing. Unlike others, he refrained from making any counter attack against Indira Gandhi or anybody else.

After the debate was over, the motion (along with amendments) was taken up for voting. The amendment moved by Bhupesh Gupta was approved by 104 to 78 votes. According to the arrangement, the Congress (I), the Congress (Urs) and the CPI voted for the amendment. All other opposition parties and groups opposed the motion and voted with the ruling party. But it wasn't too bad as, after the biennial election to the Rajya Sabha in 1978, the Congress (Urs) and the Congress (I) combine became the largest party in the Rajya Sabha. Getting the motion passed in the House posed no problem.

The amendment suggested by Bhupesh Gupta was a landmark achievement since it recommended a parliamentary committee to guide the government in matters of alleged corruption. The government was caught in a bind: they couldn't accept the recommendation nor reject it outright. Embarrassed by this turn of events, they could not even give a focused response to the resolution adopted by the House.

However, the text of the amended resolution left some leeway for both the Chairman of the House and the government to take advantage, and the latter took advantage of this leeway and sat on the resolution. I had apprehended this situation but our hands were tied. On 15 August 1978, *The Hindu* reported that the Chairman of the Rajya Sabha was consulting the Law Minister on the motion adopted in the House: 'Motion on Graft, Jatti Consults Law Minister'.

There was strong reaction to this delay in the Rajya Sabha, with Bhupesh Gupta, Kamalapati Tripathi, Bhola Paswan Shastri, Somen Bhattacharya and Kalpnath Rai speaking up strongly and saying that Parliament had been taken for a ride. I pointed out that the government was buying time, knowing that the Rajya Sabha would be adjourned shortly and it was unfortunate that the Chairman of the House was also assisting the government in delaying the matter. Finally, on 24 August 1978, Prime Minister Morarji Desai spoke, and essentially regretted the government's inability to agree to either of the two lines of action suggested in the motion. And, subsequently, the Chairman indicated that he would have to go by the fact that the government chose not to adopt either of the two alternatives.

While this issue was being battled in Parliament, the ruling Janata Party decided to go on the offensive in a bid to isolate a combative Congress (I) and possibly also to divert attention. It claimed that the Congress (I) was deliberately disrupting the House proceedings so as to stall the passing of the 44th Amendment to the Constitution (by this amendment, the Janata government sought to reverse the changes brought about by the 42nd Amendment which had been passed during the Emergency). Our stand on the 44th Amendment was clear: we were not opposed to it per se, but had reservations regarding some of its provisions. To say that we were trying to stall its passage in Parliament was incorrect.

The reaction to this decision was obvious. Except for the

CPI(M) and a few smaller groups, all major opposition parties reacted sharply. All of us opposed the Chairman's contention. But insofar as the House was concerned, the curtain was drawn on the issue. Even though we could not make the government agree to our proposal, we had scored a point over them. The attempt to isolate the Congress (I) in the House had been thwarted, and we emerged as the principal opposition party on the floor of the House and outside. The activities of the party outside the Parliament grew substantially, too.

# CHAPTER TEN

# BACK IN THE SADDLE: INDIRA GANDHI'S RETURN TO POWER

A series of by-elections—to state assemblies as well as the Lok Sabha—after the 1977 Lok Sabha election clearly signalled Indira Gandhi's return to power. Indira Gandhi had decisively demonstrated her strength in the south, and now it was time to turn north and showcase her strength in the Hindi belt where the party had been routed in the earlier general elections. Congress (I) won the Azamgarh Lok Sabha seat, in addition to Manakpur and 7 assembly seats in Uttar Pradesh and the Khedbrahma assembly seat in Gujarat. In the Lok Sabha constituencies of Karnal in Haryana and Samastipur in Bihar, the Congress (I) was very close to victory. This was not only a demonstration of the strength of the party led by Indira Gandhi but also a clear indication that people had no confidence in the Congress led by Chavan and his followers. Their candidates, including Chandrajit Yadav and Shanti Bhushan, were decisively defeated in all the by-elections: they won only one—the Joypur seat in Purulia, West Bengal—of all the by-election seats contested during this period.

The CWC, while congratulating the electorate, observed:

They have given a clear verdict symbolizing the unmistakable trend in the thinking of the vast masses of people in areas where they had, only a year ago, turned away from Congress... Having been catapulted into power, more as a political accident than a positive political achievement, it was no surprise that the Janata Party should have totally failed to deliver the goods and should have rapidly lost the confidence of the masses. As already reiterated by the Congress on several occasions in the past, the people have, quite naturally, again begun to look to the Congress for providing the leadership and delivering them from the morass of problems arising out of the commissions and omissions of the Janata Party government.[74]

The most significant victory of the party, however, came from the relatively lesser-known Lok Sabha constituency of Karnataka—Chikmagalur—which returned Indira Gandhi to Parliament in November 1978. Someone had suggested that she be elected to the Rajya Sabha from Karnataka, and her name was quietly registered from Chikballapur. However, she did not like the idea, preferring to contest elections for the Lok Sabha instead. And as the Chikmagalur Lok Sabha seat fell vacant, an opportunity presented itself.

We did not announce her candidature. It was apprehended that the central government may, on some pretext or the other, stall the by-election to prevent her re-entry into the Lok Sabha. The decision was, therefore, kept a closely guarded secret. As soon as the time schedule of the by-election was made public, the party announced her candidature. It came as a shock to the Janata Party, which frantically started looking for a suitable candidate to field against her. However, none of the opposition

---

[74]Resolution of the Congress Working Committee, 15 May 1978.

stalwarts of the party were willing to fight the election against her, even though all of them agreed to oppose her.

George Fernandes, the Industries Minister in the Janata government, belonged to this area. He was put in charge of the campaign and election management. Leveraging his goodwill in the state, Veerendra Patil, former Karnataka Chief Minister, was fielded as the Janata Party candidate. George Fernandes and other Janata Party leaders put their entire might into the campaign to ensure Indira Gandhi's defeat. Union Home Minister Charan Singh went to the extent of telling voters not to waste their vote on a candidate who would rot in jail for the rest of her life, even if she was elected. Some newspaper groups, particularly the Indian Express Group, intensified the detailing and reportage on the depositions before the Shah Commission. Thousands of copies of these newspapers were distributed for free. A young woman named Nandana, who was the daughter of noted artist Snehalata Reddy, demonstrated with a group of girls at every public meeting Indira Gandhi addressed. The motive was clear. They wanted to provoke the police into taking action against such disturbance. If the police took the bait, they would pass the buck on to the state administration, then run by our party, and allege that they had been obstructed from conducting free and fair elections. Devaraj Urs had a tough job. He instructed the police to exercise utmost restraint.

The campaign management and election work had been carried out efficiently. All eight assembly segments were placed in charge of responsible leaders—state ministers, former Union ministers, MPs and MLAs. K. Lakkappa, the MP from Tumkur, actively worked for Indira Gandhi. Though he did not join our party, veteran Congress leader K. Hanumanthaiah supported Indira Gandhi and spoke at some public meetings. R. Gundu Rao, Devaraj Urs and Margaret Alva all worked very hard during this election.

The public euphoria surrounding Indira Gandhi had reached its zenith, with some sections of women worshipping her as a deity. Hundreds and thousands of people from the oppressed sections of society turned up at her meetings. While a section of the Indian media continued to find fault, foreign journalists covering the election were impressed with her hard work and professional expertise during the campaign. London-based Indian author Sasthi Brata, who was covering the election for the BBC and who was otherwise very critical of the Emergency, was all praise for Indira Gandhi's professional electioneering.

Janata Party leaders, aided by a section of the media, alleged that our party was spending money like water. One newspaper reported that, as a close confidante of Indira Gandhi, I was especially entrusted with the protection of the party's cash chest. George Fernandes enacted a drama by going door-to-door to raise small collections. He was snapped by newspapers, bucket in hand, collecting donations from shopkeepers. The picture they tried to portray was that while the Janata Party was strapped for cash, Indira Gandhi's party was flush with truckloads of it. All major Janata Party leaders, except the Prime Minister, visited the constituency and addressed meetings. But their collective strength was not enough to prevent Indira Gandhi's re-entry into Parliament. She won the Lok Sabha seat of Chikmagalur by a margin of over 80,000 votes over her nearest rival.

The history of contemporary India took another turn with her re-entry into the Lok Sabha. The reaction of the ruling Janata Party and some others was less than dignified. The Janata Party (as also a section of the media) tried to explain away her success by attributing it to the popularity of Devaraj Urs. Talk of her 'money power' also figured among the popular public slander. S.A. Dange, veteran leader of India's communist movement, was at his sarcastic best when he lambasted the self-styled crusaders

of democracy by sending a 'condolence' telegram to the Janata
Party election manager George Fernandes.

■

After the victory at Chikmagalur, Indira Gandhi decided to visit
England on invitations from various organizations, including the
Indo-British Friendship Society. For this week-long visit, Lord
Swraj Paul took the responsibility of coordinating her itinerary.
Her passport had been impounded earlier, but permission was
granted and a diplomatic passport was issued to her. The other
invitees accompanying Indira Gandhi, apart from Geeta and
myself, were Sonia Gandhi, A.P. Sharma, C.M. Stephen (leader
of the opposition in the Lok Sabha), Darbara Singh and Madhav
Singh Solanki. We took an Air India flight on 10 November.
Indira Gandhi, Sonia Gandhi, Geeta and I stayed at the Claridges.

A small group of Indians were demonstrating against her
when we landed, but adequate security arrangements had been
made. A large number of press correspondents posed many
questions; a section of the British press had already made up
its mind against her and advised public figures in the UK to
be cool in their response to her. The *Sunday Times* editorial
called her 'a thoroughly corrupt person and an unwelcome
visitor...' It observed: 'Unlike Mrs Gandhi's India, this is a free
country. Therefore, anyone who wants to come here on a visit
should be free to do so. This does not mean, however, that
Mrs Gandhi should be welcomed, celebrated, honoured or in
any way acknowledged by politicians with a claim to represent
the people of this country.' The *Sunday Telegraph* advised that a
'cool politeness is probably the wisest attitude for British public
figures to adopt towards the former Indian dictator.' The *Economist*
reminded people that 'she should not be allowed to win the

international approval she was seeking.'

However, all the advice and reminders had no effect. Her visit was received with considerable enthusiasm by the British public and politicians. She was invited by the British Prime Minister, James Callaghan, to 10 Downing Street for tea. She called on Lord Mountbatten and met Margaret Thatcher, the then leader of the opposition, who later became Prime Minister. Michael Foot, the British Deputy Prime Minister, described her as the 'unifier of India' and 'champion of liberty' by referring to her contribution to the liberation of Bangladesh. In the speech delivered at the annual dinner of the Indo-British Friendship Society, Michael Foot went to the extent of remarking that the 'life of Indira Gandhi is not a closed chapter. Many more glorious achievements are yet to be added to it'. The years that followed proved how prophetic he was. Four years later, in 1982, I met Michael Foot again at the annual dinner of the same society. He was then the leader of the opposition. I reminded him of his prophecy about Indira Gandhi, much to his delight.

The reaction among Janata Party supporters in London was sharp. They organized demonstrations against Indira Gandhi almost everywhere, with those at Southall being particularly ugly and violent. Even before her arrival, the pro-Janata association, The Friends of the Indian Society International, had distributed letters all across the UK asking people to tell her that 'she was an unwanted person'.

Her visit to Wales was remarkable. At the inauguration of a spiral steel mill owned by Swraj Paul, her emotional speech swept the audience off its feet. Wales is the place where Aneurin Bevan had made his historical speeches to further the cause of socialism. Bevan was a personal friend of Pandit Jawaharlal Nehru. Against this historical backdrop, the followers of Bevan and the daughter of Nehru made a pretty picture together and evoked intense spells of nostalgia. Moved by her speech, a worker commented that she was sure to win the parliamentary seat if she chose to contest from Wales. The Wales story was distorted by some Indian journalists, and a yarn also spun regarding her 'investment of money' in the steel mill.

On the way back to India, she decided to meet some important Soviet leaders at the Moscow airport. Arrangements were made, but nothing was disclosed, not even to other party members. I was the only one accompanying her. (Sonia Gandhi had gone to Italy to meet her relatives and extended her stay in Europe. My wife, Geeta, had decided to stay on in England for another four weeks.) We decided to leave for India by Aeroflot airlines; there was no passenger in the first-class cabin of the aircraft except the two of us. A CPI leader from Uttar Pradesh travelling from London on the same aircraft recognized Indira Gandhi.

We were taken to the reserved lounge at the Moscow airport. Indira Gandhi was taken to another room where she met the Soviet dignitary; I stayed with the other Soviet officials and had dinner with them. Nobody came to know what actually happened at the airport. Later, the CPI leader who had recognized Indira Gandhi spread the news that Indira Gandhi and I had got off at the Moscow airport, but that he had no idea who she had met. The Indian embassy, too, had no knowledge about this visit. Some press persons, later, wanted me to disclose the name of the Soviet leader; nobody believed me when I pleaded ignorance. But the media soon lost interest in the subject, since more important developments were taking place in Parliament at that time.

Indira Gandhi took oath as a member of the Lok Sabha on 20 November. Having been elected from Karnataka, she took the oath in Kannada. Janata Party and CPI(M) members like Jyoti Basu stated that with her, 'evil has come back to Parliament'.

Other than that, most members welcomed her warmly. But it wasn't for long that she was an MP.

The question of breach of privilege against her and some other persons was raised on the floor of the House by two Janata members, Madhu Limaye and Kanwar Lal Gupta, in November 1978, and was referred to the Privilege Committee by the Speaker. The Janata Party held a majority within the committee, and she was accused of obstruction, intimidation, harassment and institution of a false case against certain officials who were collecting information in connection with Maruti Udyog Limited during the fifth Lok Sabha. Indira Gandhi gave them her version of the story. It was pointed out that the officers concerned were not officers of Parliament, and thus could not claim parliamentary privilege. They were government officials and were asked to do a job which was, by nature, within their regular duties. But logic found no home, and she was found guilty. The committee came to the 'inescapable conclusion' that Indira Gandhi had misused her position as Prime Minister to protect the interest of Maruti Udyog Limited, which was controlled and managed by her son. She was held guilty of a 'serious breach of privilege and contempt of the House'. Along with her, R.K. Dhawan, her former Additional Private Secretary, and D. Sen, former Director of the CBI, were held guilty. However, according to practice, the committee left to it to the 'collective wisdom of the House to award such punishment as it may deem fit'.

The motion was moved in the House by Prime Minister Morarji Desai, as leader of the House. Janardan Thakur in his book, *Indira Gandhi and Her Power Game*, has mentioned that there were both hawks and doves in the Janata Party.[75] Some wanted her to be punished severely while others wanted to play

---

[75]Janardan Thakur, *Indira Gandhi and Her Power Game* (New Delhi, 1979), pp. 90-91.

soft. Morarji Desai and Charan Singh were, for once, united on the need for 'stern action'. Atal Bihari Vajpayee suggested that a 'reprimand' would be enough.

The hawks won, and the motion was carried: she was to be expelled from the House and was to be imprisoned till the House was prorogued. Many political parties opposed this severe punishment. Even the CPI(M) in its politburo resolution advised against stern action. It said, '…there has been a lot of dithering and softness when hard political decisions had to be taken. In such a situation, to strike heroic and militant poses on the privilege issue and demand extreme action will be counter-productive in the struggle against authoritarianism and give an excuse to opponents to appear as martyrs and claim the sympathy of the people.' The Congress led by Chavan also opposed the extreme step. But to no avail. The hawks in the Janata Party were determined to eliminate her.

Some feelers were sent to us indicating that if Indira Gandhi apologized she would not be expelled or jailed. The idea was repugnant to her and she rejected it outright. Her speech on this occasion was inspiring and prophetic (see Appendix 13). She said that she was prepared to go to jail to vindicate her principles and ideals. She had been prepared for an eventuality like this for many months. Warning the government, she said, 'The failures of this government are leading to its isolation from people everywhere. The ineptitude of this government has destroyed the cohesiveness of the administration and created a situation of uncertainty and insecurity. If this situation is not reversed, it will provide fertile soil for the growth of fascism.'

After adopting the motion, the House was adjourned at 5.05 p.m. on 19 December. She had to wait in the House for nearly three hours. We waited with her, as did Sonia and Maneka Gandhi and the children. She consoled everyone and quoted a line from an English poet that read: 'Say goodbye, not with tears but with smiles.'

The Janata Party did not stop at expelling her from the Lok Sabha and sending her to jail. A Bill was passed in the Lok Sabha seeking to set up special courts to try certain cases and organize summary trials, with the obvious target being Indira and Sanjay Gandhi, and some of their followers. There were mass agitations on the issue of setting up special courts. The party organized a nationwide protest against this judicial persecution. In Delhi, a massive rally was organized on 16 May at Ramlila Maidan, attended by a large number of people from different parts of the country.

The reaction to Indira Gandhi's expulsion from the House and subsequent imprisonment was spontaneous. The party gave a call to all workers and sympathizers of the party to rise to the occasion and to protest against the most savage outrage on democracy. The Congress (I) Working Committee met on 20-21 December 1978 in New Delhi and passed a resolution condemning the action, and laid the grounds for the response.

The movement launched throughout India gathered momentum and thousands of satyagrahis across the country courted arrest. The response was so spontaneous that the AICC had to issue circulars from time to time to ensure that the movement continued in a disciplined manner. In one such circular (No. 34, 21 December 1978), AICC General Secretary Buta Singh pointed out: 'In such a situation, discipline becomes the life line of our organization. It has also to be ensured and followed by every Congressman vigorously. Breach of discipline will not only weaken our organization but it will also harm the satyagraha itself.'

Reports of more and more satyagrahis courting arrests started reaching the AICC office. Many refused to be released on bail, leading to a situation where some prisons had to erect tents in maidans to house the detainees. Even the North Indian winter did not dampen their spirits. However, after a while, the 'jail bharo' movement was discontinued; on 27 December 1978, the CWC directed Congressmen to henceforth concentrate on organizing public meetings, rallies, and undertaking padayatras.

An eventful 1978 came to an end. It had started uncertainly for us, precipitated by the split in the Congress, but ended with hope and renewed strength. Demonstrating her mass appeal and her calibre as the only leader with a pan-India appeal, Indira Gandhi had decisively established her Congress as the 'real' Congress. Indira Gandhi was a confident and far-sighted leader, insightful regarding people as well as electoral politics—a combination which made her a rare politician. Not only that, her short period in the political wilderness revealed her strength. For one used to a comfortable life, she wasn't fazed at having to sleep under the open sky during the Azamgarh election campaign or when, during her electioneering in Andhra Pradesh, her circuit house reservation was found to be cancelled, or, indeed, when she had to travel on the back of an elephant to Belchi. Under her inspiring leadership, it took Congress workers just a year to regain courage, conviction and confidence in the future. The non-performing conglomeration known as the Janata Party started counting its days. Fraught with inherent contradictions, it had no stamina to face the opposition provided by a strong and determined Congress under the leadership of Indira Gandhi. The writing was on the wall, though some simply refused to read it. At the beginning of the year, the Congress faction led by Chavan had deserted Indira Gandhi and chosen to recede into oblivion. When the year ended, the Janata Party dug its own grave by expelling her from the Lok Sabha and sending her to jail.

# CHAPTER ELEVEN

# NEW CHALLENGES FACE CONGRESS (I)

The year 1979 dawned with new challenges. The ambitions of Charan Singh, who wanted to become the Prime Minister of India, the ever-increasing influence of the RSS and the Jana Sangh in the administration, the increasing dependence of the Prime Minister on that group, and the internal factional quarrel among the socialist groups in the ruling clique had already destroyed the cohesion of the Janata Party. The only cementing force which kept them formally together was the lurking fear of the emergence of Indira Gandhi.

The attacks on Congress leaders and workers went on unabated. In Punjab, Giani Zail Singh was brutally attacked; and in West Bengal, Barkat and many other state congress leaders were beaten up by the police. In Bhubaneswar, Indira Gandhi's convoy was assaulted, as were important Congress leaders like K.C. Lenka and B.M. Mohanty. Even ordinary workers of the party faced such attacks, but no eventuality was enough to daunt them, such was the level of their enthusiasm.

■

The issue of dual membership—Janata Party and the RSS—was highlighted by leaders like Madhu Limaye, and a section of the Janata Party members demanded that Jana Sangh members snap ties with the RSS. A section of the Janata Party, particularly the socialists, felt that the dominance of RSS elements in both the state and central administrations was costing the party its Muslim vote bank. In addition, the ineffectiveness of various state governments to tackle communal riots in Uttar Pradesh, Bihar, Madhya Pradesh, Gujarat and other states had seriously eroded the Janata Party's base among Muslims. The Janata Party had already lost the support of the Harijans and other weaker sections, since vested interests and upper castes in the states ruled by the Janata Party deprived them of the gains received during Congress rule. The virtual dismissal of Charan Singh and Raj Narain from the government, the mutual trading of charges between the Prime Minister and the former Home Minister, the massive kisan rally in support of Charan Singh to demonstrate his power, all were symptoms of the fissures appearing in the ruling party. The electoral success and the massive popular support received by Congress (I) in 1978 worried these warring factions and made them realize that they had to bury their differences in the interest of survival. The Janata Party tried to deal with their internal contradictions, and hence it started a patch-up bid, along with vindictive action against Indira Gandhi.

■

Meanwhile, we went on strengthening our party through mass agitation and other public programmes. Indira Gandhi started touring the length and breadth of India and pulled mammoth crowds everywhere she went. Even the hostile press had to admit that she was the real opposition and alternative to the

Janata Party. Every day, important leaders were quitting Chavan's Congress to join us. In both Houses of Parliament, we were now the main opposition party. C.M. Stephen and Kamalapati Tripathi were recognized as leaders of the opposition in the Lok Sabha and Rajya Sabha respectively.

Initially, making a big dent in Northeast India seemed to be an impossibility. I was working hard at this and ultimately it was possible to rope in some important Congress leaders of that region: Captain Williamson Sangma and P.A. Sangma joined our party, along with their entire group in Meghalaya. Others who joined us were Raj Kumar Dorendra Singh and Rishang Keishing of Manipur, Chiten Jamir and S.C. Jamir of Nagaland, P.K. Thungan and Gegong Apang of Arunachal Pradesh, Lal Thanhawla of Mizoram and N.B. Khatiwada of Sikkim. Leaders like S.K. Patil and K. Hanumanthaiah also joined us by early 1979.

Some organizational changes were also made in the parliamentary party and the mother organization, both at the state and central levels. After these changes, Congress (I) launched political programmes highlighting the failures of the Janata Party in protecting the interest of the Harijans and the minorities. The debacle that the Congress had suffered in the general elections of 1977 owed largely to the erosion in these powerful bases. Indira Gandhi concentrated on addressing these two issues, regarding which there was sustained agitation at various levels through the year. The first AICC session of the year was held in Delhi on 21-22 April 1979, and its political resolution focused on adopting an action programme. From the action plan, it was evident that the principal opposition party, Congress (I), espoused the cause of the downtrodden and the suffering weaker sections of the country.

We were facing acute financial constraints. While newspapers spun yarns about Indira Gandhi's unlimited resources, it was becoming extremely difficult to manage day-to-day organizational expenses. As treasurer of the party, I found it difficult to make both ends meet. I suggested to Indira Gandhi that she should appeal for funds during the rallies and mass meetings. She did just that and the response was good. We instructed all PCCs and other subordinate bodies to collect funds through coupons, which yielded encouraging results.

■

Since the Chikmagalur election, Devaraj Urs had taken a peculiar position. He thought of himself as a leader and that he was the reason for Indira Gandhi's election win and popularity— even repeating on the floor of the state assembly J.B. Kriplani's remark that he (Urs) could have got even a schoolgirl to win the election from Chikmagalur.

The final report of the Grover Commission was submitted on 17 March. Before this, in January, the interim report had been submitted in which Urs was charged with nepotism, among other things. We had not taken any cognizance of it, and people, unaffected by its constant mention in election campaigns, voted overwhelmingly for Indira Gandhi's party. Devaraj Urs, however, felt that he should have his second line of defence ready and started courting the Janata Party. After the final report was submitted, Urs met with Janata Party leaders Chandra Shekhar and George Fernandes, and Congress leaders Rajni Patel and Sharad Pawar at the penthouse of Goenka's Express Towers in Bombay. This meeting explored the idea and possibility of former Congressmen, wherever they were, coming together, but without Indira Gandhi.[76]

■

---

[76]Janardan Thakur, *Indira Gandhi and Her Power Game* (New Delhi, 1979), p. 104.

Simultaneously, efforts were made for all factions of the Congress to unite. Formal talks were initiated, and Indira Gandhi deputed P.V. Narasimha Rao to talk on behalf of Congress (I). Swaran Singh, who became the President of Congress (O) after Brahmananda Reddy, was eager to forge unity between the two Congresses too. So were Congressmen like Devendra Dwivedi, Bipin Pal Das and others. Indira Gandhi gave a public call for such unity and this was endorsed in the AICC resolution of 21 April.

On 26 February, Swaran Singh met Indira Gandhi at her residence. A joint statement was issued saying that steps to unite the two parties were being taken: 'We hope nothing would be done to hamper the progress.'[77] At a press conference on the following day, Swaran Singh expressed hope of this unity being actioned shortly. In fact, it was his own party that posed the maximum challenge, as the hawks were intent on destroying Indira Gandhi and Swaran Singh's attempt. Some of this ilk, like D.K. Barooah, Unnikrishnan, Saugata Roy and Dadasaheb Rupwate, met at the residence of Dinesh Goswami and proclaimed that the Indira-Swaran joint statement was a camouflage to entrap Congressmen into a position where they would be used by Indira Gandhi to further her ulterior and selfish motives. The hawks said that Indira Gandhi wanted unity primarily because she was scared of the Special Courts Bill and the imminent conviction of Sanjay Gandhi in the 'kissa kursi ka' case. They wanted the unity talks to stop at once. 'No surrender' was their slogan. With Y.B. Chavan's blessings, Sharad Pawar launched a full-scale attack against the unity move and, ultimately, on 12 March, the Congress (O) finally declared that this chapter was over and there would be no more talk of unity.

There was nothing new about the unity talks which we

---

[77] *Times of India*, 27 February.

had suggested. We said that instead of compromising our stand regarding the anti-people policies of the Janata Party government, we should confront them, unitedly, through mass movements. But our efforts were frustrated. We were sad, but some of us already knew that the unity talks would not materialize and that the other Congress (O) would soon be rendered ineffective.

▪

Close on the heels of this came trouble in Karnataka. As I mentioned, Devaraj Urs had started moving on the sly. During those days, some people believed that there was the need for a third front comprising the non-RSS outfits, the Janata Party and the non-Indira Congress. At a dinner with Chandra Shekhar, Y.B. Chavan said that there was a possibility of cooperation between the Janata Party and the anti-Indira group in the Congress. Urs elaborated this view in a meeting of the CWC: 'Let people stop going surreptitiously to Mr Sanjay Gandhi,' he said, 'else, I will expose such people... I believe in the policies and programmes of the Congress and in the leadership of Mrs Gandhi...but do not mistake me for a sycophant.'[78] Uncalled for and in bad taste, this observation left many members of the CWC stunned.

Another member who fired her salvo at Sanjay Gandhi at this AICC session was Tarkeshwari Sinha. 'Some people have formed a Saturn's ring around you,' she told Indira Gandhi. When she was asked to speak further on the subject, she left the meeting agitated. Fortunately, members attending the meeting were unaffected by these melodramatic fireworks.

Devaraj Urs was appointed President of the ad hoc PCC in Karnataka in January 1978. When he became Chief Minister,

---

[78] AICC session, 21 April.

it was expected that he would step down from the state Party President's post on his own, in keeping with the convention of one-man one-post. But Urs wanted to keep both offices. He was asked a number of times to recommend someone of his choice as the PCC President but he kept avoiding the issue. Finally, on 8 May 1979, C.K. Jaffer Sharief publicly demanded Urs's resignation as the state Party President. Indira Gandhi was scheduled to visit Karnataka during that period. She requested that a PCC meeting be called on 11 May to discuss the question of the PCC President. At the meeting, Urs expressed his desire to step down from the office of PCC President but insisted that the PCC President be elected, which was against the rules and constitution of the party. The Congress President and all other organizational units are elected according to the Constitution of the party. However, during the split, we got Indira Gandhi elected as President of the INC by the members assembled in January 1978. Indira Gandhi was authorized to nominate all bodies, including the CWC, the CPB and state units. Urs refused to appreciate this simple issue. He was determined to stage a showdown against the Congress high command on this issue. When Indira Gandhi was asked at the press conference to comment on the matter of the PCC President, she replied that the subject would be discussed further.

At the parliamentary board we took a firm stand and maintained that we would not succumb to pressure from Devaraj Urs. Urs had to follow the usual convention and he was told clearly that the President of the ad hoc PCC would be nominated by the CWC, as had been done with every PCC. Urs did not like this approach and went on to criticize the leadership both directly and obliquely in the press. Addressing a convention of Congressmen at Ahmedabad, he said, 'Personalities are no doubt important, but the party's policies and programmes are more important than personalities.' Prima facie, this observation seemed perfect, but in view of the context of his speech, it would clearly appear to be a dig at Indira Gandhi. He was trying to create a larger-than-life image for himself. Come rain or shine, Bangalore walls and streets were full of his life-size cut-outs.

As things started deteriorating, Indira Gandhi asked me to go to Karnataka and contact local leaders. First, I contacted B. Janardhana Poojary, the MP from Mangalore and a total devotee of Indira Gandhi. We had decided not to put Gundu Rao and his friends at the forefront since they were very close to Sanjay Gandhi, and Sanjay Gandhi was a red flag for Urs. I spent the whole of May and a part of June in Karnataka. C.M. Stephen and Kamalapati Tripathi also came to Bangalore and had talks with Devaraj Urs, but to no avail. He was determined to part ways. He thought that by being firmly saddled in office for five years and with powerful friends in the ruling Janata Party, he could part ways with Indira Gandhi who, to him, had become 'dispensable' by then. His cup of confidence was brimming when he remarked before reporters immediately after the Chikmagalur election: 'I do not want to tell you what all I did. Do you call this a victory? Where is her charisma? Tell me.'[79]

After crossing the river, he forgot the ferryman.

I toured the districts of Karnataka extensively and contacted important Congressmen. I was accompanied by Janardhana Poojary, Veerappa Moily, S. Bangarappa, Jaffer Sharief and K. Mallanna. Back in Delhi from Karnataka, I reported to Indira Gandhi that we should think in terms of building the party unit there without Urs, if necessary. When the question of the appointment of the ad hoc PCC came up at the CWC meeting,

---

[79]Janardan Thakur, *Indira Gandhi and Her Power Game* (New Delhi, 1979), p. 100.

many members suggested that we make one more attempt to reconcile with Urs before taking this extreme step. They pointed out that there were only two oases in the desert and we should not allow one of them to dry up. I was firm in my assessment and I gave them my impression of the situation there. I told the committee that appeasing Urs would not brighten the image of the leadership and if we could not assert ourselves now, we may never be able to do so. Stephen and Antulay strongly supported me. Ultimately, on 7 June 1979, the CWC appointed the ad hoc Karnataka PCC committee consisting of the following members: S. Bangarappa (President), B. Shankaranand, D.K. Naicker, M. Veerappa Moily, Janardhana Poojary, A.K. Samad, Blasius D' Souza, Sahur Shivanna, Dharam Singh, B.N. Kenge Gowda and Devaraj Urs (ex-officio).

B. Basavalingappa had first agreed to serve on the committee and gave his consent in Delhi. But when he returned to Bangalore he changed his stand and issued statements against the decision of the CWC. He then joined Devaraj Urs's bandwagon. Urs's reaction was as expected. He launched a scathing attack against the Congress high command. He gathered his group and orchestrated hysteria against the party leadership at a joint meeting of the dissolved PCC and legislature party. As if that was not enough, he demanded the resignation of R. Gundu Rao from the cabinet, in the most undignified manner. Gundu Rao's only fault was that he was a loyal supporter of Indira and Sanjay Gandhi. It seemed like a personal vendetta and nothing short of a retaliatory measure, because Gundu Rao was not even a member of the newly appointed ad hoc committee.

Devaraj Urs and his followers started issuing open statements condemning the Congress (I) leadership. The ruling Janata Party and Congress (O) started believing that the end was very near for Indira Gandhi and her party. A section of the national press, so long critical of Devaraj Urs, suddenly rediscovered great virtues in him and was all praise for him.

The Congress high command could not remain a silent spectator. A show cause notice was issued to Urs who, instead of explaining his conduct and expressing regret, sent a nasty reply which clearly indicated that he was itching for disciplinary action.

The repercussions of the CWC's decision were to be expected. Urs formed his own 'Karnataka Congress'. He neither resigned nor took steps to reconcile with the leadership. However, he had no immediate worry as the majority of the MLAs were with him and a large number of MPs continued to remain loyal to him. He had succeeded in pushing them into a make-believe world in which it appeared that Devaraj Urs was more popular than Indira Gandhi in Karnataka. He believed that his own image as a benefactor of the poor was brighter than that of Indira Gandhi. This view was supported by the anti-Indira forces within the country and, thanks to a few members of the national press, Devaraj Urs came to be considered a national leader by many.

Our task was not easy. There were those in the party who believed that I had wrongly advised Indira Gandhi and that I should not have taken a hard line. But, except for a few chronically disgruntled elements like N.K. Tirpude from Maharashtra and Maganbhai Barot from Gujarat, no one complained publicly. So we set about rebuilding the party in Karnataka. While the leaders were not with us, we had party support from the grassroots. Accompanied by Bangarappa, Moily, Sharief and Poojary, among others, I went back to Karnataka and toured the districts extensively: Hassan, Chitradurga, Tumkur, Mandya, Chikmagalur, Karkala, Belthangady, Mangalore and Udupi. At the end of this extensive tour, we decided to hold a convention of Congressmen at the Glass House in Bangalore. It was fixed for 15 July 1979.

Indira Gandhi reached Bangalore the night before the

convention and was warmly welcomed. The road from the airport to the Kumara Krupa guest house was lined with people. Attended by a huge number of Congress workers from all parts of the state, the convention was a success. The news of Morarji Desai's resignation reached us when Indira Gandhi was addressing a public meeting organized after the convention. We returned to Delhi immediately. The twists and turns in the Janata Party's destiny were now leading to its inexorable collapse.

Devaraj Urs was by no means sitting pretty while we launched our offensive in Karnataka. He had already formed his Karnataka Congress, and his divorce from Congress (I) was a shot in the arm for Congress (O), which was fast running out of steam. Their reaction was hysterical. Not satisfied with congratulating Urs for his 'bold step', they offered him party leadership on a platter. Overnight, Congress (O) became Congress (Urs), with Devaraj Urs at its helm.

But it was the beginning of the end. Within just six months of parting ways with the Congress (I), Urs was wiped out from the state in the Lok Sabha elections, while Congress (I) won 27 of the 28 seats (with only 1 seat going to the Janata Party).

■

Trouble had started in Maharashtra, too. The coalition government of the Congress (I) and Congress (O) under Vasantdada Patil collapsed. Sharad Pawar, with a section of Congress (O) MLAs and the support of the Janata Party, now formed the government. N.K. Tirpude developed cold feet and joined the Devaraj Urs camp.

While all this was going on, the nation's eyes were trained on Delhi. There, the Janata Party had started counting its last days.

# CHAPTER TWELVE

# THE 1980 LOK SABHA ELECTIONS AND AFTER

Indira Gandhi headed into the 1980 elections strong and confident as ever. Demonstrating that she clearly had her finger on the pulse of the nation, she predicted a rousing victory. This was evident in an interaction I had with her on the choice of party candidates for election. While I was all for choosing core and loyal Congressmen to contest, Indira Gandhi advised me to 'choose people who could run the government'—so confident was she of electoral success. And her confidence was well-founded.

She had strongly advised me against contesting the Lok Sabha election in 1980, but gave in at my insistence. I contested the election from the Bolpur constituency, and was defeated by a margin of 68,629 votes. The CPI(M) candidate retained the seat (he had been elected from this constituency in 1962, 1971 and 1977). Since the delimitation in 1962, this seat had been won by the Congress only once in 1967. The decisive defeat demoralized me. I had worked hard and secured nearly 200,000 votes but the CPI(M) was superior in organization. Moreover, infighting within the Congress (I), lack of organizational enterprise and, worst of all, sabotage by some local Congress leaders were some of the key factors for my defeat. In the rest of the country, the performance of the Congress (I) was good: it secured more than a two-thirds majority in the Lok Sabha but in West Bengal, it bagged only 4 out of 42 seats. Barkat was elected from Malda by a margin of nearly 12,000 votes. The other three successful candidates were Ashoke Kumar Sen, Ananda Gopal Mukherjee and Dr Golam Yazdani.

My wife, Geeta, had already left for Delhi when the results came out. She called me on the same day and said I should return to Delhi immediately as Indira Gandhi wanted to meet me. I returned to Delhi by the evening flight and went straight to 12 Willingdon Crescent to meet Indira Gandhi. It would not be an understatement to say that she was unhappy about my insistence to contest the election. Sanjay Gandhi told me she had been upset ever since she had heard of my defeat, and she made her displeasure evident when I met her. I was unambiguously chastised. It was about 9 p.m. and Indira Gandhi was sitting in the dining room at one end of the long dining table. She had a bad cold and was soaking her feet in a tub of warm water. Standing at the other end of the dining table, I received a vociferous dressing-down for what seemed to be an interminable span of time. I was rebuked for taking the ill-advised decision of contesting from Bolpur, against her advice, and was told that such imprudent decisions nullified all my other hard work. Having recognized my folly, I could do nothing but stand there till she calmed down. She then sent me home with a basket of fruit.

The media was rife with speculation about the proposed cabinet. Various names were suggested but no one mentioned mine. Everyone had taken it for granted that my electoral defeat would cause me to be left out of the government. Bengali newspapers started projecting Barkat, and his supporters also went about saying that he was tipped for an important portfolio. So much so that Congressmen from West Bengal came to Delhi and started flocking around Barkat, who stayed at Jeet Paul's Park Hotel in New Delhi in those days. At my invitation, some of them came to my residence for dinner. Though I refrained from discussing it with them, they seemed to rather enjoy my predicament. Congress leaders from Assam, Orissa, Karnataka and Andhra Pradesh, however, came and told me they would talk to Indira and Sanjay Gandhi about my inclusion in the cabinet. I told them to leave matters where they were and not to lobby for me. But they were insistent. I do not know for certain but I believe they did take the matter up with Indira Gandhi.

On 10 January, Indira Gandhi was elected leader of the party at the meeting of the Congress (I) Parliamentary Party. I attended the meeting as usual. Indira Gandhi's name was proposed by B. Shankaranand, elected to the Lok Sabha from Chikkodi in Karnataka, and seconded by Jamil-ur-Rehman, a member from Purnea, Bihar.

On 11 and 12 January, I was mostly at my residence. A stream of visitors—Congress leaders from the states and the centre as also newly elected MPs from Orissa, Andhra Pradesh, Tamil Nadu, Karnataka, Kerala, Maharashtra and Gujarat came and met me. One senior leader told me that Indira Gandhi had advised him to see me, and a few others reported similarly. I still cannot reason why, but perhaps Indira Gandhi felt that my defeat should not bog me down. When the Sikkim Chief Minister Nar Bahadur Bhandari and the Assam Chief Minister Jogendra Nath Hazarika met Indira Gandhi, she instructed them to talk to me since I was looking after the Northeastern region. On the afternoon of 12 January, Kamal Nath came to see me, and told me of some likely inclusions in the cabinet. I thought there might be some truth in the information since Kamal Nath was close to Sanjay Gandhi. He said he was trying to induct Barkat as a Cabinet Minister. He then asked me if I had had a word with Indira Gandhi or with Sanjay Gandhi about my inclusion in the cabinet. (I had a hunch that Kamal Nath wanted to know my mind.) I apprised him in the negative, and he left, saying that he was going to meet Sanjay Gandhi. Sanjay Gandhi called me in the evening and asked me to meet him. When I reached Indira Gandhi's residence, Sanjay Gandhi told me clearly that he was sorry to know that I was upset about the possibility of my non-inclusion in the government. I told him he was incorrectly informed because, frankly, I did not mull over that matter at all after my defeat and that I knew it would be quite embarrassing to approach Indira Gandhi for my inclusion in the government. To this, Sanjay Gandhi told me, 'It was already decided to include you in the government with the cabinet rank as Commerce Minister.' But he had no idea whether I would be among the first lot to be sworn in, or the second. He asked me to speak to Indira Gandhi. I told him I didn't think it appropriate to speak to her on this matter.

Meanwhile, I was informed that Indira Gandhi wanted to speak to me. When I met her, she told me to talk to the Sikkim Chief Minister Nar Bahadur Bhandari and work out a scheme for the merger of his party with the Congress. After this, she sought my opinion regarding certain individuals, without citing any specific reason for such inquiry. I gave her my account of those individuals: the names she had mentioned kept appearing in newspapers as likely entrants into the cabinet. After some twenty minutes of discussion, she told me to carry some fruit back home for my wife and children, and a servant was asked to carry a basket to my car. At her residence gate, I met Barun Sengupta, a good friend of mine. Barun babu was anxious to know if I had had any conversation with the Prime Minister designate about the formation of the cabinet. I told him we had only spoken of the Sikkim organization which, in any case, was true. The next day, on 13 January, I had several visitors at my residence, many of whom wanted to know if I was going to be included in the government. I disappointed all.

On the morning of 14 January, the date fixed for the swearing-in ceremony, newspapers were agog with speculation. At about 9.30 a.m., I received a call from R.K. Dhawan requesting me to be at Rashtrapati Bhawan by 11 a.m. He told me that I need not wait for any message or call from the Cabinet Secretariat. Accompanied by Mr Abrol, Member of Customs and Chairman of CBEC (Central Board of Excise and Customs) during my tenure from 1975 to 1977, I drove to Rashtrapati Bhawan. When I reached the Ashoka Hall[80] there was no seat for me in the row of the ministers to be sworn in. I looked at Indira Gandhi, who immediately realized that something was amiss. R.K. Dhawan came up to me and asked me to wait. He went to the Cabinet Secretary and then consulted the President's Secretary, only to discover that in the letter recommending the names of ministers to be appointed, my name had been handwritten, not typed. The President's Secretariat had inadvertently missed it as a consequence. Naturally, no seat had been earmarked for me. Indira Gandhi immediately wrote another letter by hand and got it delivered to the President's Secretary. I was asked to sit between R. Venkataraman and P.V. Narasimha Rao. The swearing-in papers were handed over to me but, not being in possession of the list of ministers, I did not know my portfolio. I asked P.V. Narasimha Rao and R. Venkataraman but they told me that they were not privy to any details, except their respective portfolios.

---

[80]When I was entering the Ashoka Hall, I met Bhagwat Jha Azad who was leaving in a huff. Later I learnt that he had refused to be sworn in as a Minister of State. Azad joined the cabinet as a Minister of State a few months later and remained a Minister of State for the rest of his tenure.

Indira Gandhi was sworn in first, followed by Kamalapati Tripathi. The names that followed his were called out alphabetically. A total of twenty-two members were sworn in as the Council of Ministers.[81] The state-wise break-up of the Council of Ministers was thus: UP: 2; West Bengal: 2; Andhra Pradesh: 3; Tamil Nadu: 2; Bihar: 3; Karnataka: 2; Maharashtra: 1; Gujarat: 1; Punjab: 1; Haryana: 1; Assam: 1; Orissa: 1; Rajasthan: 1; and Madhya Pradesh: 1.[82] There was no one in the cabinet who was not a member of either of the two Houses of Parliament; I was the only person defeated in the Lok Sabha election, though I continued to be a member of the Rajya Sabha.

*The Tribune*, published from Chandigarh, commented on my inclusion: 'A last minute addition to the cabinet was Mr. Pranab Mukherjee who has just been defeated in the election for Lok Sabha in West Bengal. He is a member of the Rajya Sabha. His name was added quite some time after Mrs Gandhi had sent the final list to the President N. Sanjiva Reddy.' Media rumours had it that Indira Gandhi wanted to have a team of twenty-two, an astrologically auspicious number, and since Bhagwat Jha Azad had refused to be sworn in, I was included. Rumours stemming from fertile imaginations indeed, since I had already explained the sequence of events leading to my inclusion.

■

---

[81]Indira Gandhi, Kamalapati Tripathi, Giani Zail Singh, B. Shankaranand, Vasant Sathe, A.B.A. Ghani Khan Choudhury, Rao Birendra Singh, P.C. Sethi, Bhishma Narain Singh, A.P. Sharma, P. V. Narasimha Rao, R. Venkataraman, J.B. Patnaik, P. Shiv Shankar and I were sworn in as full cabinet ministers, and R.V. Swaminathan, P. Venkatasubbaiah, Jagannath Pahadia, Nihar Ranjan Laskar, Yogendra Makwana, C.K. Jaffer Sharief and Kartik Oraon were sworn in as Ministers of State.

[82]Out of the twenty-two ministers sworn in, four were from the Rajya Sabha, including myself, and the rest from the Lok Sabha. Two were Muslims, four represented the scheduled castes and one the scheduled tribes.

During this period, UNIDO (United Nations Industrial Development Organization)-III was hosted in Delhi. The Prime Minister decided that I should preside over the conference, which was to be attended by a large number of the heads of government. R. Venkataraman was to lead the Indian delegation as the Minister of Industry. S. Rangachary, who was a member of the Central Board of Excise and Customs during my previous tenure as Minister of State for Revenue and Expenditure and Minister of State for Revenue and Banking, was in charge of this conference. He came to brief me. By now, I was appointed leader of the House in the Rajya Sabha. Two days before this, Indira Gandhi had asked me who should be the leader of the Rajya Sabha. Of the three other MPs from the Rajya Sabha—A.P. Sharma, Bhishma Narain Singh and I—A.P. Sharma was desirous and had already started lobbying. I told Indira Gandhi that A.P. Sharma was senior to me in age and made it quite clear that I was not entirely keen for the position. But, at the end of the day, she decided to nominate me, and a communication to this effect was sent to the Chairman of the Rajya Sabha. I was nominated by Indira Gandhi on 18 January 1980 and again in August 1981, and held that office till 31 December 1984.

Since now I was leader of the House in the Rajya Sabha and, given that we had been reduced to a hopeless minority in the Rajya Sabha, my presence in the House was of absolute necessity. I explained my predicament to Indira Gandhi. She appreciated my concern and decided that R. Venkataraman would preside over this prestigious international conference.

■

At that time the Congress (I) had only 69 members in a House of 244. The position was awkward but not unusual. The ruling party had lost the majority in the Rajya Sabha for the first time since the 1969 split in the Congress. This deficiency was made up for during the biennial elections in 1972, 1974 and 1976. Again, when the Janata Party came to power in 1977, it formed a minority in the Rajya Sabha; the Congress had 165 members in the House at that time. But in 1978, the Congress split again and in the biennial elections of 1978 the strength of the Congress got reduced substantially.[83] In none of the state assemblies, except Andhra Pradesh and Karnataka, did the Congress have a majority. In Maharashtra, the Congress (I) and the Congress (Urs) had equal strength.

I continued to be the leader of the House for a full term of five years till 31 December 1984, when I was dropped from the government. I had then the second longest tenure as the leader of the Rajya Sabha, second only to Govind Ballabh Pant. Later, however, Prime Minister Manmohan Singh had the longest tenure as leader of the House (Rajya Sabha) that lasted for ten years, from 2004 to 2014.

When the Rajya Sabha session started, I had anticipated trouble and had discussions with leaders of the opposition in the House in an effort to prevail upon them not to press for a division. I told them that during the Janata Party rule we had a majority in the Rajya Sabha but we had extended support to the ruling party on the Motion of Thanks to the President, even though in that address our (outgoing) government's policies were bitterly criticized. I also highlighted that a similar situation may crop up in the future and hence there should be some

---

[83]The party-wise break up in the Rajya Sabha was as follows: Congress (I): 69, Congress (Urs): 43, Janata: 45, Janata (S): 19, CPI: 9, AIADMK: 9, CPI (M): 7, DMK: 2, ML: 2, and the FB, PWP, RWP, Akali Dal, RPI, Kerala Congress, National Peoples Conference and Socialist Party with 1 each. There were 9 nominated members, 12 independents and 10 vacant seats.

understanding among the parties in the Rajya Sabha not to play a confrontational role to the majority party in the Lok Sabha. The opposition leaders, however, did not buy this argument. They insisted that the government should give a categorical assurance that the state assemblies would not be dissolved as they had been in 1977. They were prepared to cooperate with the government only on such an assurance, which they said must come from the Prime Minister while replying to the debate on the Motion of Thanks. I told them that the government could not bind itself by giving any such blanket assurance. Later, when I discussed this issue with the Prime Minister, she agreed with me. A group of ministers, including myself, started reviewing this situation.

The Congress was accused of promoting defections, and examples of Haryana, Himachal Pradesh and Karnataka were cited by the opposition parties. The cases of defection in Haryana and Himachal were outright, as the members to these assemblies were elected on non-Congress tickets. But the case of Karnataka was different. In the Karnataka assembly elections in 1978, the Indira Gandhi-led Congress (I) had won hands down, defeating the Congress led by Chavan and Brahmananda Reddy as also the Janata Party. In 1979, Devaraj Urs, the Chief Minister of Karnataka, was expelled from the Congress (I) but he remained the Chief Minister as a majority of the Congress (I) MLAs continued to support him. That is when the party split. After the 1980 Lok Sabha elections, all of Devaraj Urs's candidates were defeated and the majority of the Congress (I) MLAs returned to Indira Gandhi's Congress, which formed the government under the chief ministership of Gundu Rao. This, in fact, was a split and a rejoining of the Congress (I) in a matter of just six to seven months, something that could hardly be treated as defection. Of course, in Haryana we made a mistake by allowing Bhajan Lal to switch over to the Congress (I) with his team.

The first six months were a rough ride for me since we had no majority in the House. The first encounter was during the Motion of Thanks to the President for his address to the joint session of Parliament. Bhupesh Gupta and others moved the following amendment to be added at the end of the Motion of Thanks: 'But regret that the Address does not take notice of the disturbing attempts to engineer defections on a large scale in the Assemblies in flagrant violation of all federal principles, nor does it give any assurance that the government will not, in any manner, encourage, directly or indirectly, such attempts at subverting the Constitution and flouting democratic norms and standards.'[84]

The issue, naturally, was a complex one and we could not give a straightforward commitment that we would not dissolve the state assemblies to appease the opposition. We stood our ground and informed the opposition leaders that the government was unable to give any such assurance. Whips were issued to all party members and I tried to get the support of some unattached independent members too. But we lost the motion.

This amendment was passed by 79 votes against 75. Margaret Alva, Amarjit Kaur, K.C. Pant, Dinesh Singh and Narendra Singh were among those who voted in favour of the amendment and ensured the defeat of the government. Margaret Alva and K.C. Pant were later included in the Rajiv Gandhi Cabinet; Amarjit Kaur was given the post of Joint Secretary of the AICC. We got some votes from the independents such as R.K. Poddera, Dinesh Goswami, B.P. Maurya and Devendra Dwivedi.

I felt small at this defeat suffered by the party at the very first encounter, all the more because some of our party members had defied the Whip and absented themselves. Indira Gandhi

---

[84] *Rajya Sabha Debates*, vol. CXII, no. 6, 30 January 1980, pp. 349.

told me to take it easy.

Nevertheless, I asked Bhishma Narain Singh, Minister for Parliamentary Affairs and the Chief Whip of the party to call for an explanation from each absentee member. Over the following two days, all four absentee members met me and expressed regret. My stern attitude yielded effect: in subsequent years I barely ever faced such a problem, though the Whip had to be used at times to keep the attendance steady.

During the same session, I had to cross another hurdle, an even more difficult one. An Ordinance had been proclaimed by the outgoing caretaker government, seeking to provide the central and the state governments with preventive detention powers to deal with black marketers and to maintain essential supplies. At that time, the Leftist chief ministers of West Bengal, Tripura and Kerala as well as the Congress (I) opposed the Ordinance, though for different reasons. While the former opposed it as a matter of principle, the Congress (I)'s objection was on the technical ground that a caretaker government could not assume such sweeping powers on the eve of elections. Now, after assuming office, we had to decide the fate of the Ordinance.

When we assumed office in January 1980, the wholesale price index had risen to 22.7 per cent, the highest in the 1980s. The government, hence, had decided to replace the Ordinance by a regular Bill—the Prevention of Black Marketing and Maintenance of Essential Supplies Bill—with the aim of adequately checking black marketers and hoarders and thus the prices. It was my responsibility to pilot the Bill in Parliament.

I faced stiff opposition in the Lok Sabha. In the Rajya Sabha, the Bill was discussed on 1 February and passed easily. It generated enormous interest in the media, as was evident in the headlines the next day across almost all national and regional newspapers. A few editorial comments were also made. While the parties of the Left maintained their principled opposition to the Bill, other parties took a peculiar stand. They opposed the Bill on the ground that the Congress (I) under Indira Gandhi could not be trusted with the power of preventive detention. They were certain that it would be misused as she had 'misused' MISA during the Emergency, despite an assurance given by her that it would not be used against political opponents. The stand taken by the Congress (Urs) and Lok Dal was amusing because they (the Charan-Chavan government) were the ones responsible for the promulgation of the Ordinance in the first place.

I appealed to opposition members not to be subjective and unduly obsessed with past experience. I explained the provisions of the Bill and pointed out that adequate constitutional safeguards had been incorporated to protect individual liberty. I also assured them that the government would ensure that the provisions were not misused. Jyoti Basu, in his characteristic manner, challenged the government and boasted that the communist governments in three states would not implement the law. I firmly pointed out that it was the constitutional responsibility of the central government to ensure the implementation of the law passed by Parliament, the highest national forum of the country. And that it was not sensible for any member to encourage non-implementation.

My reply to the debate was sharp and hard-hitting. I told the Janata Party members that if they were opposed to preventive detention on principle they could have removed the provisions from the Constitution when they introduced the Constitution Amendment Bill (48th Amendment). I asked the members belonging to the Lok Dal and the Congress (Urs) to explain the contradiction between their promulgation of the Ordinance in October 1979 and opposing the same provisions in January 1980. The Bill was passed by 188 to 56 votes in the Lok Sabha.

The CPI(M) saw the shadow of authoritarianism in the passage of this Bill. The party's leader in West Bengal, the late Promode Dasgupta, criticized my observations in the Lok Sabha and drew the conclusion that authoritarianism was raising its head. Chief Ministers Jyoti Basu of West Bengal, E.K. Nayanar of Kerala and Nripen Chakraborty of Tripura reiterated their unwillingness to implement the law. However, they pinned their hopes on the Bill getting defeated in the Rajya Sabha due to the numerical strength of the opposition parties in that House.

The Bill came to the Rajya Sabha for discussion on 4 February. Though the opposition tried to postpone the discussion, I requested the Chairman to start the discussion rather than set a new precedent. Bhupesh Gupta made a hard-hitting speech. I was the butt of his attack but, as usual, his attack had no malice. My reply to the debate was equally hard-hitting as it demolished all the arguments of the opposition speakers. All sections of the House congratulated me after my speech. Eminent lawyer and former Law Minister Shanti Bhushan quoted a number of jurists while opposing preventive detention on principle. I responded by saying that while I had no eminent jurist to back my argument in favour of continuing preventive detention, if I could, I would quote one authority and that would be Shanti Bhushan himself. I quoted a few lines from his speech in the Rajya Sabha in defence of preventive detention while piloting the Constitutional Amendment Bill in 1978.

The effect was telling. This had a devastating impact on the critics of the Bill, particularly the Janata Party. The attacks that came from Surjeet and Bhupesh Gupta were sharper. They contended that I was threatening the state governments which had declared their inability to implement the preventive detention law. One of my remarks at a press meet in Calcutta as well as an observation in the Lok Sabha had been interpreted as a warning to the state governments. While replying to the debate, I said that I had not threatened any state government; rather, I had merely explained the constitutional responsibility of the Union government in implementing a law passed by the Parliament. The session went into the evening and, as a matter of common courtesy, I invited all members to dinner. Bhupesh Gupta was cryptic in his remark when he said: 'Sir, gastronomically we have been enthused, because provision has been made for our dinner but that will not make any change in our stand.'[85] Being in a numerically better position in the Rajya Sabha, the opposition parties were confident of success, more so as they had defeated a government motion just a few days before—on 30 January. Besides, they had combined and decided to support a motion moved by Purabi Mukherjee of Congress (Urs) to refer this Bill to the Select Committee.

The confidence of the opposition parties about defeating the government on the motion also became obvious from the comments made by various members—in Parliament and outside. Not wishing to take a chance, I talked to all like-minded members and parties to garner their support: the DMK and the AIADMK were approached who assured us of their support, and a large number of unattached/independent members, too, promised their support. Not only that, a few members who were loath to support us openly agreed to absent themselves at the time of voting. I also ensured that all our party members presented themselves for the vote, and both my office and that of the whips were fully geared to meet the situation.

I succeeded. Purabi Mukherjee's motion was put to vote, and was rejected (87 votes cast in favour, 101 votes against). The main motion moved by me was then carried by voice vote. The

---

[85] *Rajya Sabha Debates*, vol. CXII, no. 9, 4 February 1980, pp. 251-252.

opposition was totally demoralized. Indira Gandhi personally congratulated me. She was present in the House at the time of voting, and jokingly told me, 'Though I have no voting in this House, I have to render you support.' She smiled when the electronic switchboard flashed the results. 'Congratulations,' she said.

The passage of this Bill became the lead news item in many national and regional dailies.

The *Times of India* (Delhi) reported:

The Congress (I) government secured a major victory in the opposition dominated Rajya Sabha today (04.02.1980), when the House adopted the controversial Prevention of Black Marketing and Maintenance of Essential Supplies Bill, rejecting an opposition amendment. The amendment which stood in the name of Mrs Purabi Mukherjee, Congress (U) sought to refer the Bill to an 18-member Select Committee of the House. It was turned down by 101 votes to 87.

Last week the government suffered a defeat when the opposition succeeded in amending the Motion of Thanks on the President's Address. Then the opposition amendment was carried by 80 votes in favour and 75 against. Congress (I) has only 79 members in the House having an effective strength of 232. It however seemed to have received the support of DMK and AIADMK parties having respective strength of five and seven. A few others including some independents supported the passage of the Bill. A total of 188 members were present, all voting either way, with no abstention.

My third confrontation with the opposition in the Rajya Sabha was in the context of the biennial elections to the Rajya Sabha due in March 1980. One-third of the members were to retire by

2 April 1980. The assemblies were dissolved on 17 February. Consequently, the assemblies of Bihar, Uttar Pradesh, Madhya Pradesh, Rajasthan, Gujarat, Punjab, Orissa, Tamil Nadu and Maharashtra were not in a position to fill the vacancies caused by the retirement of members from these states. While the Congress (I) did not have more than one member each from these states, the opposition parties had many. So out of the retiring members Congress (I) did not have more than 10-15 members while the opposition parties were to lose 60-70 members. The composition of the House would change radically after 2 April, and Congress (I) would not have to endure what it had to on earlier occasions. The President's proclamation of dissolution of the state assemblies and imposition of President's Rule was to be approved by the House within two months from the date of proclamation. The opposition parties demanded that the proclamation should be considered before 2 April. That is when they would still be in a position to vote out the proclamation and create a constitutional crisis. Indira Gandhi appointed a small group to discuss the issue of dissolving state assemblies which included me, Giani Zail Singh, P.V. Narasimha Rao, Bhishma Narain Singh and R. Venkataraman to examine this issue from various angles. We talked with senior state leaders of the party as also with some senior AICC leaders, including Kamalapati Tripathi, Stephen and others. The consensus was that these assemblies should be dissolved and fresh elections held. Someone suggested that we should win over the parties ruling in the states, as had been the case with Haryana and Himachal Pradesh. I did not approve of this line of action and told Indira Gandhi that it would be desirable to have a clear mandate from the people. It was also felt that, without a fresh mandate, the political smokescreen would not clear up. Accordingly, we recommended the dissolution of these assemblies, except for those in Karnataka, Haryana and Himachal Pradesh.

On the day of dissolution, I had gone to a nearby tourist spot in Haryana and spent the morning there, along with my family members and friends. Dharamvir Sinha and Sheikh Hasina Wajed (daughter of Mujibur Rahman), with her family, had also joined us at the picnic. Knowing that the formal announcement would be made in the evening, I returned by late afternoon.

When Parliament reassembled on 11 March 1980, there was a furore in both the Houses of Parliament. In the Rajya Sabha, the entire opposition came down heavily on the government. They wanted discussions on the resolution moved by the government to seek the approval of the House before 2 April. L.K. Advani, the leader of the opposition, Bhupesh Gupta and other opposition leaders spearheaded the attack. They described the move of the government as unconstitutional and undemocratic. After prolonged discussions on the points raised by opposition leaders, I rose to reply. I observed that since the Constitution provided that the approval of the House had to be sought within two months of the date of proclamation, the government was well within its rights to seek the approval any time before 17 April, the expiry of the two-month period. I disagreed with the main contention of the opposition leaders that after 2 April, the composition of the House would change as one-third of the members would retire rendering those seats vacant till the elections to state assemblies and the biennial elections to the Rajya Sabha. My argument was that the vacancies in some seats would not debar the House from discharging its constitutional duties and responsibilities. All states would have their representations in the House, since two-thirds of the members would remain and states like Andhra, Karnataka, Assam, West Bengal and Gujarat would have full representation, since the time for their biennial elections to the Rajya Sabha had yet to come. Secondly, the Supreme Court judgement had made it abundantly clear in the

1977 dissolution case that the theory of mandate was relevant. As a political party, we had accepted the judgement in this case despite our reservations at the initial stages when we challenged the government's order in 1977 in the Supreme Court. Shanti Bhushan pointed out that the verdict of the people in Uttar Pradesh and Bihar was not so decisive. Two states had given the ruling party some seats in the Lok Sabha election of 1980 and none to Congress in the election of 1977. I pointed out that, in 1977, assemblies had been dissolved in states like West Bengal, Orissa and Gujarat, too, though the Congress had got some Lok Sabha seats from these states. I pointed out that we were just following a precedent set by the Janata Party in 1977. When the members insisted on being informed of the exact date on which the resolution would be placed for approval, my answer was: 'At the appropriate time.' I did not yield to the pressure of the opposition leaders and ultimately they walked out. Their walkout was highlighted by the national and regional newspapers. The *Indian Express* (Delhi, 12 March) reported:

> The opposition members in Rajya Sabha today staged a walkout protesting against the government's refusal to commit itself to a firm date for seeking the approval of the House on the imposition of President's rule in nine States. Opposition members, exception [sic] a few independents and a DMK member, walked out when the Commerce Minister Pranab Mukherjee, who is the Leader of the House, said that the government would seek the approval of the House for the Presidential proclamation under Article 356 at an 'appropriate time'.
>
> Earlier, the members belonging to all the opposition parties had strongly criticized the government for its action dissolving nine state assemblies despite the concern shown

by the House when it passed an amendment to the Motion of Thanks to the President.

Pranab Mukherjee justified the dissolution of the nine state assemblies on the ground that the government in those states had lost the confidence of the people as reflected in the Lok Sabha poll. His own party which had opposed the dissolution of state assemblies in 1977 had accepted the Supreme Court verdict on the issue. 'It is wrong to call it an undemocratic act since people in these states are being given an opportunity to choose their rulers again,' he said. Mr Mukherjee also disputed the point made by some members that the House will not be fully representative if the government sought the approval on the Presidential proclamation after 2 April. 'This House is a continuing House even if some states are not fully represented,' he said.

L.K. Advani, who led the opposition walkout said that the Minister was straying from the basic issue. Disregarding of the views of the House on the dissolution issue was an affront to the House. He said, 'He has added insult to injury by indicating that the approval might be sought after 2 April when one-third of the members retire, leaving the House not wholly representative.'

Raising the issue immediately after the Minister of State for Home, Yogendra Makwana placed the proclamation of dissolving nine state assemblies on the Table of the House at the end of the Question Hour. The opposition members utilized the opportunity to criticize the government for its action and saw in it a threat to the federal structure of the country as well as revival of authoritarian trends.

Bhupesh Gupta and P. Ramamurthy had also strongly criticized the government's action. The Chairman, M. Hidayatullah, found it difficult to control the House. Chaos prevailed the next day as well and continued on the days that followed. The Chairman suggested that I agree to have discussions before 2 April. I told him that I would let him know on 19 March the exact date when the government would move the resolution for approval. I decided to move the resolution before 2 April as almost every member belonging to Congress (Urs) had started crossing the floor and swelling our ranks. Moreover, I was sure of the support of a few independents and the DMK members. The attitude of the Congress (Urs) members in the Rajya Sabha in the past was similar. After the split in the party in January 1978, we had only 15 members in the Rajya Sabha, and almost the same number in the Lok Sabha. When the Rajya Sabha met in February 1978, Kamalapati Tripathi was replaced by Bhola Paswan Shastri as the leader of the Congress Party. He led the majority party in the Rajya Sabha because the ruling party (Janata Party) had hardly any strength before the biennial elections in 1978. The scene underwent a dramatic change after 6 March when elections to the Andhra Pradesh, Karnataka and Maharashtra assemblies decisively established the popularity of Indira Gandhi over her detractors. Within weeks, the strength of Congress (I) rose from 15 to 65. The same story was repeated in the Lok Sabha and C.M. Stephen, the leader of our party, was recognized as the leader of opposition.

But this time, both Indira Gandhi and Sanjay Gandhi wanted to be selective in admitting members from the Congress (Urs) into our party. At one stage, I had advocated admitting the members liberally because of the compulsion of getting the resolution passed by the House. Both of them saw reason in my view but insisted that no commitment should be made to re-nominate them in the next biennial election. I fully agreed with this and made it quite clear to those seeking admission to our party that they should not expect any price for their support. The allegations made by the leaders of the opposition that Congress (I) had won over the Congress (Urs) members by promising them re-nomination in the next election or otherwise were baseless and unfounded. However, Congress (Urs)'s desire to return to the mainstream brought them back to the Congress. I was confident of winning in the Rajya Sabha. But while I did not like to be bullied by the opposition, I did not like the Chairman to exercise the exclusive right of determining the agenda of the House either. The Chairman had a desire to assume total power with regard to the business of the House. This role of a Presiding Officer may have been theoretically correct but was practically not possible. The House is a political institution, not merely a debating club. It has to transact the business of the nation initiated, and be guided by prevailing political forces. The Rajya Sabha was to play a balanced role in transacting business. It was not a secondary chamber but, at the same time, it could not take advantage of the numerical position of a party to play an obstructionist role against the wishes of the ruling party, which had come to power with the mandate of the people. So, the handling of a delicate situation by maintaining a balance required political judgement, not always available with persons otherwise eminent and competent.

I am of the view that offices such as those of the President and Vice President should not be held by people other than politicians, and the role of presiding officers in legislative chambers has to be similarly viewed. In India, presiding officers are elected with the support of political parties and, as such, one cannot expect them to be free of political inclination altogether. Though they must strive to remain neutral, their neutrality cannot be stretched to a ridiculous extent.

When the issue was raised again on the floor of the House on 12 March, I had to point out that the leader of the House had a say in deciding the business of the House. When the opposition leaders failed to get any firm date, they used their parliamentary skills to push the government into an awkward position. Bhupesh Gupta and others tabled a motion under rule 170 (Rules of Procedure and Conduct of Business in the Rajya Sabha) and A.C. Kulkarni moved a non-official resolution as his name was approved in the ballot under Rule 157. Both these motions had the same objective of discussing the proclamation and expressing disapproval of the government's action. It was a clear move on the part of the opposition and they were perfectly within their rights to resort to these methods by putting the government on the mat.

I consulted the whips and assessed the strength of the party as on that date. I also discussed with Indira Gandhi and assured her of getting the majority on the floor of the House. I also told her it would be desirable to settle the issue before 2 April, so that we could claim to have defeated the combined opposition even after honouring their wishes. Indira Gandhi saw logic in my suggestion. She told me not to be complacent but to work hard to ensure victory on the floor of the House. We admitted a large number of members from the Congress (Urs) who were only too eager to join the ruling party.

When the issue came up again before the House on 12 March, we made our position clear. I pointed out that with regard to government business, under Rule 23 the leader of the House, in consultation with the Chairman of the House, should indicate the date and time to be allocated in the Business Advisory Committee. The government business should get priority over other business. With regard to the admissibility of the motion, the Chairman's view was final. So I appealed to the members to keep in mind that mutual cooperation and understanding among the parties were necessary for the conduct of business in the House. On

19 March, I informed the Chairman and the Business Advisory Committee of the House that the government intended to move the resolution seeking approval of the Presidential proclamations in respect of nine states on 27 March. There was no need to admit any parallel motion by private members. This was agreed to in the Business Advisory Committee represented by all the political parties and presided over by the Chairman. Thus, the bitterness created in the House was done away with and the Chairman found it easier to have a smooth session in the House. By this approach, I also built up a good rapport with opposition leaders.

With an understanding among parties in the House, tackling situations becomes much easier. During my five-year period as Leader of the House, I received cooperation from opposition parties and leaders. Though it was not always smooth sailing, I sailed through some of the most challenging situations because of this.

When the government resolution seeking approval to the presidential proclamation in respect of nine states was moved and debated on 27 March, the opposition parties knew that they had no chance. A large number of members belonging to Congress (Urs) had already joined our party. Out of the eight Congress members from West Bengal, only Purabi Mukherjee, Sankar Ghosh, Jawaharlal Banerjee, Pratima Bose and Phani Hansda were in Congress (Urs). The rest, i.e., D.P. Chattopadhyaya, Ahmed Hossain Mondal and Prasenjit Barman voted with us. The statutory resolution of Bhupesh Gupta was negated by 95 to 119 votes and the government resolution moved by Giani Zail Singh, the then Home Minister, was carried by voice vote. After their resolution was voted out, the opposition parties walked out of the House. Before walking out, L.K. Advani observed, 'Sir, I and my colleagues regard this as a dark day of democracy... We cannot be a party to the approval of this resolution... These proclamations are anti-democratic...'[86] Other opposition groups, except the DMK and the Muslim League, and a few independents also walked out. Bhupesh Gupta once again showed his debating skills and ability in opposing the government's motion and in moving his own. His was one of the best speeches delivered on that occasion. While formally replying to the debate as the mover of the statutory resolution, he observed: 'Sir, we have fought a very important battle, that is our satisfaction. Many of us will be out of this scene some time or the other but the arguments, the logic, the reasons that have been advanced by us in support of our motion will remain just as theirs also will remain. It will be for the posterity to judge as to which side was speaking the voice of the people and of democracy, probity and integrity in public life and who was speaking the voice of a fanatic, frenzied, limitless lust for consolidation and extension of authoritarian personal power...' The sincerity with which he spoke was ringing loud and true. Unfortunately, the same could not be said of the other opposition leaders. They showed the path in 1977. What was done in 1980 was just a facsimile of the 1977 action. If the first was wrong in 1977, then it was wrong in 1980. But no one could claim what was justifiable for other parties was wrong for the Congress (I). In 1980, the Janata Party was paid back in its own coin. Some journalists attempted to explain that the grounds during the Janata Party rule were different and therefore justified. Most of the state assemblies then were continuing on an extended period, they said, as their five-year term was over in 1977 (elections took place in 1972). They continued because their life was extended by amending the Constitution during the Emergency. The press argued that the Janata Party had an additional ground to dissolve the state

---

[86]*Rajya Sabha Debates*, vol. CXIII, no. 12, p. 389.

assemblies, apart from the 'theory of mandate'. But there was one chink in this armour of argument. It was factually incorrect to say that all the state assemblies dissolved in 1977 had outlived their five-year term. The assemblies in Uttar Pradesh and Orissa were not supposed to have been dissolved until 1979, as election to these state assemblies had taken place in 1974. The Gujarat assembly was elected in 1975 and had its term up to 1980. The fact of the matter was that, in 1977, the Janata Party wanted to win elections to the state assemblies while the wave of popular support continued to flow in their favour. In 1980, the Congress wanted to do the same.

# EPILOGUE

*To safeguard democracy the people must have a keen sense of independence, self-respect, and their oneness.*

*The spirit of democracy cannot be imposed from without. It has to come from within.*

—Mahatma Gandhi

Mahatma Gandhi's observations have a prescient ring to them if we study the dramatic decade of the 1970s. Indira Gandhi, India's first woman Prime Minister, and one who had her finger on the pulse of the masses, was voted out by an unforgiving populace after the Emergency. But then, reminded of her vision of development and progress, her commitment to the cause of the poor and the disadvantaged and her ability to equally take the rough with the smooth and not waver, the people of India decisively brought her back to power in 1980. This was a true marker of the wisdom of the democratic set-up, and the sagacity of a people who could look beyond slander campaigns and innuendo, and stand by a leader's conviction of purpose. Those who had predicted the end of Indian democracy with the onset of the Emergency were proven wrong, as were those who had written off the political career of Indira Gandhi.

Indeed, this was the age when democracy matured. It all began with the Janata Party—an outfit that emerged in opposition to the Emergency, comprising the Congress (O), the Bharatiya Lok Dal, the Jana Sangh and the Socialists. While the Janata Party collapsed in a little over two years, plagued as it was by internal dissent and rivalry, its significance lay in signalling the advent of multiple political parties, particularly regional ones, and the emergence of coalition politics in the Indian political landscape.

In the subsequent decades, the 1980s and 1990s, the political play in India—with multiple parties and remarkable alliances— would not only mature but also grow wise with experience. I intend to explore these developments in greater detail in the next two volumes.

But no matter which period of history we study in India, there are few decades more significant than the 1970s. For this is the epoch that made India the vibrant democracy it is today.

# MUJIB'S 6-POINT CHARTER OF DEMANDS

- Point 1: Pakistan shall be a federal state. There shall be a parliamentary government formed by a legislature elected on the basis of universal adult franchise.
- Point 2: The federating units or the provinces shall deal with all affairs except foreign relations and defence.
- Point 3: There shall be two separate but easily convertible currencies for the two wings of Pakistan. Or, alternatively, there may be a single currency with the provision that the Federal Bank shall take adequate measures to stop the siphoning off from East Pakistan to West Pakistan.
- Point 4: The federating units or provinces shall reserve the rights to levy taxes. The central government, of course, shall have some share of the tax proceeds.
- Point 5: Separate accounts shall be maintained for the foreign exchange earnings of the two wings. The foreign exchange earned from foreign trade shall be under the control of the respective wings. The federating units shall be independent in conducting trades with foreign countries.
- Point 6: The federating provinces shall be able to raise para-militia or para-military forces for their own defences.

*Source:* http://www.albd.org/index.php/en/party/history/116-the-6-point-programme-magna-carta-of-bangalees (the official website of the Awami League). Accessed on 26 April 2014.

# PRESS STATEMENT ISSUED BY TAJUDDIN AHMAD, 11 APRIL 1971

[*This press statement has been reproduced in the third volume of the documents of the independence struggle of Bangladesh.*]

### TO THE PEOPLE OF THE WORLD

Bangladesh is at war. It has been given no choice but to secure its right of self-determination through a national liberation struggle against the colonial oppression of West Pakistan.

In the face of positive attempts by the Government of Pakistan to distort the facts in a desperate attempt to cover up their war of genocide in Bangladesh, the world must be told the circumstances under which the peace-loving people of Bangladesh were driven to substitute armed struggle for parliamentary politics to realise the just aspirations of the people of Bangladesh.

The Six Point Programme for autonomy for Bangladesh within Pakistan had been put forward in all sincerity by the Awami League as the last possible solution to preserve the integrity of Pakistan. Fighting the elections to the National Assembly on the issue of Six Points, the Awami League won 167 out of 169 seats from Bangladesh in a House of 313. Its electoral victory was so decisive that it won 80 per cent of the popular votes cast. The decisive nature of its victory placed it in a clear majority within the National Assembly.

The post election period was a time of hope, for never had a people spoken so decisively in the history of parliamentary democracy. It was widely believed in both Wings that a viable constitution based on Six Points could be worked out. The Pakistan people's party which emerged as the leading party in Sind and Punjab had avoided raising the issue of Six Points in their election campaign and had no obligation whatsoever to its electorate to resist it. In Baluchistan, the dominant party, National Awami Party, was fully committed to Six Points. In NWFP, the NAP, dominant in the Provincial Assembly, was also a believer in maximum autonomy. The course of the elections, which marked the defeat of the reactionary parties, therefore, gave every reason to be optimistic about the future of democracy in Pakistan.

Preparatory to the convening of the National Assembly talks were expected between the main parties in the political arena. However, whilst the Awami league was always willing, preparatory [sic] to going to the Assembly, to explain its constitutional position and to discuss alternative proposals from the other parties, it believed that the spirit of a true democracy demanded that the constitution be debated and finalised in the National Assembly rather than in secret sessions. To this end, it insisted on an early summoning of the National Assembly. In anticipation of this session, the Awami League worked day and night to prepare a draft constitution based on Six Points and fully examined all the implications of formulating and implementing such a constitution.

The first major talks over Pakistan's political future took place between General Yahya and Sheikh Mujibur Rahman in mid-January. In this session General Yahya probed the extent of the Awami League's commitment to its programme and was assured that they were fully aware of its implications. But contrary to expectation Yahya did not spell out his own ideas about the constitution. General Yahya gave the impression of not finding anything seriously objectionable in Six Points but emphasised the need for coming to an understanding with the PPP in West Pakistan.

The next round of talks took place between the PPP and the Awami League from 27th January, 1971 in Dacca where Mr. Bhutto and his team held a number of sessions with the Awami League to discuss the constitution.

As in the case with Yahya, Mr. Bhutto did not bring any concrete proposals of his own about the nature of the constitution. He and his advisers were mainly interested in discussing the implications of Six Points. Since their responses were essentially negative and they had no prepared brief of their own it was not possible for the talks to develop into serious negotiations where attempts could be made to bridge the gap between the two parties. It was evident that as yet Mr. Bhutto had no formal position of his own from which to negotiate.

It must be made clear that when the PPP left Dacca there was no indication from their part that a deadlock had been reached with the Awami League. Rather they confirmed that all doors were open and that following a round of talks with West Pakistani leaders, the PPP would either have a second and more substantive round of talks with the Awami League or would meet in the National Assembly whose committees provided ample opportunity for detailed discussion on the constitution.

Mr. Bhutto's announcement to boycott the National Assembly therefore came as a complete surprise. The boycott decision was surprising because Mr. Bhutto had already been accommodated once by the President when he refused Sheikh Mujib's plea for an early session of the Assembly on 15th February and fixed it, in line with Mr. Bhutto's preference, for 3rd March.

Following his decision to boycott the Assembly, Mr. Bhutto launched a campaign of intimidation against all other parties in West Pakistan to prevent them from attending the session. In this task, there is evidence that Lt. Gen. Umer, Chairman of the National Security Council and close associate of Yahya, with a view to strengthening Mr. Bhutto's hand, personally pressurised various West

Wing leaders not to attend the Assembly. In spite of this display of pressure tactics by Mr. Bhutto and Lt. Gen. Umer, all members of the National Assembly from West Pakistan, except the PPP and the Qayyum Muslim League, had booked their seats to East Pakistan, for the session of 3rd March.

Within the QML itself, half their members had booked their seats and there were signs of revolt within the PPP where many members were wanting to come to Dacca. Faced with the breakdown of this joint front against Bangladesh, General Yahya obliged Mr. Bhutto on 1st March by postponing the Assembly, not for finite period, but sine die. Moreover he dismissed the Governor of East Pakistan, Admiral S. M. Ahsan, who was believed to be one of the moderates in his administration. The Cabinet with its component of Bengalis was also dismissed so that all power was concentrated in the hands of the West Wing military Junta.

In these circumstances, Yahya's gesture could not be seen as anything but an attempt to frustrate the popular will by colluding with Mr. Bhutto. The National Assembly was the only forum where Bangladesh could assert its voice and political strength, and to frustrate this was a clear indication that Parliament was not to be the real source of power in Pakistan.

The reaction to the postponement in Bangladesh was inevitable and spontaneous and throughout the land people took to the streets to record their protest at this arbitrary act. People now felt sure that Yahya never really intended to transfer power, and was making a mockery of parliamentary politics. The popular mood felt that the rights of Bangladesh could never be realised within the framework of Pakistan, where Yahya could so blatantly frustrate the summoning of an Assembly proclaimed by his own writ and urged that Sheikh Mujibur Rahman must go for full independence.

Sheikh Mujib however continued to seek a political settlement. In calling for a programme of non-cooperation on 3rd March he chose the weapon of peaceful confrontation against the army of occupation as an attempt to bring them to their senses. This was in itself a major gesture in the face of the cold blooded firing on unarmed demonstrators on the 2nd and 3rd March which had already led to over a thousand casualties.

The course of the non-cooperation movement is now a part of history. Never in the course of any liberation struggle has non-cooperation been carried to the limits attained within Bangladesh between 1st and 25th March. Non-cooperation was total. No Judge of the High Court could be found to administer the oath of office to the new Governor, Lt. General Tikka Khan. The entire civilian administration including the police and the Civil Service of Pakistan, refused to attend office. The people stopped supply of food to the army. Even the civilian employees of the Defence establishment joined the boycott.

Non-cooperation did not stop at abstention from work. The civilian administration and police positively pledged their support to Sheikh Mujibur Rahman and put themselves under his orders.

In this situation the Awami League without being a formally constituted Government, was forced to take on the responsibility of keeping the economy and administration running whilst non-cooperation lasted. In this task they had the unqualified support not only of the people but the administration and business community. The latter two subordinated themselves to the directives of Awami League and accepted them as the sole authority to solve their various problems.

In these unique circumstances the economy and administration were kept going in spite of the formidable problems arising out of the power vacuum which had suddenly emerged in Bangladesh. In spite of the lack of any formal authority, Awami League volunteers in cooperation with the police maintained a level of law and order which was a considerable improvement on normal times.

Faced with this demonstration of total support to the Awami League and this historic non-cooperation movement, General Yahya appears to have modified his tactics. On the 6th March he still seemed determined to provoke a confrontation when he made his highly provocative speech, putting the full blame for the crisis on the Awami League and not even referring to the architect of the crisis, Mr. Bhutto. It seems that he expected a declaration of independence on 7th March. The Army in Dacca was put on full alert to crush the move and Lt. Gen. Tikka Khan was flown to replace Lt. Gen. Yakub to signify the hardening of attitudes within the Junta.

Sheikh Mujib, however, once again opted for the path of political settlement in spite of massive public sentiment for independence. In presenting his 4-point proposal for attending the National Assembly he not only had to contain the public mood but to leave a way open for Yahya to explore this last chance for a peaceful settlement.

It is now clear that Yahya and his Generals never had the slightest intention of solving Pakistan's political crisis peacefully but were only interested in buying time to permit the reinforcement of their military machine within Bangladesh. Yahya's visit to Dacca was a mere cover for his plan of genocide. It now becomes clear that contingency plans for such a crisis had already begun well in advance of the crisis.

Shortly before 1st March tanks which had been sent north to Rangpur to defend the borders were brought back to Dacca. From 1st March the families of Army personnel were being sent off to West Pakistan on a priority basis along with the families of West Pakistani businessmen.

The military build-up was accelerated after 1st March and continued throughout the talks upto 25th March. Members of the armed forces dressed in civilian clothes were flown in PIA commercial flights via Ceylon. C-130s carrying arms and provisions for the garrisons flew into Dacca. It is estimated that upto one division, with complementary support, was brought into Bangladesh between 1st and 25th March. To ensure security, the airport was put under strict airforce control and heavily guarded with artillery and machine-gun nets whilst movement of passengers was strictly supervised. An SSC Commando Group specially trained for undercover operations in sabotage and assassinations was distributed in key centres of Bangladesh and were probably responsible for the attacks on Bengalis in Dacca and Saidpur in the two days before 25th March to provoke clashes between locals and non-locals so as to provide a cover for military intervention.

As part of this strategy of deception Yahya adopted the most conciliatory posture in his talks with Mujib. In the talks beginning on 16th March, he expressed regrets for what had happened and his sincere desire for a political settlement. In a crucial meeting with Sheikh Mujib, he was asked to positively state the Junta's position on the Awami League's 4-point proposal.

He indicated that there were no serious objections and that an interim constitution could be worked out by the respective Advisers embodying the four points.

The basic points on which agreement was reached were:

1. Lifting of Martial Law and transfer of power to a Civilian Government by a Presidential proclamation.
2. Transfer of power in the provinces to the majority parties.
3. Yahya to remain as President and in control of the Central Government.
4. Separate sittings of the National Assembly members from East and West Pakistan preparatory to joint session of the House to finalise the constitution.

Contrary to the distortions now put out by both Yahya and Bhutto the proposal for separate sittings of the Assembly was suggested by Yahya to accommodate Mr. Bhutto. He cited the practical advantage that whilst 6-points provided a viable blueprint to regulate relations between Bangladesh and the Centre its application would raise serious difficulties in the West Wing. For this reason West Wing MNA's must be permitted to get together to work out a new pattern of relationships in the context of a Six-Point constitution and the dissolution of one-Unit.

Once this agreement in principle had been reached between

Sheikh Mujib and Yahya there was only the question of defining the powers of Bangladesh vis-à-vis the Centre during the interim phase. Here it was again jointly agreed that the distribution of power should be as far as possible approximate to the final constitution approved by the National Assembly which it was expected would be based on 'Six Points'.

For working out this part of the interim settlement Mr. M.M. Ahmed, the Economic Adviser to the president, was specially flown in. In his talks with the Awami League advisers he made it clear that provided the political agreement had been reached there were no insuperable problem to working out some version of Six Points even in the interim period. The final list of three amendments to the Awami League draft which he presented as suggestions, indicated that the gap between the Government and Awami League position was no longer one of principle but remained merely over the precise phrasing of the proposals. The Awami League in its sitting of 24th March accepted the amendments with certain minor changes of language and there was nothing to prevent the holding of a final drafting session between the advisers of Yahya and Mujib when the interim constitution would be finalised.

It must be made clear that at no stage was there any breakdown of talks or any indication by General Yahya or his team that they had [a] final position which could not be abandoned.

The question of legal cover for the transfer of power is merely another belated fabrication by Yahya to cover his genocide. He and his team had agreed that, in line with the precedence of the Indian Independence Act of 1947, power could be transferred by Presidential Proclamation. The notice that there would be no legal cover to the arrangement raised subsequently by Mr. Bhutto and endorsed by General Yahya was never a bone of contention between Sheikh Mujib and Yahya. There is not the slightest doubt that had Yahya indicated that a meeting of the National Assembly was essential to transfer power, the Awami League would not have broken the talks on such a minor legal technicality. After all as the majority party it had nothing to fear from such a meeting and its acceptance of the decision for a separate sitting was designed to accommodate Mr. Bhutto rather than a fundamental stand for the party.

Evidence that agreement in principle between contending parties had been reached is provided by Mr. Bhutto's own Press Conference on 25th March. It is not certain what passed in the separate session between General Yahya and Mr. Bhutto but there is evidence that deliberate falsehoods about the course of the talk with the Awami League were fed to the PPP who were told that Sheikh Mujib was determined to have a showdown and was daily escalating his demands. Needless to say not the slightest indication of these misgivings had been raised in the meetings between the Awami League team and General Yahya's advisers where amicability and optimism prevailed to the end.

Whilst hope for a settlement was being raised, more ominous signs of the intentions of the army were provided by their sudden decision to unload the munition ships M.V. Swat berthed at Chittagong Port. Preparatory to this decision, Brigadier Mazumdar, a Bengali officer commanding the garrison in Chittagong, had been suddenly removed from his command and replaced by a West Pakistani. On 24th night he was flown to Dacca under armed escort and has probably been executed. Under the new command notice was given to local authorities of the decision to unload the ship inspite of the fact that the army had abstained doing so for the last 17 days in the face of non-cooperation from the port workers. The decision to unload was a calculated provocation which immediately brought 1,00,000 people on the streets of Chittagong and led to massive firing by the Army to break their way out. The issue was raised by the Awami League with General Peerzada as to why this escalation was being permitted whilst talks were still going on. He gave no answer beyond a promise to pass it on to General Yahya.

Following the final meeting between General Yahya's and Awami League's advisers on 24th March where Mr. M.M. Ahmed passed on his amendments, a call was awaited from General Peerzada for final session where the draft could be finalised. No such call materialised and instead it was learnt that Mr. M.M. Ahmed who was central to the negotiations, had suddenly left for Karachi on the 25th morning without any warning to the Awami League team.

By 11 P.M. of the 25th all preparations were ready and the troops began to take up their positions in the city. In an act of treachery unparalleled in contemporary history a programme of calculated genocide was unleashed on the peaceful and unsuspecting population of Dacca by midnight of 25th March. No ultimatum was given to the Awami League by Yahya, no curfew order was even issued when the machine guns, artillery and cannon on the tanks unleashed their reign of death and destruction.

By the time the first Martial Law proclamations issued by Lt. General Tikka Khan were broadcast the next morning some 50,000 people, most of them without offering any resistance, and many women and children, had been butchered. Dacca had been turned into an inferno with fires raging in most corners of the city. Sleeping inhabitants who had been drawn from their homes by the fires started by the military, were machine-gunned as they ran to escape the flames.

Whilst the Police, EPR and armed volunteers put up a heroic resistance, the main victims remained the weak, the innocent and the unsuspecting who were killed at random in their thousands. We are compiling a first hand account of the details of genocide committed by the Pakistan Army on the orders of the President of Pakistan which we will publish shortly. The scale and brutality of the action exceeds anything perpetrated in the civilised world.

Yahya himself left Dacca on the night of 25th March after having unleashed the Pakistan Army, with an open licence to commit genocide on all Bengalis. His own justification for this act of barbarism was not forthcoming till 8 P.M. the next day when the world was given its first explanation for the unleashing of this holocaust. The statement was self-contradictory and laced with positive lies. His branding of a party as traitors and outlaws, with whom he had only 48 hours ago been negotiating for a peaceful transfer of power, bore no relationship to the situation in Bangladesh or the course of the negotiations. His promise to hand over power to the elected representatives of the people after banning the Awami League which was the sole representatives of Bangladesh and held a majority of seats in the National Assembly was a mockery of the freely recorded voice of 75 million Bengalis. The crudity of the statement was clear evidence that Yahya was no longer interested in taking shelter behind either logic or morality and had reverted to the law of the jungle in his bid to crush the people of Bangladesh.

Pakistan is now dead and buried under a mountain of corpses. The hundreds and thousands of people murdered by the army in Bangladesh will act as an impenetrable barrier between West Pakistan and the people of Bangladesh. By resorting to pre-planned genocide Yahya must have known that he was himself digging Pakistan's grave. The subsequent massacres perpetrated on his orders by his licensed killers on the people were not designed to preserve the unity of a nation. They were acts of racial hatred and sadism devoid of even the elements of humanity. Professional soldiers, on orders, violated their code of military honour and were seen as beasts of prey who indulged in an orgy of murder, rape, loot, arson and destruction unequalled in the annals of civilisation. These acts indicate that the concept of two countries is already deeply rooted in the minds of Yahya and his associates who would not dare commit such atrocities on their own countrymen.

Yahya's genocide is thus without political purpose. It serves only as the last act in the tragic history of Pakistan which Yahya has chosen to write with the blood of the people of Bangladesh. The objective is genocide and scorched-earth before his troops are either driven out or perish. In this time he hopes to liquidate our political, intelligentsia and administration, to destroy our industries and public amenities and as a final act he intends to raze our cities to the ground. Already his occupation Army has made substantial progress towards this objective. Bangladesh will be set back fifty years as West Pakistan's parting gift, to a people they have exploited for twenty-three years for their own benefit.

This is a point of major significance to those great powers who choose to ignore this largest single act of genocide since the days of Belsen and Auschwitz. If they think they are preserving the unity of Pakistan, they can forget it because Yahya himself has no illusion about the future of Pakistan.

They must realise that Pakistan is dead murdered by Yahya— and that independent Bangladesh is a reality sustained by the indestructible will and courage of 75 million Bengalis who are daily nurturing the roots of this new nationhood with their blood. No power on earth can unmake this new nation and sooner or later both big and small powers will have to accept it into the world fraternity.

It is, therefore, in the interest of politics as much as humanity for the big powers to put their full pressure on Yahya to cage his killers and bring them back to West Pakistan. We will be eternally grateful to the people of the USSR and India and the freedom loving people of all the countries for their full support they have already given us in this struggle. We would welcome similar support from the People's Republic of China, USA, France and Great Britain and others. Each in their own way should exercise considerable leverage on West Pakistan; and were they to exercise this influence, Yahya could not sustain his war of aggression against Bangladesh for a single day longer.

Bangladesh will be the eighth most populous country in the world. Its only goal will be to rebuild a new nation from the ashes and carnage left behind by Yahya's occupation army. It will be a stupendous task because we are already one of the world's poorest nations. But we now have a cause and a people who have been hardened in the resistance, who have shed their blood for their nation and won their freedom in an epic struggle which pitted unarmed people against a modern army. Such a nation cannot fail in its task of securing the foundations of its nationhood.

In our struggle for survival we seek the friendship of all people, the big powers and the small. We do not aspire to join any bloc or pact but will seek assistance from those who give it in a spirit of goodwill free from any desire to control our destinies. We have struggled far too long for our self-determination to permit ourselves to become any one's satellite.

We now appeal to the nations of the world for recognition and assistance both material and moral in our struggle for nationhood. Every day this is delayed a thousand lives are lost and more of Bangladesh's vital assets are destroyed. In the name of Humanity, act now and earn our undying friendship.

This we now present to the world as the CASE of the people of Bangladesh. No nation has a greater right to recognition, no people have fought harder for this right.

Joy Bangla!

Tajuddin Ahmad
Prime Minister of Bangladesh
17 April 1971

# INDIRA GANDHI'S LETTERS TO THE SHAH COMMISSION

*In her letter dated 21 November 1977, Indira Gandhi stated:*

'I should further like to point out that the terms of reference of this Hon'ble Commission are one-sided and politically motivated. While they empower the Hon'ble Commission to enquire into the excesses committed during the emergency, they are silent about the circumstances which led to its declaration. This country is vast and beset with deep-rooted and wide-ranging problems. The administrative machinery is fragmented. Urgent measures have to be taken. Programmes are implemented at various levels and by different individuals and agencies. Some excesses in their implementation cannot always be avoided nor do they always come to notice at that time. I have publicly expressed regret for any unjust hardship caused to any individual. But if the professed purpose of the inquiry is to check abuse of power in the future, it is equally imperative that the circumstances which created chaotic conditions in the nation before the emergency should also be enquired into and not allowed to be repeated. For two years preceding the emergency, the country was in the grip of grave crisis. The economic situation had deteriorated due mainly to internal and international causes beyond our control. Interested parties and groups wished deliberately to aggravate the situation for their own gain.

Freedom of speech and expression were used to spread hatred and parochial regional sentiments. Noble institutions of learning were turned into hot-beds of political intrigue. Public property was destroyed at the slightest excuse. A Minister in the present cabinet is reported to have proudly claimed, "In November last year [1975] in the Union state of Karnataka alone, we caused derailment of 52 trains." The attempt was to paralyse national life. The dissolution of Gujrat [sic] assembly was forced by undemocratic means. Duly elected legislators were beaten and intimidated into resigning from their seats in the Assembly.

Relying upon the judgment of the Allahabad High Court the demand for my resignation was made in the name of democracy and morality. But what was the morality and how did democracy come in? If at all, moral considerations were on my side as nothing had been found by the High Court against me which smacked of moral turpitude. I had lost on a legal technicality but law also gave me the right to reconsideration of the judgment by the highest court. And the act of seeking to remove a duly elected leader of the majority party through threats to gherao me and with a call to the Army and Police to revolt could not be justified in the name of any known democratic principles. A chaotic state of affairs similar to that in India before July 1975 prevailed in France when de Gaulle came to power. His major response was constitutional reform and the introduction of Article 16 in the new Constitution goes a long way to show how necessary it became for my government to resort to the emergency provisions in the Constitution if India were to pull herself out of the impending disaster. The new Article provided *inter alia* that "When the regular functioning of the constitutional governmental authorities is interrupted, the President of the Republic shall take the measures commanded by the circumstances" to restore order.

It must also be borne in mind that it would be impossible for a democratically elected government to function effectively if it is to live under the fear of politically inspired inquisitorial proceedings against its policies and decisions by a subsequent government.'

*In her letter dated 2 December 1997 she observed:*

'In fact, that the declaration of Emergency, according to this Hon'ble Commission, might be an excess and therefore calls for an inquiry, is a matter which does not fall within the purview of this Hon'ble Commission. The proclamation of Emergency by the President was a Constitutional step. It was approved by the Cabinet and duly ratified by both the Houses of Parliament in terms of Article 352(2) of the Constitution. After the ratification, the proclamation, which was political in character, became an Act of Parliament. In the United States the exercise of political power by the President has been held to be beyond challenge. Chief Justice Marshall observed in Marbury Vs Madison:

> By the constitution of the United States the President is invested with certain important political powers in the exercise of which he is to use his own discretion, and is accountable only to his country in his political character and to his own conscience...The subjects are political. They respect the nation, not individual rights and being entrusted to the Executive, the decision of the Executive is conclusive.

Under the Indian Constitution, on the other hand, the proclamation of Emergency has been made subject to ratification by parliament. No authority in this country, not excluding any commission appointed under the Commission of Inquiry Act, can sit in judgment over such an Act of Parliament. For any political decision, the Government under our Constitution is answerable only to Parliament. If this Hon'ble Commission arrogates to itself the power to determine that the declaration of Emergency was an excess, this Hon'ble Commission will not only be stultifying the Constitutional Scheme, but also establishing a precedent which will make serious inroads into Parliamentary supremacy with disastrous consequences to Parliamentary freedom. Even the terms of reference of this Hon'ble Commission do not warrant such an inquiry. They are strictly confined to the determination of the alleged excesses during the emergency or in the days immediately preceding it.

But apart from this, I should like to bring to the notice of the Hon'ble Commission that while making its pronouncement on my submission that the terms of reference were one-sided and politically motivated and that it was equally imperative that this Hon'ble Commission should go into the circumstances which led to the declaration of Emergency. This Hon'ble Commission observed as follows:

> But one thing I propose to bring to the notice, I am only concerned with the declaration of Emergency, if it amounts to an excess and not otherwise. If on consideration of the material before me, I am *prima facie* of the view that the declaration of Emergency could be regarded as an excess, an inquiry in open will be made. If, however, there is no such view formed by me, no such inquiry will be made.

This observation of the Hon'ble Commission, I most respectfully submit, is not sustainable. In the first place it is tantamount to saying: There shall be an inquiry into the declaration of Emergency if I can be damned in the process, but there shall be no inquiry if others whose actions justified the declaration of Emergency, are likely to be damned. Secondly, it is difficult to imagine how this Hon'ble Commission can take any decision regarding the declaration of Emergency without full consideration of the range of circumstances and the incidents which had accumulated for a long time preceding the proclamation, into an imminent threat to paralyse the duly elected government at the Centre and in the States.

During the period, ostensibly the attacks were concentrated upon me. In reality, the political opposition had been using this strategy to weaken the Central Government and subvert its socialist and progressive programmes for quite some years. It was a question of change versus the status quo. Secular democratic socialism on the one hand and the retrograde, communal and capitalistic forces on the other had been struggling against each other to gain the upper hand. The split in the Congress in 1969 gave an edge to this confrontation. The nationalisation of banks and other measures which disturbed the entrenched privileges and the vested interests, and offered opportunity and help to the poor and the weaker sections of our society, created such tremendous popular upsurge that the communal and capitalistic elements probably lost all hope of being able to successfully fight on an ideological plane. Hence they changed their methods. Similar[ly], such political phenomenon was not peculiar to India. Recent history is replete with such instances.

The vicious campaign of character assassination and denigration waged by the political opponents denuded Indian politics of all ideological debates. Even in the 1971 Lok Sabha elections, the opposition did not put forth any alternative economic or social programme. I was the focus of attack as the first target. Ordinary human decency was lost in the process. Their decisive defeat at the polls frustrated their faith in the democratic process. There was then a short interlude during which India faced one of the gravest challenges with which any nation has been confronted. The influx of ten million refugees from Bangladesh, the aggression and the subsequent war, the unprecedented country-wide drought and the global inflationary spiral aggravated by the oil crisis, and other factors would have upset the economic balance of any rich and developed country. India was fighting for her economic survival. It was during this period that the then Opposition resorted to extra-constitutional means to paralyse of our democratic institutions. As I have explained in my previous statement, there was hardly any sphere of national life which was not sought to be disrupted.

The inevitable distress of many sections of our people was exploited to mount attacks on duly elected Governments and Assemblies of the day. We cannot forget the tragic circumstances leading to the dissolution Gujrat [sic] Assembly only a few months after its constitution.

It was in this political atmosphere prevailing in the country that the judgment of the Allahabad High Court was delivered and was seized upon by the opposition to whip up political frenzy against me. Although I was the immediate target, the real design was to dislodge the Congress Government and to capture power through extra-constitutional measures. If a duly elected Government can be allowed to be pulled down by threats of violence and demonstrations in the streets and by incitement of the army and police to revolt, the democratic structure of the nation would collapse. In 1958, while putting the case for constitutional reforms, the French Prime Minister, Mr Gallard said: "Democracy is only a consequence and if those who hold power by the will of the majority do not also enjoy an authority corresponding to the responsibilities which they assume..."

As the Prime Minister of the country, I could not abdicate my responsibility to stem the impending disaster merely for the fear that my motive in proclaiming the emergency could be suspected. When the democratic institutions of a nation are held to ransom and the Government of the day rises to the occasion to meet the challenge, certain freedom of some individuals might be affected. That in fact is the rationale behind Article 352 of the Constitution which authorizes the declaration of Emergency. Emergency was not intended to cause sufferings and I have expressed deep sorrow for any hardship caused.

It may not be out of place to draw the attention of this Hon'ble Commission to the present Prime Minister, Shri Morarji Desai's recent observations in the Rajya Sabha that there was "nothing like absolute right to anybody... Every right is subject to the right of the whole society. If the rights of the whole society are in danger, the Government is bound to take action to prevent that danger."

In these circumstances, the Hon'ble Commission's predetermination, of certain dates while circumscribing the scope of its inquiry belies the reality. It has been repeatedly proclaimed by the members of the present Union Government that it was allegedly because of the Allahabad High Court judgment of 12th June, 1975 and the qualified stay given by the Supreme Court on [the] 22nd of June, that the Emergency was declared for personal reasons, namely to stultify the judgment by extra-legal means and to maintain my position as the Prime Minister by extra-constitutional methods, I have to point out with utmost respect, that the Commission appears to have projected the theory propagated by my political opponents.

By putting the inquiry beforehand into a pre-determined chronological matrix, the evidence would naturally proceed under the conditioning of this predetermined matrix, and this untested material will be systematically publicised to make it appear as proof. This, in my humble opinion, directly defeats the ends of justice.'

# EXTRACTS OF SPEECHES IN PARLIAMENT
## CRITICAL OF THE EMERGENCY

Though the Press was under censorship during Emergency, MPs of the opposition parties used the floor of the House to express their views on the existing political situation.

Mohan Dharia was a member of Lok Sabha elected on Congress (R) ticket in 1971. He was a Minister of State in Indira Gandhi's government from 1971 to 1974 but was later suspended from the party. Dharia was detained under MISA in December 1975, and became Minister of Commerce (1977-1979) in the Morarji Desai government. On 22 July 1975, Dharia said in his Lok Sabha speech:

Sir, the 26th day of June 1975, the day when the Emergency was declared, when my colleagues, several political workers and leaders were barbarously put behind bars, when the freedom of Press and civil liberties were surrendered to the bureaucrats, that day will be treated as the blackest day in Indian Democracy and in the history of our country.

I would at the outset like to condemn this monstrous operation. I have no doubt that it is the Prime Minister and a few of her colleagues who are responsible for it. I am not charging the whole Cabinet [Dharia was an ardent follower of Y.B Chavan, a senior member of Indira Gandhi's cabinet] because I know that even the Cabinet was not told about it [till] after the operation was already initiated...

A systematic propaganda is being carried on that it is because of the opposition parties, it is because of the right reactionary forces, it is because of the extremists, that the economic programme could not be implemented. Is it true?...

I know things from close quarters. In 1969 in Bangalore my amendment was supported by 170 members of the AICC, an amendment to nationalize the banks, it was not done. But no sooner was the political life of the Prime Minister was at stake than the banks were nationalized. The Party welcomed it. The Party did not split on programmes, the party split for personalities. But even then we welcomed it, because we felt that it would accelerate the whole process of the politics of commitment. Unfortunately, it did not happen. After the massive mandate nobody prevented us from implementing that. It is we who faltered... let me be allowed to say that when I look at the '21 Point Programme', the basic decisions are not there... All these programmes could have been implemented without declaration of Emergency. To say that an Emergency was necessary is a blatant lie, if I may be allowed to use that word, no other word could be found fit for it.

On 21 July 1975, Krishan Kant, another Congress Member of the Upper House of the Parliament who was subsequently expelled from the party, had observed on the floor of the Rajya Sabha:

It is very difficult to associate my Congress colleagues Chandra Shekhar and Ram Dhan with rightist conspiracy. Chandra Shekhar had remained radical and leftist and a fighter for the poor... However these two friends can turn overnight right reactionary conspirators? I have always been a Congress Socialist who believes that socialism in India has to be brought about by application of Gandhian principles... Nobody stopped the Congress party from carrying out radical restructuring of the economy of the country and taking the measures to eradicate poverty. The rightists outside the Congress were too weak to stop us from carrying out the programme. It is certain forces in the party which were too strong to allow us to implement them. Today, unfortunately, it is not the obstructionist forces who have been arrested but Chandra Shekhar and Ram Dhan. Chandra Shekhar's leftism and nationalism is [sic] too visible to be recounted here. Ram Dhan, a leader of the weaker sections, has been fighting for the causes of the downtrodden and poor. What prevented the Congress and the Government to follow up the bank nationalization and election manifestos of 1971 and 1972 with vigorous measures? Which opposition obstructed the Prime Minister and the Government in 1971, '72, '73 and early months of 1974? Even though we had the biggest majority, yet we did not have the will to act and implement radical measures. Besides passing some legislations on paper and making some amendments to the Constitution what have we done?

I would like to ask who amongst the Congress leaders have been punished for sabotaging the Congress programme during the last five years? Only Krishna Kant, Chandra Shekhar, Mohan Dharia and Ram Dhan. Their only crime known to the people in the country was their total commitment to the continuous insistence upon implementing party programmes and policies both in letter and spirit. If we agitated against malpractices and corruption it was in the high tradition of the Congress. Today, who are the supporters and enthusiasts of the 20-point programme? Read the censored newspapers. The daily retinue to the Prime Minister's house will show that the saboteurs of the Congress economic programme are now the enthusiastic supporters of the Emergency.

Those who have been profited by inflation and sabotage of Government Policies have turned overnight into loud mouthed supporters of the 20-point programme. Let me warn you against such time servers who are supporting her programmes as [the] noose supports the persons to be hanged...

Bereft of ideology, this nation is drifting towards a personality cult, into slogan shouting, gimmickry and into total immobilization. Cabinet colleagues have not been taken into confidence, senior partymen who have spent their lifetime in the party are not with us today. The men dedicated to the values of Gandhi, Nehru and socialism have been put under arrest. In this situation, who is going to implement the 20-point programme?

Next comes an extract from the speech of A.K. Gopalan, Leader of CPI(M) in the Lok Sabha on 21 July 1975:

I rise to speak in an extraordinary and most distressing situation in which thirty-four members of Parliament are not here, not on their own volition, but because they have been detained without trial, and Parliament itself has been reduced to a farce and an object of contempt by Shrimati Gandhi and her party... On behalf of the CPI (M) I totally oppose the new declaration of Emergency and its ratification in this House. We know fully well that in the present situation no one is free from arrest and detention. There are hundreds of persons inside the jail including Congressmen. There was a rumour—when I was inside jail—that Jagjivan Ram and Shri Chavan were under house arrest. I do not know how far it is correct or not. Many leaders of opposition as well as thirty-nine members of Parliament including some Congress leaders are inside the jail. We cannot betray the interests of people and cannot give our assent to the obliteration of all vestiges of democracy in India—freedom of the person, freedom of speech, freedom of press, freedom to criticize the Government and work for its replacement by a Government of the people's choice, freedom to form association, freedom to approach the courts... Every day Constitutional changes are coming... Every day, every hour.

Our such suspension means that there is not even equality before the law. Any discrimination can be practiced by the executive. Any person arrested need not be produced before the Court. The news of his arrest, whereabouts condition can be kept completely secret. He may be physically liquidated by the police and nobody need know anything about it. This is the position today. The camouflage of the Emergency being used only against right reactionary parties, has been fully exposed by indiscriminate arrests of the thousands of CPI (M) and other left and democratic party leaders and workers. The police have been left loose on the people. In Kerala, for example, thousands of political workers belonging to the Opposition parties including the CPI(M), the Kerala Congress, the Socialist Party and so on were arrested and large number brutally beaten...

The industrialists in the name of productivity can impose any workload and retrench workers and any protest will be crushed. Wage cuts and DA cuts can be resorted to and any resistance shall be crushed. Working conditions can be worsened and the least protest will be met by summary dismissal. No movement against this exploitation will be allowed. In the rural areas too, the agricultural workers fighting for better wages, tenants fighting against evictions, all will meet the same fate. That is why these measures virtually amount to dictatorship of the bourgeois and landlords against all other sections of the people...

Who will believe that by suppressing the popular forces fighting against the monopolies and landlords and by denying them all democratic rights, Indira Gandhi is fighting against right reaction?

Source: Lok Sabha Debates, vol. LIII, 22 July 1975, pp. 258-259.

# EXTRACTS FROM THE CPI(M)
# MANIFESTO

On 1 May (May Day) 1976, the CPI (M) issued a manifesto which runs as follows:

Comrades! Workers! Employees! Toilers of India!

Raise the flag of working class unity on May Day! Raise the flag of solidarity of workers of India with the peasants, with the agricultural workers, with all toiling people. Comrades! Never since Independence has such an offensive been waged by the big capitalists and landlords against the working class and people. Never have the working class and people of India been deprived of every semblance of right by the regime of the capitalists and landlords as after the declaration of Emergency on June 26, 1975.

The Indira Gandhi regime, under the signboard of fighting reaction, launched a wholesale attack on the liberties of all sections of the people, on peasants, on the middle class, on the working class. Its purpose is to ensure unbridled exploitation of the people of India by the capitalists and landlords. The anti-people regime has deprived the people and the working class of the right to hold meetings and demonstrations. It has banned all strikes and trade union agitations. Through the Press censorship law and other measures the regime has brought the entire Press under its control. It has stifled every criticism of its anti-people actions. It has banned all news of working class strikes and struggles, all news of the suffering of the common people. No trade union can issue a leaflet or a poster calling the workers to action, or criticizing the regime.

Comrades! What has the Emergency brought to the workers and employees in India?

A regime which suppresses the people, robs them of their democratic rights, facilitates the designs of foreign imperialists is undermining national freedom.

The working class has a special role to play in the struggle of the entire people against tyranny of Emergency rule. It is very powerful class, a class which has seen many heroic battles. It must take up the challenge boldly and on a growing scale.

# REPRESENTATION TO THE PRESIDENT ON POLITICAL PRISONERS AND AMENDMENT TO THE ELECTION LAW

August 5, 1975,
President of India,
Rashtrapati Bhawan,
New Delhi.

Dear Rashtrapatiji,

We feel very much concerned at the information and reports which we are receiving, regarding the high handed and inhuman treatment of the jail authorities and executive towards the Political prisoners who have been arrested since the second proclamation of Emergency and seek your personal intervention.

The political prisoners are now being treated in a much worse manner than during the British rule. Their whereabouts are kept a closely guarded secret from their relatives. Even in case of Members of Parliament the news of their arrests and whereabouts are being published in the Parliamentary Bulletins and not in the Press, and their relatives are not being informed.

From the reports which we are receiving, it appears that Jaya Prakash Narayan, Morarji Desai, Jyotirmoy Basu K.R. Malkani, Chowdhury Charan Singh and many others in different parts of the country are kept in solitary confinement. Most of them are not even allowed to meet their relatives and lawyers.

The jail codes of various States are not being complied with in respect of political prisoners and they refuse even to have a look at the jail codes and jail regulations.

We are surprised and shocked to receive information and reports, the authenticity of which we have no reasons to disbelieve, third degree methods are being applied on many prisoners in jails and police lock ups. In their connection, the recent statement of Brahmananda Reddy to the effect that the police are not to use third degree methods is significant,

Reading materials and other amenities are not being allowed to the political prisoners. In many cases, food in accordance with jail code and regulations is not being allowed to the political prisoners, and letters written by or to them are being withheld for unreasonably long time.

We request you to see that the authorities concerned are prevailed upon to treat the political prisoners in a normal manner and notify the fact of their arrest and whereabouts to their relatives within the shortest possible time and treat them in a human way.

We would further request you to advise the Government to allow an all party delegation of Members of Parliament to visit jails to look into the condition of the detenues.

Thanking you,
Yours faithfully,

Signed by the non-CPI Opposition Leaders
4, Parliament House, New Delhi

August 5, 1975
The President of India
Rashtrapati Bhawan New Delhi

Dear Rashtrapatiji,

We the undersigned members of Parliament, on behalf of
ourselves and also the various political parties we represent,
have to submit this memorandum before you in connection
with the Election Laws (Amendment) Bill 1975, introduced
in the Lok Sabha on the 4th August 1975. We request you
not to give your assent to the above Bill, if passed by both
Houses of Parliament, for the following reasons:

The whole purpose of the Election Law (Amendment)
Bill 1975, is to prevent the Supreme Court from deciding
the Prime Minister's appeal in the pending election appeal,
according to the law prevailing. The change of law during
the pendency of the appeal is obviously for the purpose of
helping the Prime Minister to succeed in the appeal. Such
a Bill if passed is bound to destroy whatsoever faith the
people have in the rule of law. Since the rule of law is the
very basis of democracy, it is desirable that the President
may not give assent to the Bill.

Moreover, the clause 2 and 4B of the Bill, if passed are
bound to make fair elections virtually impossible. One of the
main reasons, which makes the present election procedure
unfair, consists of the assistance which the ruling party is able
to have by utilizing government fund[s], and Government
machinery for furthering its own election prospects. Clauses
2 and 4B of the Amendment Bill will always favour the
party in power against the Opposition parties, because the
party in power will be able to secure both official assistance
as well as Government machinery for its electoral success.
These provisions, therefore, do not deserve to be assented

to by the President.

It would be recalled that a Joint Committee of Parliament on Electoral Reforms had made [a] certain recommendation. Thereafter, the Government made a definite commitment to discuss with the Opposition parties various suggestions for electoral reforms before bringing any Bill for change in the electoral laws. The discussion had started, the Opposition parties had submitted their written views on various amendments which were necessary for bringing about reform in electoral process. One of the points emphasized by the Opposition parties in their memorandum was that necessary alterations should be made in the law so as to prevent any party from utilizing Government funds and official machinery for the success of the candidates. The amendments sought to be made in the Amending Bill are contrary to the memorandum submitted by the Opposition parties unanimously and also contrary to the promise made by the Government to consider the recommendations so made, as well as contrary to the unanimous views of the Joint Select Committee.

Regarding the remaining provisions of the Amendment Bill and the amendments proposed thereto by the Government after introduction of the Bill, they are obviously intended to help the Prime Minister in her pending appeal and as stated above, it is not proper that a law which is otherwise fair and just should be altered merely for the purposes of helping an individual to litigate to success in the court.

In this connection it may be mentioned that the amendments proposed by the Government to section 8A of the Representation of the People Act, particularly the proposed sub-section 3 thereof which makes it obligatory on the part of the President to obtain the opinion of the Election Commission and also to act according to such opinion, is against the spirit of the Constitution and derogatory to the high position the President occupies.

Thanking you,
Yours Sincerely,

Signed by the non-CPI Opposition leaders

# EXTRACTS FROM PRANAB MUKHERJEE'S SPEECH ON ALL INDIA RADIO, ON THE VOLUNTARY DISCLOSURE SCHEME, 2 JANUARY 1976

Friends!

I have great pleasure in reporting to the nation that the Voluntary Disclosure Scheme launched by the Government of India about three months ago has proved a resounding success. According to information compiled up to date, the total value of the income and assets disclosed under the scheme has crossed Rs. 1,450 crores. This has proved wrong the prophets of despair. This also speaks volumes for the administrative acumen and understanding of the Government of India, particularly the Ministry of Finance and the Department of Income Tax. According to the latest information, the break-up of the total disclosures of Rs 1,450 crores is: Disclosed income-Rs 700 crores and disclosed wealth-Rs 750 crores. This involves a total revenue of Rs 250 crores by way of taxes on income and wealth. In addition to this, Rs 40 crores has been invested in Government securities.

Before I proceed to analyse the benefits and advantages flowing from the legitimisation of such a big chunk of black money I would like to describe the background under which the Government decided to launch this scheme. You are aware of the parallel economy that has been undermining our society for such a long time. It was not only the breeding ground of all kinds of economic evil but it also disturbed the day to day life of the ordinary citizen who had to cope with the galloping rate of inflation. The Government was deeply concerned about the evil practices which prevailed in the parallel economy such as understatement of the sale price of properties, violation of price controls and foreign exchange regulations and smuggling. You may recall when the Emergency was declared the Prime Minister enunciated a new 20-point socio-economic programme to ameliorate the lot of the backward sections of the society and tone up the economy.

Prevention of tax evasion was one of the points included in the revolutionary programme of action.

It was as a part of the implementation of this programme that the Income Tax Department declared an open war against the tax evaders and intensified surveys, searches and seizures in the entire country. The Government also came down with a heavy hand on the smugglers and foreign exchange racketeers. This resulted in the creation of a changed atmosphere in which the black money holders felt panicky and realised in full measure the inevitability of the punishment that awaited them at the hands of the administration. The drive was organised in such an effective manner that the tax evaders felt that detection of concealed income and wealth was only a question of time.

The Government, however, thought it desirable to give the beleaguered tax evaders their last chance to come clean and turn a new leaf. It was against this background that the idea of voluntary disclosure of hidden income and wealth subject to taxation on reasonable basis and without any penalty or prosecution, was conceived.

The objectives of the scheme were first to offer an opportunity to persons who have evaded tax in the past to declare their undisclosed income and wealth and return to the path of rectitude, and secondly, to secure canalisation of black money so disclosed into productive fields in the overall interest of the economy.

The benefits of the scheme were not made available to persons detained under the Conservation of Foreign Exchange and Prevention of Smuggling Activities Act. A noteworthy feature of the scheme was that, in addition to the income tax and wealth tax payable on the disclosed income and wealth, the declarer was required to invest 5 percent of the disclosed income and wealth, respectively in notified Government securities. I have already mentioned that as a result of this scheme there would be an additional revenue of Rs 250 crores. It is obvious that this addition to the exchequer would go a long way towards covering the Budget deficit. Moreover, the conversion of Rs 1,450 crores of black money into white money is likely to have a massive changing effect on various facets of the national economy.

In the first place it would help us contain the inflationary pressure in so far as expenditure on ostentatious living would be curbed. Secondly, the income from assets which have now been disclosed would result in a recurring gain to the revenue in the shape of additional taxes on increased income in the coming years. Likewise, there would be a sizable addition to the revenue from wealth tax also. Thirdly, the disclosure of assets would increase the declarability of future transactions and would ultimately result in larger revenues from such sources as stamp duty, sales tax and licenses.

Last but not the least, all this money which was previously utilised only to disrupt and distort the national economy would now be canalised into productive efforts. I may also mention that the Government intends to utilise the proceeds of the national secmities for projects of high social priority like slum clearance and housing for low income groups...

Though the time limit of the Voluntary Disclosure Scheme expired on December 31, I may bring to the notice of the citizens that even under the normal provisions of the tax law, a disclosure of income and wealth can be made. Though no concessional tax rates are applicable to such disclosures, the authorities have the power to give immunity to the declarer in respect of penalty and prosecution.

What I mean to emphasise is that those persons who have somehow not been able to avail of the Voluntary Disclosure Scheme have still some avenues open to them for making a clean breast of their affairs. Having accorded such a liberal treatment to all those who have evaded tax in the past, the Government now proposes to cry halt to this policy of forget and forgive. The machinery of the Income Tax Department is being geared up once again to deal with those offenders who have not co-operated with the Government. Tax laws have already been amended drastically with a view to dealing effectively with cases of tax evasion.

The Government is also taking adequate steps to strengthen the Income Tax Department so that the administration of these new laws is as effective as possible. The tax evaders have only two options open to them now: (i) to come clear and pay taxes due from them under the normal law of the land, or (ii) to face inquiries, investigations and consequent penalties and prosecution, I have no doubt that they will take the first option.

With my New Year's good wishes I thank you. Jai Hind.

# EXTRACTS FROM THE STATEMENT OF THE CONGRESS WORKING COMMITTEE, 1977

(i)    The Congress Working Committee has been studying in depth the reasons for the electoral defeat of the Congress Party in some areas of the country particularly in the Northern States. The people of this country gave to the Congress continued support and helped to secure electoral victory in few general elections and gave it an opportunity to serve them. In the recent general elections, the Congress failed to return as a majority party to the Lok Sabha. The Congress respects this verdict of the people with humility. The Congress thanks the millions of people, its workers, supporters and sympathizers who had helped the Congress during the election.

(ii)   Our esteemed leader Indira Gandhi has taken upon herself the entire responsibility for the defeat. While this is in the highest tradition of public life, we should like to tell the people that we too share with her the blame for what happened. As we reflect on the situation that faces us, we remember our mentors Mahatma Gandhi and Jawaharlal Nehru who never hesitated to admit publicly any error that they committed.

(iii)  In analyzing the reasons for this verdict, we have to turn the search lights on the functioning of our Party organization and our Government.

(iv) It is true that some unfortunate events during the Emergency contributed to the defeat of the Congress. It would, however, be wrong to relate our defeat simply to the Emergency. During the Emergency many steps were taken to revitalize the economy and introduce long neglected social reforms, especially relating to the poor farmers and the scheduled castes and the scheduled tribes. At the same time, it has to be recognized that things happened during the Emergency in a manner which alienated the people from the Congress organization and the Government. The Congress will fully ensure the democratic functioning of the party as also the evolution of collective leadership within the organization.

(v) What is now important is to utilise the present opportunity for self introspection and revitalize and strengthen the Congress Organisation. This can be done only by going back to the people, particularly to the poor and the down-trodden in humility, sincerity and earnestness.

(vi) This is not a time for mutual recrimination. What is needed today is unity in the Congress backed by discipline and clarity of goals. It is this great and challenging task that is before us.

(vii) We rededicate ourselves to strive for the realization of our national objective for which the Congress has always stood. They are national integration, democracy and socialism. To these we are irrevocably committed. The common endeavour is to build a strong and united India and bring about social transformation by consent and involvement of the people. The social objective is to remove inequalities and improve the left of the people, particularly the weaker sections of the society. As responsible opposition in Parliament, we shall offer constructive cooperation to the Union Government to serve the national purpose and the interests. This role, as an opposition party, casts a heavy responsibility on us to safeguard the interest of the people, particularly of the poor, the oppressed and the minorities. We should not hesitate to the take up the cause of the people, resist injustice and work for the legitimate rights of the people.

(viii) States where we are in government should vigorously pursue the implementation of our election manifesto and ensure clean, just and effective administration.

(ix) Congress Working Committee notes with alarm the trends in the ruling coalition at the Centre to start a process of destabilization of the State Governments under one pretext or other. If constitutionally established governments are toppled by the ruling coalition at the Centre, it would be purely for political advantage for them to go to polls on the basis of premises only and not on the basis of performance. This would lead to confrontation, instead of national reconciliation for which we stand.

(x) We can best fulfill the historic role of Indian National Congress by recapturing the spirit of service to the people and being sensitive to their feelings, aspirations and needs.

Source: *The Encyclopaedia of the Indian National Congress,* vol. XXIV, pp. 264-266.

## RESOLUTION OF THE CONGRESS WORKING COMMITTEE ON THE HOME MINISTER'S STATEMENT ASKING FOR THE DISSOLUTION OF CONGRESS-LED STATE ASSEMBLIES, 19 APRIL 1977

The doctrine of sovereignty enunciated by the Home Minister is wholly out of place and out of date. Even in U.K. there is no instance in modern times of the sovereign attempting to dissolve parliament without or against the advice of the Ministry. The conventions governing the exercise of the prerogative power of the King in the United Kingdom to dissolve Parliament are now clearly established and there are no exceptions to them. These conventions are:

(a) The Sovereign should dissolve Parliament when advised by the Prime Minister to do so.

(b) The Sovereign should not dissolve Parliament unless advised by the Prime Minister to do so.

(c) The Prime Minister has the right to choose the time of dissolution, within the five year period prescribed by the Parliament Act 1911. This power of timing is a weapon of great political importance in the hands of the Government and especially of the Prime Minister.

(d) If the government is defeated in the House of Commons on a question of policy, the government must either ask for a dissolution or resign.

Apart from this, ours is a written Constitution envisaging a federal structure. The power of the President or the Governor to dissolve the assembly is specifically provided for in the Constitution and there can be no other ground on which the President could dissolve the Assembly. The source of this power is the Constitution and the Constitution alone. As pointed out by the Leader of the opposition, Shri Y.B. Chavan, in his statement, in a written Federal Constitution such as ours, the Centre and the State are fully competent to function within their respective spheres. To argue that when every time elections to the Parliament are held, the State must automatically fall in line with the result is totally untenable. Instances can be cited in the past when the verdict of parliamentary elections was completely in favour of a party opposed to that of the State Government. For example in 1971 in Karnataka, the Indian National Congress won all the 27 seats. At that time the Ministry in Karnataka was headed by Shri Veerendra Patil of Congress (O). Similar situations had arisen on 1971 and even earlier in other States. Nobody raised the question at that time that the State Government had no legal or moral right to continue in power. The only ground on which the Assembly could be dissolved or the State Government dismissed would be under the provisions of Article 356, that is to say, if the conditions in any State are such that the State Government cannot be carried on in accordance with the provisions of the Constitution. This position does not exist in any of the nine States. Therefore the question of dissolution does not and cannot arise.

Two factors cannot be dismissed from the minds of the people while dealing with the statement of the Home Minister:

(a) The Presidential election is to be held by the middle of August and the State Assemblies, which they are seeking to dissolve, are important electoral colleges for this election.

(b) The Central Government has already introduced a Bill in the parliament for the reduction of the life of the present State Assemblies to five years.

It will not be wrong on the part of anybody if he were to suggest that the motive of the Central Government to dissolve the nine State Assemblies simultaneously at this juncture is:

(a) to affect vitally the coming Presidential election.
(b) to by-pass the Constitutional amendment which has been introduced in Parliament.

The charge that this move on the part of the Central Government is politically motivated cannot be brushed aside lightly.

If the Home Minister's argument is taken to its logical conclusion, it is bound to lead to absurd situation. The States of Tamil Nadu, Andhra Pradesh, Karnataka and Kerala voted overwhelmingly against the Janata Party in the recent Parliamentary election. Does that mean that the few MPs elected from these State with Janata Party tickets have no right to sit in Parliament or to participate in the Central Government?

The Prime Minister today is charged with heavy responsibility of living up to his assurance that he would give a fair deal to all the State Governments. The Working Committee still hopes that partisan considerations would not dilute or distort the basis of our federal polity.

At this juncture it is the responsibility of all Congressmen to unitedly meet this challenge not only in the interest of the party but in the broader national interest. Congressmen should immediately take steps to mobilize public opinion on the Constitutional monstrosity which is attempted to be perpetrated on the people of India by the Central Government within a month of assuming power.

# AICC'S STATEMENT AFTER THE DISSOLUTION OF NINE STATE ASSEMBLIES, 1 MAY 1977

The dissolution of the nine Assemblies by the Central Government is totally undemocratic contrary to all norms of constitutional and political propriety, it impairs the federal structure and erodes the autonomy of the States. The Jana Sangh always had the intention that India should have a unitary government. However, to mislead the people, their election manifesto mentions as under.

*Move to amend article 356 to ensure that the power to impose President's Rule in the States is not misused to benefit the ruling party or any favoured faction within it.*

This unmasks the undemocratic pretense of the Janata Party and exposes the true nature of this amalgam of various groups, which do not seem to have belief in democracy.

The time chosen for holding the election by the Janata Party is inconvenient to the people and will deprive many of them of their right of franchise, as agricultural operations and drought relief work are on in some of the States.

While the Government ought to have devoted their full energies in combating the price rise and the drought situation, they have chosen to go in for election to serve their narrow party ends. It is obvious that they are trying to alter the electoral college for the Presidential election for partisan purpose. Instead of combating the price rise, implementing drought relief work and fulfilling their promises given to the government employees and the industrial labour in regard to the CDS and Dearness allowance, they are now trying to divert the attention of the people from the above promise by forcing the elections. It is clear that they have not implemented their manifesto and other tall promises.

We should face the situation with courage and confidence. Congressmen at all levels should show unity and determination.

The people of India, who have already seen through their game of false promises, will give a befitting reply and will vote for and rally around the Congress-Indian National Congress, the known servant of the common man. The authoritarian and the dictatorial trends of the ruling coalition party have to be curbed by the people.

# TEXT OF THE RESOLUTION PASSED BY THE CONGRESS WORKING COMMITTEE CONDEMNING THE ARREST OF INDIRA GANDHI AND THAT OF FOUR CONGRESS LEADERS, 3 OCTOBER 1977

The Congress Working Committee strongly condemns the Janata Party Government's action in arresting Indira Gandhi. Her arrest is politically motivated and betrays highly vindictive, revengeful attitude on the part of the Government. It is an attempt by the Janata Party to side track the people's attention from its total failure to [stem the] slide-back in the economy and to arrest the price rise and the deteriorating law and order situation. The Janata Party will fail to hoodwink the people by this kind of gimmickry. That a party and a Government, which shouts from the house top its commitments to civil liberties and the rule of law, should try to trump up such flimsy charges to malign and seek to destroy the Congress Party poses a great threat to the functioning of the party system in this country. The arrest of Smt. Gandhi is a challenge to all those who cherish democratic values and the Working Committee calls upon the people, and the Congressmen in particular, to meet this challenge with determination, faith and unity by organizing an effective protest through peaceful, democratic methods.

This meeting of the Congress Working Committee condemns

the vindictive and politically motivated arrests of K.D. Malaviya, P.C. Sethi, H.R. Gokhale and D.P. Chattopadhyay.

This emergency meeting was convened at the initiative of Kamlapatiji and the Congress President also readily agreed.

# TEXT OF THE RESOLUTION PASSED BY THE CONGRESS WORKING COMMITTEE ON THE ARREST OF CONGRESSMEN DEMONSTRATING PEACEFULLY, 4 OCTOBER 1977

This meeting of the Congress Working Committee views with grave concern and anxiety the rent trend of the Janata Party Government in ruthlessly launching false, frivolous and flimsy prosecutions to humiliate the Congress and harass its leaders. The illegal, unwarranted and unjustified arrest of Smt. Gandhi yesterday unmistakably demonstrates the extent to which the present Government can go in instituting motivated, malicious, malevolent complaints. The release of Indira Gandhi today by the court vindicates the stand taken by the Congress Working Committee at its meeting yesterday that her arrest was vindictive and politically motivated. The assault by the Janata Party Government on our democratic values and ideals and the rule of law, particularly in putting behind bars Smt. Indira Gandhi, an ex-prime Minister of this country and one of the acknowledged leaders of the nation, has to be resisted peacefully everywhere with all our might. In this connection, it is worth mentioning that the learned magistrate Shri Dayal, New Delhi dealing with Indira Gandhi's case today has categorically stated as follows:

It is obvious that the forwarding of the accused under Section 167 is founded on the existence of grounds for believing that the accusation or the information is well founded. The fact that no prayer has been made under section 167 indicates that even according to CBI, there was no ground for believing that the accusation is well founded. Further, the facts that even the source has not been disclosed and no evidence, either documentary or oral, has been collected till now further indicate that there is nothing to show the existence of such grounds. Thus there being no reasonable ground for detention of the accused Indira Gandhi, she is released forthwith.

The Congress Working Committee congratulates the Congress workers and the people for their spontaneous expression of and resentment against the illegal and high handed action of the Janata Government. We condemn the repressive measures used by the Government against the peaceful demonstrators in Delhi and various other parts of the country. Any unreasonable restrictions on our rights to peacefully demonstrate and express ourselves are not acceptable.

There has to be persistent and purposeful resistance to all attempts by the present Government to misuse its police power and to turn our country into a police State. Any such attempt has to be strongly resisted.

This meeting, therefore, calls upon the people in general, and Congressmen in particular, to continue to hold protest rallies and meetings culminating in the observance of the 9th October as decided earlier as 'Anti Repression Day'.

# TEXT OF INDIRA GANDHI'S DEFENCE ON THE FLOOR OF THE HOUSE, FOLLOWING THE FINDINGS OF THE PRIVILEGES COMMITTEE, 13 DECEMBER 1978

[Shri K. Mayathevar]

country. With great respect, I submit that yesterday the hon. Prime Minister made a very short speech. In that speech, he told the House that this House is the supreme body and nobody can question it. This House is democratically speaking, a sovereign body. No body is disputing it. Neither the Supreme Court nor the High Court nor any other court nor you nor I is denying it. But the supreme sovereignty lies rests with the people of India. and not with this House; it rests with the people of India outside this House, not here. Sovereignty is in the hands of the people. Therefore, I request the Government to consider the feeling and reaction of the people outside the House and not do something because you are having a brutal majority at present. It is purely temporary. Therefore, don't have total faith in your temporary majority. Don't proceed further with the charges and punish the former Prime Minister. The 65 crores of the people of India think now there is a fight between the present Prime Minister and the former Prime Minister. They think it is a politically motivated fight between the two, which would not be welcomed by the people of India outside the House. Therefore, in your interest, in the interest of the Janata Government, in the interest of the Janata Party and in the interest of the people of India, I request the Government to withdraw it and drop the further proceedings against the former Prime Minister.

SHRIMATI INDIRA NEHRU GANDHI (Chikmagalur): Mr. Speaker, Sir, and hon. Members, I am grateful for this opportunity of participating in the debate.

The Committee of Privileges submitted their report to the House on November 21, 1978. The report was taken up for consideration on December 7, 1978. I had thought that the ulti-

mate decision about the correctness of the findings of the Privileges Committee rested with this hon. House and that, until this hon. House had fully considered the report dispassionately—each member giving his opinion in the context of the views expressed by fellow members—no member with a sense of fair-play and justice, would finally conclude that I was guilty.

My hopes were belied when I read the report in the newspapers of the proceedings of the Janata Parliamentary Party's meeting, where the only point of debate was reported to be the quantum of punishment which should be inflicted upon me.

The Janata Party, with its absolute majority, had adjudged me guilty even before the House commenced its debate on the report. Would it be unfair to conclude that the Party in power is trying to convert this House into a medieval "Star Chamber" by raising (Interruptions) the question of Privilege in what is essentially a question of Party politics? This is hardly conducive to a calm, judicial and impartial consideration of the merits of the case.

(Interruptions)

MR. SPEAKER: Order order. I beg of the hon. Members to patiently hear the Member. After all, she is in the position of an accused. She is making a statement. Please hear her patiently

(Interruptions)

SHRI RAM JETHMALANI (Bombay North-West) : Is she making a statement in the position of an accused?

SHRI VASANT SATHE (Akola): They are confirming the statement about Star Chamber.

293   *Motion re.*   AGRAHAYANA 22, 1900 *(SAKA)*   *Third Report* 294
*of Committee of Privileges*

SHRI JYOTIRMOY BOSU: She is reading the statement. Only Ministers can read written statements.

MR. SPEAKER: There is no such rule that only Ministers can read. Ministers can read a policy statement and not others. This is an important debate. The Prime Minister has also read his speech. Kindly hear her patiently. *(Interruptions)*

SHRI SHYAMNANDAN MISHRA: Sir, I rise on a point of order. She is casting reflections on the proceedings of the House in the sense that she says that the majority that we command is trying to convert the House into a Star Chamber. That is a serious reflection on the proceedings of the House. *(Interruptions)*. Mr. Speaker, it should be the concern of the Chair to take objection to the House being characterised as a Star Chamber. Therefore, it falls upon us to do so, if the Chair does not protect the dignity and majesty of the House. The Member also has to perform his own duties. Sir, she can say anything about the majority, but she cannot say that the majority is trying to convert the House in a Star Chamber. In fact, Mr. Speaker....*(Interruptions)* it was Mrs. Gandhi's Party, which converted it into a Star Chamber during the course of the Emergency....*(Interruptions)* by imposing the Emergency to run the country....*(Interruptions)*. Would you persuade yourself to accept such a characterization of the House?

MR. SPEAKER: I have not seen anything out of order.

SHRI SHYAMNANDAN MISHRA : How do you say it is not out of order? Would you say that the House is a Star Chamber?

MR. SPEAKER: No, she did not say that.

SHRI SHYAMNANDAN MISHRA : What did she say?

MR. SPEAKER: She said the Janata Party is trying to convert the House into ....*(Interruptions)*

SHRI SHYAMNANDAN MISHRA : Is it a court of the Janata Party?.... *(Interruptions)*. It is enough that the Privileges Committee did not take note of it when Mrs. Gandhi went to the Privileges Committee and stated there that the Janata Party was trying to bring in all kinds of considerations. At that time, the Privileges Committee should have taken objection to that kind of remarks against the Janata Party. And you also did not direct the Privileges Committee..

MR. SPEAKER: I have heard you.

SHRI SHYAMNANDAN MISHRA : What have you heard? It is a lapse on the part of the Chair.

MR. SPEAKER: That cannot be helped. You cannot help it. You cannot give me intelligence.

SHRI SHYAMNANDAN MISHRA : She had been casting aspersions and reflections on the Janata Party in the forum of the Privileges Committee and to cast asperations....*(Interruptions)*.

MR. SPEAKER: No, no. Please go on.

SHRI M. SATYANARAYANA RAO (Karemnagar): Sir, I rise on a point of order....*(Interruptions)*. The Member spoke without your permission. Whatever he spoke should not form part of the proceedings.

MR. SPEAKER: Please go on.

SHRIMATI INDIRA NEHRU GANDHI: If the ensuing deliberations by the entire House were considered by the Janata Parliamentary Party as an empty formality, my plea of in-

[Shrimati Indira Nehru Gandhi]

nocence no doubt would be futile, so far as the hon. Members of the Janata Party are concerned..

But this cannot dissuade me from opposing the action which the Janata Party with its overwhelming majority in this hon. House is proposing against me. As the former Prime Minister as well. I owe an explanation to the people and to posterity—the future generations of men and women who will follow us and ponder over the traditions of this House.... *(Interruptions).*

SHRI VASANT SATHE: Unless you control the House, it will be impossible.... *(Interruptions)*

SHRI BHAUSAHEB THORAT (Pondharpur) : Sir, I rise on a point of order. I am a member of this House and I have to decide whether one of the hon. Members has committed a breach of this House or not. So, I am entitled to hear the hon. Member peacefully. Any Member who does not allow me to hear whatever evidence or statement the hon. Member is making is committing a contempt of the House, because that Member is not allowing me to hear the statement of the hon. Member.... *(Interruptions)*

MR. SPEAKER: There is no point of order.

SHRIMATI INDIRA NEHRU GANDHI: ...the future generations of men and women who will follow us and ponder over the traditions of this House when the passions of the present times will have died. May I therefore reiterate emphatically and categorically that in point of fact...

*(Interruptions)*

AN. HON. MEMBER: Sir, what is this running commentary?

MR. SPEAKER: What about yesterday?

*(Interruptions)*

SHRIMATI INDIRA NEHRU GANDHI: May I, therefore, reiterate emphatically and categorically, that in point of fact, I have not committed any breach of privilege of the House...

SHRI JYOTIRMOY BOSU: She never speaks the truth.

*(Interruptions)*

SHRIMATI INDIRA NEHRU GANDHI: ...and that the charges levelled against me in this regard are totally untenable.

It is alleged that I was guilty of harassment of certain officers because they were collecting information in connection with a parliamentary question. It has been alleged that I intiated the action against them by calling Shri R. K. Dhawan in the presence of Shri T. A. Pai and directing him that Shri D. Sen, the Director of the C.B.I., should be called and the houses of those officers be raided.

*(Interruptions)*

SHRI C. M. STEPHEN (Idukki): May I ask of the Leader of the House: Is it the policy decision that Mrs. Indira Gandhi should not be heard? Is it your policy decision? If that is so... *(Interruptions)* It is an elementary courtesy that has got to be given.

THE PRIME MINISTER (SHRI MORARJI DESAI): May I say...

SHRI C. M. STEPHEN: I have not finished. I have got the floor of the House, I have not finished. Let me complete my question to you.

I have put the question. What I am saying is, it is an elementary courtesy that a person against whom certain charges have been levelled, when she is a Member of this House, when she has made some attempt to put up her defence, the House must give her a patient hearing whatever be the observations coming. Therefore, I am asking whether, finding the atmosphere in those benches, that behaviour has got the sanction of the Party and the Leader of the House, whether he has allowed it or not. Otherwise, he must condone it.

SHRI MORARJI DESAI: May I say that if my hon. friend had set a good example, all this would not have happened. I do not, therefore, in any way, agree to any noise being made. Let my friends have some prudence. It is no use imitating a wrong thing and we must hear Shrimati Gandhi patiently and quitely. There is no question about it. Whatever may be the provocation, one should not be provoked by it. This is deliberately done to provoke people. Why are you getting provoked? I would appeal to my hon. friends not to get provoked by anything that they say and bear it in dignity and silence.

SHRIMATI INDIRA NEHRU GANDHI: Sir, I have a bad cold and it seems that even clearing my throat is a provocation to the House.

15.00hrs.

The sole testimony in this regard is that of Shri T. A. Pai. Did I play any role in the formulation of the reply to be given in the House? It is not the case of Shri Pai or any other person that I did. Shri Pai admits, "at no time when I met her and she ever discussed with me the affairs of Maruti." He also admitted, "I did not get the impression (when he met me on the 15th April) that she wanted me to withhold the information or be careful at the time of answering the question."

A very large number of questions involving the collection of information on many matters, including Maruti, were constantly being asked in the House and were answered by various officers of different ministries before and after this particular question. There was never any allegation about obstruction or harassment on this score.

Besides, even a cursory examination of the evidence will clearly reveal that not all the officers who were collecting information for the Parliamentary question were proceeded against by the CBI. Government records show that no action was initiated against those officers who were actually deputed to collect information from Maruti. It is clear from this that the CBI cases had nothing whatever to do with the collection of information for the Parliamentary question and that they only came in handy to the Janata Party Government to implicate me in this proceeding.

What is even worse, the sanctity of this House is being used to prejudge the criminal trial that I am facing in a Court outside this House. The Janata Party Government has by that criminal case gagged me and made it impossible for me to put forth my defence in the present case. Can this be described as a reasonable opportunity of defence? I have been cribbed and confined in my defence before the House and later I shall be facing the criminal trial with an overbearing shadow of this House looming large over those proceedings. Here is a sample of the rule of law by which the Janata Party and its leaders profess to abide.

Sir, I shall not go into the minute details of the evidence placed before the Committee on Privileges, which my colleagues Shri C. M. Stephen and Shri Venkatasubbiah have already covered. I only urge emphatically that even on the one-sided record, there is not a shred of evidence to hold me guilty of breach of privilege. The findings of the Committee, I submit, are totally unjustified and unsistainable.

The facts leave no manner of doubt that the motive which is actuating the Janata Party and its Government is not their respect for the privileges of the House but their personal vendetta against me.

[Shrimati Indira Nehru Gandhi]

The entire procedure followed by the Privileges Committee suffered from constitutional infirmities. It also sought to compel me to become a witness against myself in total violation of my fundamental rights under the Constitution. My refusal to take the oath in these circumstances is now being alleged to be another breach of privilege. I humbly submit that this is not so. I meant no disrespect whatsoever to the hon. Members of the Privileges Committee. Had it been consistent with my defence in the Court cases, I would not have hesitated to depose before the Committee in greater detail.

I also maintain that the conclusion drawn by the Privileges Committee from the text of my statement submitted to them on June 16, 1978, is not warranted. In that statement I particularly mentioned my great respect and high regard for the hon. Members of the Privileges Committee. Thereafter I pointed out the well known fact of the Janata Party's disposition towards me, a disposition which has been demonstrated by thought, word and deed, times without number. Finally, I gave expression to a reasonable apprehension about the influence of the Janata Party on its members. I respectfully submit that the difference between the expression of a reasonable apprehension on the one hand, and positive allegation of bias or prejudice on the other, has not been appreciated Incidentally, the fact that different political parties *qua* political parties are now considring this matter and formulating their respective stands even before this hon. House has taken a decision, this fact, I submit, only confirms my views. This is how political parties functioned and therefore, my observations in the said statements cannot be construed as imputations of bias.

SHRI SHYAMNANDAN MISHRA: Only your party is innocent of such deliberations.

SHRIMATI INDIRA NEHRU GANDHI: To the Shah Commission, I had said, 'Corruption in some areas of Governmental functioning especially involving commercial dealings with the public, has always been a matter of serious concern. As Prime Minister, I received many complaints in writing or orally alleging corrupt practices on the part of various Officers of the Government. These I used to forward to the concerned authorities or departments and occasionally to my staff for appropriate action...'"

"I received complaints fom some persons, including MPs about these officers, amongest others. I told Mr. Dhawan to pass on the complaints to the authorities concerned in order to verify whether there was any thruth in the allegations. There was nothing special or unique about this. When such complaints were repeated or conveyed verbally to me, I sometimes directed similar action through a member of my staff." I repudiate the allegation that I ever ordered searches or raid against these officers.

My alleged involvement in the alleged harassement of these officers was used by the Government and the Shah Commission for public denigration and character assassination. It is being used by the Janata Party to punish me for breach of privilege of this House and it is further going to be used by the Government to prosecute me in the court of law and seek my conviction. What else is political persecution? But if the Janata Party thinks that acts of persecution and victimisation can destroy the ideals for which I stand, it is cherishing false dreams.

SHRI SHYAMNANDAN MISHRA: Ideals of Emergency.

SHRIMATI INDIRA NEHRU GANDHI: It is my proud privilege and the privilege of the Party which I have the honour to lead, to fight for the ideals of secularism and socialism for which Gandhi, Jawaharlal Nehru and we all have been struggling for more than half a century.

Never before in the history of any democratic country has a single individual, who leads the principal political opposition, been subjected to so much calumny, character assisintation and political vendetta of the ruling party. *(Interruptions)*

SHRI RAM DHAN    (Lalganj): What about us ?

SHRI B. SHANKRANAND (Chikkodi): By going to jail, one cannot become a leader.

SHRIMATI INDIRA NEHRU GANDHI: I give below a few instances of the views expressed publicly by leaders of the Janata Party who are or have been also leaders of the Government.

(a) When I was released by the learned Magistrate in Delhi on 4-10-1977, Shri Morarji Desai publicly declared that the Magistrate had committed impropriety in releasing me.

(b) In a letter to Prime Minister, the former Home Minister stated that members of the Cabinet of the Janata Party were being looked upon as a band of impotent men for not having already put me behind bars.

(c) In the Chikmagalur constituency, one hon. Minister declared that my place was in jail. Another bemoaned that the Janata Party had lost the electoin because the people were angry for not having punished me.

The Parties and groups which have combined to form the Janata Party had been conducting a campaign of vilification first against my father and for more than decade against me. When I decided to espouse more strongly the cause of secularism and

democratic socialism, when I nationalised the banks and took other measures to offer opportunity and help to the poor and weaker sections, there was a tremendous popular upsurge. This disturbed the privileged and vested interests and the communal and obscurantist elements, which the Janata Party today represents, and they felt it impossible to fight me and my party on an ideological plane. Therefore, they changed their strategy and turned their fury against me personally. *(Interruptions)* In the historic phase of India's development, one would have expected a fierce ideological debate, but nothing of the sort happened. On the contrary, political and ideological issues were deliberately side-tracked by these elements. They accused me of having flouted political morality by causing a split in the Congress. Those who had been bitter political enemies before the split and had professed strong ideological differences with one another suddenly discovered a new mutual kinship in their common hostility towards me. *(Interruptions)*.

Some people have suffered during Emergency. At no time was it my intention to harass or harm anyone.

*(Interruptions)*

MR. SPEAKER: Please don't interrupt.

SHRIMATI INDIRA NEHRU GANDHI: Sir, are you guiding the House or is it being guided from some other place?

For hardship caused, I am deeply sorry. I have already expressed my regret in many public forums and do so again. Not all actions came to my notice since it is just not possible for the Head of the Government or even others to keep in touch, as the present administration well knows. *(Interruptions)*.

MR. SPEAKER: No interruptions please. You are unnecessarily taking away the time of the House.

SHRIMATI INDIRA NEHRU GANDHI: It was I who decided to go to the people again and hold elections in 1977. This act of my Government re-asserts my abiding faith in democracy and totally disproves the accusation of authoritarianism made by the Janata Party and its allies. They continue to chant slogans of dictatorship versus democarcy in order to hide the sinister character of the political forces which dominate them.

I may be annihilated in the course of my struggle for the ideals of socialism and secularism, but those ideals will live on and the time is not far off when they will overcome the forces of communalism, casteism, regionalism, obscurantism and capitalism which the Janata Party and its Government have unleashed...... (Interruptions) in a period of less than two years of their misrule.

It is obvious that the motivation of the ruling Party is to divert public attention from their inability to implement (Interruptions) their high sounding but hollow promises of February-March, 1977. (Interruptions)

SHRI JYOTIMOY BOSU: Is that all relevant?

SHRIMATI INDIRA NEHRU GANDHI: I charge the ruling party of failure to check divisive forces, thus endangering our unity, of inaction in the face of mounting lawlessness and disorder and of callously neglecting the interests of Harijans (Interruptions) and Adivasis, Muslims, Sikhs, Christians and weaker sections. (Interruptions).

It is not an accident that the Prime Minister does not feel uncomfortable to survive and be sustained in power by those who were full of hate for Mahatma Gandhi. (Interruptions).

बौधरी बलबीर सिंह (हाजियारपुर) : प्रिबलेज कमेटी की रिपोर्ट के खलाबा और कुछ नहीं यहां कहना चाहिए ।

MR. SPEAKER: Whom am I to reply to?

SHRI SHYAMNANDAN MISHRA: I would very respectfully submit to you to tell the House whether you would have permitted any other Hon. Member to go into extraneous things as the Hon. Member Mrs. Gandhi is doing. Please consult your own conscience. This is an occasion when the Chair must be asked to consult his own conscience as to whether, on such occasions, you would have permitted the House to be exploited by bringing in extraneous considerations.

MR. SPEAKER: Please! I have heard you.

SHRI SHYAMNANADA MISHRA: How is the Government. ....

MR. SPEAKER: Mr. Mishra.....

SHRI SHYAMNANDAN MISHRA: No Sir. The most important thing for you to consider is that a debate in the House must not become irrelevant; that is, no Member is allowed to bring in things which have no relavance to the matter. But here the Hon. Member is trying to bring in extraneous things and the Chair must not allow it to be done.

SHRI C. M. STEPHEN: Yesterday's speeches may be referred to. You are politicking.

MR. SPEAKER: Many comments were made about the Emergency excesses yesterday. As you know, many Members made comments about the Emergency. In a debate of this character, one cannot possibly hold oneself; they went out of the subject and made speeches about Emergency yesterday. (Interruptions).

SHRI SHYAMNANDAN MISHRA : Pages after pages she has been reading.... (Interruptions).

MR. SPEAKER: Particularly, when a person is standing in the position of an accused, she has more liberty than other Members have got.

SHRI RAM DHAN (Lalganj): On a point of order.

MR. SPEAKER: What is your point of order? (*Interruptions*)

AN HON. MEMBER: She is not yielding.

श्री राम धन: अध्यक्ष महोदय, मेरा प्वाइण्ट ऑफ ऑर्डर यह है कि इस समय हम प्रिविलेज कमेटी के विषय पर विचार कर रहे हैं और मिसेज गांधी को इस समय अपने डिफेंस में बयान देने की जरूरत है । यह इरलेवेण्ट स्पीच यहां पर, सेनेट की फोरम बनाकर, जैसे चिकमगलूर में बोल रही हैं, ऐसा मालूम नहीं होना चाहिए । (व्यवधान)..

MR. SPEAKER: Mr. Ram Dhan. it is not a point of order. (*Interruptions*)

SHRI SHYAMNANDAN MISHRA: This is not an election meeting. This is the Parliament of India.

(*Interruptions*)

THE PRIME MINISTER (SHRI MORARJI DESAI); Will you please hear me? Let me make it very clear that the whole thing is entirely irrelevant. She is an accused person, and I do not mind an accused person saying whatever she wants to. I do not mind.

(*Interruptions*)

SHRI C. M. STEPHEN: There must be complete silence on this side please. (*Interruptions*)

MR. SPEAKER: Order, order. Such of them who are feeling so excited may kindly go to the lobby and come later. (*Interruptions*)

SHRIMATI INDIRA NEHRU GANDHI : Mr. Speaker, as you have rightly pointed out, all kinds of remarks were permitted in the previous days during this debate, and nobody then considered that they were irrelevant. We had listened to them very carefully.

AN HON. MEMBER: And patiently.

SHRIMATI INDIRA NEHRU GANDHI: However, I must congratulate those members and leaders of the ruling Party whose eyes were opened by the Aligarh riots and who had the courage to tell the truth and identify the danger. High personages have warned the Prime Minister that the Government might not last for the Government's failure to hear the danger signals and to find answers to the crying problems of our people.

This Government has created conditions of civil war in Bihar and unprecedented organised communal violence in Aligarh, Lucknow, Kanpur, Amroha, Varanasi and in so many other places.

If Harijans are burnt alive, if innocent Muslims, men women and children, fall victim to the daggers of assassins and if all accepted national policies which kept this country together for the last thirty years after independence are being systematically reversed, the Prime Minister has reasons to forget his life-long association with my illustrious father, Jawaharlal Nehru.

By the toil and sweat of agricultural labour and the sustained effort of our farmers, we have been liberated from dependence on foreign aid, but neither minimum wages nor remunerative prices for produce are being ensured. Industrial workers had contributed to increased production in our factors especially in the public sector, but now the Government's attitude towards, and policies for them are threatening their fundamental righs and the existance of their organisations. (*Interruptions*).

MR. SPEAKER: Just now the Prime Minister said,

SHRI SHYAMNANDAN MISHRA: You are not there to regulate the debate? You have no duty in the matter?

SHRIMATI INDIRA NEHRU GANDHI: I charge the present government of weakening the foundations laid by Gandhiji and built upon by my father, of surrendering the sovereign right of India to use nuclear technology for our vital interests, of diluting the policy of non-alignment, of weakening the public sector, of denigrating our indigenous science and technology and of inviting multinationals, surreptitiously though in a big way, to control the commanding heights of our economy.

I accuse the present government of tarnishing our image at home and of lowering India's prestige in the world.

The failures of this Government are leading to its isolation from people everywhere. The ineptitude of this government has destroyed the cohesiveness of the administration and created a situation of uncertainty and insecurity. Cynicism is growing. If this situation is not reversed it will provide a fertile soil for the growth of fascism.

I say all this not in anger but in deep sorrow, yet say it I must in the interests of our country and our people who are the ultimate sovereign.

It is my firm conviction that the fight between the forces of fascism and socialism in India and in the world is now reaching a decisive stage and if I may quote the Prime Minister of Zambia, "the dying horse kicks harder". Only at our peril can we afford to lose sight of these trends.

Mr. Speaker, Sir, and distinguished members of this august House, I should like to submit with the utmost sincerity that I would cheerfully sacrifice even my life....

AN HON. MEMBER: After taking so many lives.

SHRIMATI INDIRA NEHRU GANDHI: .... let alone the membership of this House, if by so doing I could promote the cause of our country. As a British poet has written "All else must be sacrificed to this great cause. I fear no hardships. I have counted the cost." The Janata Party knows and the Prime Minister knows—indeed every man, women and child in India know that if the drama of a kind of impeachment of a former Prime Minister is enacted, its sole purpose is not to solve any national problem but to silence a voice which they find inconvenient.

If the government believes that by sending me to prison or banishing me from this House, the voice of protest against their wrong policies will be silenced, they are woefully mistaken. Their erroneous policies have created problem of such dimensions that no longer can the bogey of Indira Gandhi keep the government in power or their party united. We must find principled answers to the problems confronting our country. This government has landed this country into a deep crisis which it is in no position to resolve.

I am not guilty of the crimes of which I am being charged by this government. Nor do I believe that this government is concerned about such crimes. How can it be? Never in the 30 years of Independence has there been such shameless corruption, such blatant misuse of power.... (*Interruptions*) the forced retirement of some of the best amongst our civil servants, the deliberate and persistent harassment not only of political workers but of the defenceless average citizen. No, these are not what the Janata Party considers crimes. But they dare not publicly admit to what they do consider my real guilt and the guilt of my party.

My father said "We are sentenced to hard labour." And so we are. But that hard labour is a privilege for it means the service of the people. And it brought with it not the reward of riches but of something much more valuable and much more rare—the trust and affection of the people.

What have been the crimes of my party and myself in the eyes of the Janata Party?

(1) That we were able to weave the strands of our diversity into a strong national fabric, by respecting all religions, by giving full play to the personalities of the different regions, by enriching all our languages and by encouraging local pride and initiative. This was secular nationalism.

(2) That we strengthened the economy, harming none yet making every attempt to redress the imbalance of centuries by special help to the weaker and neglected sections, the minorities, the smaller men in any group. This was democratic socialism.

(3) That we held our head high in international affairs. Not imitating, not boasting, not cringing. Just being, ourselves—Indians, belonging to a very special civilisation. Self-reliant, self confident. This was non-alignment.

The pages of history are strewn with the names of innocent people who have been hounded to death or otherwise victimised for their convictions. Some of the greatest men and women have been subjected to persecution. Many many have gone before me, but I did have the honour of personally knowing a few.

I am a small person but I have stood for certain values and objectives. Every insult hurled at me will rebound. Every punishment inflicted on me will be a source of strength to me.

My voice will not be hushed for it is not a lone voice. It speaks not for myself, frail woman, and unimportant person. It speaks not for a so-called 'total revolution' involving smugglers, dacoits and other such, but for the deep and significant changes in society which alone can be the basis of true democracy and a fuller freedom, which alone can ensure justice, and help to create a better man.

The atmosphere in this House has been reminiscent of the scence in Alice in Wonderland, when all the cards rise up in the air and shout, "Off with her head"! My head is yours. My box has been packed these several months we had only to put in the winter things.

I have stated some of the points in my case. There are others equally relevant and telling. I am now in the hands of the Hon'ble members.

SHRI EDUARDO FALEIRO (Mermugao): Sir, I am on a point of order.

MR. SPEAKER: What is your point of order?

SHRI EDUARDO FALEIRO: The point of order is this. These are matters of breach of privileges. They should be tried on a judicial basis. They should not be decided on a party basis.

MR. SPEAKER: This is not a point of order.

SHRI EDUARDO FALEIRO: Everyone must be given a chance to speak. But you are making this a real Star Chamber.

MR. SPEAKER: Mrs. Gore.

SHRIMATI MRINAL GORE *rose—*

# ACKNOWLEDGEMENTS

I gratefully acknowledge the contribution of a large number of my friends and well-wishers who have helped me write this book. The list is long and I may not mention them all by name, but this book would not have been possible without their encouragement.

Even so, I would like to express my gratitude to M.J. Akbar, well-known columnist and writer, who urged me to put pen to paper after going through the notes I had prepared a while ago. Thanks are also due to three young journalists—Agni Roy, Shankadip Das and Diganto Banerjee—for researching and collecting data and information from old journals, newspapers and books. Archival material of this nature has been quoted from and acknowledged in *The Dramatic Decade*. Of these sources, I would like to especially mention Janardan Thakur. While Thakur was never an admirer of Indira Gandhi, his description of Mrs Gandhi's visit to Belchi merits retelling, and his objectivity and impartiality need to be acknowledged.

The publisher and editor of this book—Kapish Mehra and Ritu Vajpeyi Mohan respectively—have worked very hard, patiently going through each revised copy. I do not have words to thank them for their effort.

# INDEX

Additional District Magistrate
Jabalpur's case, 65
Advani, L.K., 178, 194, 239, 241
Ahmad, Tajuddin, 37, 75
Ahmed, Abul Mansur, 28
Ahmed, Fakhruddin Ali, 44
Ahmed, Hashimuddin, 29
Ali, Asaf, 20
Ali, Muhammad, 18, 25–27
Ali, Raja Ghazanfar, 21
Ali, Tofazzal, 26–27
All India Anna Dravida Munnetra
Kazhagam (AIADMK), 187,
236–237, 248
All India Congress Committee
(AICC), 8, 47, 114, 119, 121,
131, 138–139, 141, 144–145,
152–154, 165, 169–170, 210,
214, 216–217, 232
Alva, Margaret, 126, 176, 203, 232
Amin, Nurul, 28
Ansari, Abdur Rauf, 130, 170
Anthony, Frank, 169
Antony, A.K., 153
Antulay, A.R., 108, 122, 126, 140,
147, 152–153, 155, 157–159,
169, 220

Anwar, Tariq, 127
Apang, Gegong, 214
Article 39 of the Constitution, 59
Article 363 of the Constitution, 60
Auchinleck, Sir Claude, 20
Awami League, 28, 30–37, 41
Azad, Bhagwat Jha, 126, 140,
152–153, 157, 159, 228
Azad, Ghulam Nabi, 127

Bahuguna, Hemvati Nandan, 106,
178, 184, 186–187
Bakhia, Sukar Narain, 85
Banerjee, Ajit, 141, 143
Banerjee, Bijoy, 12
Bangarappa, S., 219–221
Bangla Congress, 5–9
Bangladesh, formation of, 14–15
bank nationalization, 56–57
Barooah, Dev Kanta, 73, 108–112,
114, 125, 128, 172, 216
Barua, Dhruba, 172
Basavalingappa, B., 220
Basu, Jyoti, 7, 18, 122, 207,
234–235
Basumatari, Dharnidhar, 171
Beg, Justice M.H., 74

Belchi massacre, 148–150
Bhabha, C.H., 20
Bhagat, H.K.L., 159
Bhandari, Nar Bahadur, 225–226
Bhandari, Sunder Singh, 181
Bharatiya Kranti Dal (BKD), 10, 58
Bharatiya Lok Dal (BLD), 167, 180, 183–185
Bhargava, Dr Gopi Chand, 21
Bhashani, Abdul Hamid Khan, 28
Bhatia, Madan, 169
Bhattacharya, Asoke, 171–172
Bhattacharya, Kanai, 8
Bhattacharya, Somen, 199
Bhave, Vinoba, 127, 147
'bhrashtachar hatao' (remove corruption) movement, 69
Bhushan, Shanti, 195–196, 201, 235, 240
Bhutto, Zulfikar Ali, 35–36
Biswas, Ananda Mohan, 131, 141, 170
Bose, Sarat Chandra, 16, 20, 23
Bose, Subhas Chandra, 5, 16, 20
boundary commissions of Punjab and Bengal and Partition scheme, 22–23
breach of privilege notice to Smt. Gandhi and its impact, 208–211

Callaghan, James, 206
Chakraborty, Nripen, 235
Chakravartty, Nikhil, 148
Chakravarty, Gautam, 141
Chandrachud, Justice Y.V., 74
Chandrasekar, M., 116, 152, 157–159, 169
Chattaraj, Suniti, 124

Chattopadhyaya, D.P., 44–45, 107, 125, 129, 132, 245
Chavan, S.B., 175
Chavan, Y.B., 50, 52, 72, 108–109, 115–116, 123–124, 129–130, 134, 144–146, 148, 150, 157, 165, 173, 184, 187–188, 197, 216–217
Chawla, Justice, 157
Choudhury, A.B.A. Ghani Khan (Barkat), 107, 123–124, 141, 170, 172
Chundrigar, Ibrahim Ismail, 20
Communist Party of India (CPI), 14, 59, 72, 187, 198
Communist Party of India (Marxist) (CPI[M]), 8, 187, 200, 209, 235
Congress for Democracy (CFD) group, 171, 186
Congress (I), 131, 163, 165, 169, 170, 173–175, 183, 185, 187–189, 191, 196–201, 210, 213–216, 220–225, 229–234, 237–238, 242–243, 246, 248
Congress (I), and Indian general election, 1980, 223–243
Congress (I), victory in 1978 Lok Sabha elections, 201–205
Congress (I) Parliamentary Party, 225
Congress (I) Working Committee, 210
Congress (O), 58–59, 173–174, 216–217, 220, 222
Congress Parliamentary Party (CPP), 108–109, 129, 147, 189
Congress Party, crisis post defeat in general election, 1977, 106–112, 114–122

Congress party, Karnataka debacle, 143–145
Congress party, reaction to Indira Gandhi's arrest, 133–143
Congress (R), 58
Congress (U), 237
Congress (Urs), 184, 187, 198, 222, 230, 234, 242–245
Congress Working Committee (CWC), 21, 46, 108–112, 114–117, 119–121, 123–124, 126–128, 134, 138, 144–145, 154–155, 158–159, 163, 165–166, 169, 201, 211, 217–221
Conservation of Foreign Exchange and Prevention of Smuggling Activities Act (COFEPOSA), 84–85, 87, 89, 92, 156
Constitution Amendment Bill (48th Amendment), 234–237
Cripps, Sir Stafford, 19

Dange, S.A., 135, 204
Dantwala Committee, 102
Das, Bipin Pal, 128, 216
Dasgupta, Promode, 235
Dasmunsi, Priya Ranjan, 108, 110, 116, 123–126, 129–130, 132
Dayal, Judge, R., 133
Debt Recovery Settlement Board, 17
Desai, Morarji, 55, 57–59, 89, 92, 107, 117, 137, 177–182, 185–193, 196–199, 208–209, 222
Deshmukh, C.D., 92
Deshpande, Nirmala, 135
Devi, Gayatri, 110, 121–122, 156
Dey, Nityananda, 170
Dhara, Sushil Kumar, 10
Dhawan, R.K., 132, 208, 227

Direct Action Day, 18
Dorjee, Kazi Lhendup, 117
Dravida Munnetra Kazhagam (DMK), 14, 58–59, 236–237, 246, 248
D' Souza, Blasius, 220
Dwivedi, Devendra, 129, 216, 232

East Bengal legislative assembly election, 1954, 25–29
East Pakistan political crisis, India's response to, 38–42
East Pakistan political crisis, refugee movement to India, 39–40, 68–69
Economic Administration Reforms Commission, 99
economic offences, tackling, 89–93
Emergency proclamation (1975) and political unrest, 44–53, 73–83, 106–107

Fernandes, George, 179, 184, 186–187, 197, 203–205, 215
Foot, Michael, 206
Forward Bloc, 7

Gadgil, Vitthal, 129
Gafoor, Kazi Abdul, 141
Gandhi, Indira, 5, 14, 38–49, 54–59, 62–63, 65–66, 68–79, 81, 83, 106–111, 113, 115–116, 120–121, 123, 126–129, 132–148, 150–155, 157–162, 165–166, 168, 170, 172–174, 178, 183–184, 187, 189, 196, 198, 201–211, 213–229, 232, 234, 237–238, 242, 244, 248
Gandhi, Mahatma, 5, 8, 13, 20, 23 101

Gandhi, Maneka, 126, 135, 209
Gandhi, Rajiv, 133, 135, 232, 248
Gandhi, Sanjay, 107–108, 110–113,
    122, 125–127, 129–131, 133,
    135, 151, 158, 185, 188, 210,
    216–217, 219–220, 224–226,
    242
Gandhi, Sonia, 135, 205, 207, 209
Ganesh, K.R., 52, 89
Ghosh, Atulya, 6, 54
Ghosh, Prafulla, 6, 8–12
Ghosh, Sankar, 125
Ghosh, Sato, 107
Ghosh, Surendra Mohan, 6
Giri, V.V., 57–58, 72
Gogoi, Tilak, 171
Gokhale, H.R., 63, 132
Golak Nath case judgement,
    55–56, 59, 62
Goswami, Dinesh, 193, 216, 232
Government of India Act, 1935, 15
Gowda, B.N. Kenge, 220
Gramin banks, 101–102
grand alliance and 'Indira hatao,'
    58–59
Grover, Justice, 144
Grover Commission, 215
Guha, Arun Chandra, 6
Gupta, Bhupesh, 122, 193, 198–
    199, 232, 235–236, 239, 241
Gupta, Kanwar Lal, 208

Hanumanthaiah, K., 203, 214
Haq, Shamsul, 26
Haque, Fazle, 141
Haque, Haji Lutfal, 170
Hashim, Abul, 17, 24
Hazarika, Jogendra Nath, 225
Hegde, Justice, 67
Hidayatullah, M., 241

Hossain, Khairat, 26
Huq, Fazlul, 16–17, 26, 28
Hussain, Dr Zakir, 55, 57
Hussain, Iftikar, 21

Indian biennial elections, 1978, 175
Indian general election, 1967, 7, 9,
    14, 54–55
Indian general election, 1977, 106
Indian general election, 1980,
    223–243
Indian Independence Act, 1947, 59
India-Pakistan war, 1971, 35–38
Indo-British Friendship Society,
    205–206
interim government of India, 1946,
    20–21
Ishaque, A.K.M., 141
Islam, Nurul, 108, 131, 142, 170
Islam, Syed Nazrul, 37
Iyer, Justice V.R. Krishna, 72–74

Jamil-ur-Rehman, 225
Jamir, Chiten, 171, 214
Jana Sangh, 58, 80, 137, 178–183,
    186–187, 212–213
Janata Party, 53, 81, 89, 102, 107,
    112, 117–121, 124, 128,
    133–139, 143–144, 146–148,
    150–151, 154, 160–165, 167,
    172–175, 177–180, 182–189,
    196–197, 199, 202– 222, 230–231,
    234–235, 240, 242, 246–248
Janata Party, disintegration of,
    177–200
Jatti, B.D., 119
Jha, L.K., 99
Jinnah, Fatima, 31
Jinnah, Muhammad Ali, 21–22,
    25–27, 31

Kabir, Professor Humayun, 10, 54
Kamaraj, K., 54
Kant, Krishna, 79
Kapoor, Yashpal, 132, 158
Karnataka Congress, 145, 221–222
Karunanidhi, M., 58
Kaur, Amarjit, 232
Keishing, Rishang, 171, 214
Kesavananda Bharti case, 62
Kesri, Sitaram, 109
Khaliquzzaman, Chaudhry, 27
Khan, Abdus Salam, 29
Khan, Ataur Rahman, 28
Khan, Faiz Mohammad, 108
Khan, F.M., 144, 159
Khan, General Ayub, 31–32
Khan, General Yahya, 32, 35–37
Khan, Khurshed Alam, 126
Khan, Liaquat Ali, 19, 25–26
Khan, Maulana Akram, 22, 27
Khan, Sir Shafaat Ahmad, 20
Khandelwal, Karl, 169
Khanna, Justice H.R., 74
Khaparde, Saroj, 122, 126, 148, 176
Khatun, Anwara, 26
Kidwai, Mohsina, 172
Kissinger, Henry, 41
Kripalani, J.B., 174
Krishak Praja Party (KPP), 16
Krishnamachari, T.T., 92
Kumaramangalam, S. Mohan, 63, 66

Lahore Resolution, 17
Lal, Bansi, 108, 110–112, 152, 158
Lal, Bhajan, 183, 231
Lal, Devi, 183, 185
Lenka, K.C., 212
Limaye, Madhu, 143, 180, 182, 184, 186, 208, 213
Lok Dal, 234

Mahatab, Dr Harekrushna, 9–10
Mahishi, Dr Sarojini, 85
Maitra, Arun, 124, 129–130
Maken, Lalit, 126–127, 159
Makwana, Yogendra, 241
Malaviya, K.D., 132
Mallanna, K., 219
Mandal, Jogendra Nath, 18, 21
Mandal, Sunil, 141–143
Mathai, Dr John, 20
Mathew, Justice K.K., 74
Maurya, B.P., 108, 126, 140, 147, 151–152, 157, 175, 232
Mehta, Om, 85, 108, 110, 152
Mehta, S.R., 93
Menon, Vishwanath, 193
Mirdha, Ram Niwas, 191
Mirza, Iskander, 31
Mishra, Jagannath, 149, 152
Mitra, Somen, 107, 127, 131
Mohammad, Ghulam, 25
Mohammed, Dr V.A. Syed, 129
Mohanty, B.M., 212
Moily, Veerappa, 219–220
Monopoly and Restrictive Trade Practices (MRTP) Act, 57
Mookerjee, Dr Syama Prasad, 23
Mountbatten, Lord Louis, 206
Mukherjee, Ajoy, 5–10, 54
Mukherjee, Ananda Gopal, 224
Mukherjee, Purabi, 108, 112, 116, 131–132, 134, 143, 236–237, 245
Mukherjee, Subrata, 132, 142, 170
Mukti Bahini, 38, 42, 69
Muslim League, 16–18, 21, 22–28, 246

Nag, Dr Gopal Das, 129

Naicker, D.K., 220
Narain, Raj, 70, 179–185, 188–189, 193, 213
Narasimhan, K., 100
Narasimhan Committee, 101
Narayan, Jayaprakash (JP), 41, 46, 50, 69, 71–81, 127, 137, 150, 179
Naskar, Gobinda, 141
Nasser, Gamal Abdel, 75
Nath, Kamal, 225
Nayak, V.P., 116
Nayanar, E.K., 235
Nazimuddin, Sir Khawaja, 24–25, 27
Nehru, Jawaharlal, 13–14, 20, 23, 38–39, 54, 79, 160, 175, 177, 206
Niazi, General, 38, 42
Nijalingappa, S., 54, 58–59
Nishtar, Abdur Rab, 20
Noon, Malik Sir Feroz Khan, 31
North-West Frontier Province (NWFP), 15, 33–34

Pakistan National Assembly (PNA), 14, 35
Pandey, Kedar, 149–150
Panja, Ajit Kumar, 141
Pant, Govind Ballabh, 230
Pant, K.C., 116, 123, 130–131, 134, 146, 232
Patel, H.M., 89
Patel, Rajni, 91, 108, 153–155, 215
Patel, Sardar Vallabhbhai, 20, 23
Patel, Yusuf, 85
Patil, K.H., 143–145
Patil, S.K., 54, 214
Patil, Vasantrao, 153–155
Patil, Veerendra, 203

Patnaik, Biju, 54, 182, 186
Paul, Swraj, 205–206
Pawar, Sharad, 174, 215–216, 222
People's United Left Front (PULF), 7
Poddar, Deoki Nandan, 170
Poddera, R.K., 232
5-point programme (Sanjay Gandhi), 126
10-point programme, 57
18-point programme, 7
20-point programme, 100, 104
Poojary, B. Janardhana, 219–221
Pradesh (state) Congress Committee (PCC), 124, 130–131, 145, 170, 172, 217–220
Pradhan, Pabitra Mohan, 9–10, 54
Prasad, Bishnu, 171, 173
Prasad, Dr Rajendra, 20
Prevention of Black Marketing and Maintenance of Essential Supplies Bill, 233–235
Preventive Detention Act, 90
privy purses, abolition of, 56–57, 59–62
provincial assembly elections, 1937, 15
provincial party position in 1970 elections, 33–34

Qasim, Syed Mir, 109, 115–116, 153, 159–160, 169
Quit India Movement, 20

Radcliffe, Sir Cyril, 21–22
Radcliffe Line, 15
Rahman, Mujibur, 14, 18, 23–24, 26, 28–32, 35–37, 43–44, 74, 239

Rai, Kalpnath, 127, 129, 140, 176, 191, 199
Rajagopalachari, C., 20
Raj Narain *vs* Indira Gandhi, 70
Ram, Jagjivan, 20, 72, 94, 106, 177–178, 180, 182, 185–186
Rangachary, S., 229
Rao, Chief Justice Koka Subba, 55
Rao, P.V. Narasimha, 115–116, 152, 157–159, 169, 216, 227, 238
Rao, R. Gundu, 115, 144, 203, 219–220, 231
rashtrabhasha (national language) agitation, 25–27, 31
Ray, A.N., 61, 74
Ray, Siddhartha Shankar, 45–47, 63, 66, 101, 107–108, 115–119, 130,132, 142
Reddy, Brahmananda, 47–48, 115–116, 120, 123, 130, 134, 138, 141, 143, 146, 150–153, 155, 158, 160–162, 175, 216, 231
Reddy, Dr M. Chenna, 153, 169, 174–175
Reddy, N. Sanjiva, 54, 57–59, 146, 187, 228
Reddy, Snehalata, 203
Regional Rural Banks (RRBs), 100–105
'Resignation Demand Week,' 72
Revolutionary Communist Party, 7
Revolutionary Socialist Party, 7
Roy, Kalyan, 122
Roy, Kiran Shanker, 23
Roy, Rupnarayan, 18
Roy, Santi, 170
Roy, Saugata, 216
Roy, Shanti Mohan, 141
Roy, Suhas Dutta, 141

Roychowdhury, Tapan, 19
RSS (Rashtriya Swayamsevak Sangh), 182, 212-13, 217
Rupwate, Dadasaheb, 216
rural credit arrangements. *see* Regional Rural Banks (RRBs)

Saheb, Babu, 149
Saikia, Hiteswar, 172
Salve, N.K.P., 175–176, 196–197
Samanta, Tuhin, 141–142
Sangma, Captain William, 153, 171, 214
Sangma, P.A., 214
Sathe, Vasant, 108, 115, 127, 129, 133, 139–140, 147, 151–153, 157
Sattar, Abdus, 29, 45, 124, 131–132, 141, 171
school and college days, 3–4
Scindia, Madhav Rao, 61
Selbourne, David, 81
Sema, Hokishe, 171
Sen, Ashoke Kumar, 224
Sen, Bholanath, 124
Sen, Prafulla Chandra, 6
Sengupta, Barun, 8, 226
Sethi, P.C., 132
Shah, Justice J.C., 81, 138, 156–157
Shah Commission, 45, 47, 128, 154–157, 168–169, 203
Shankar, P. Shiv, 63, 65
Shankaranand, B., 126, 220, 225
Sharief, C.K. Jaffer, 218–219, 221
Sharma, A.P., 108, 115–116, 140, 152, 155, 158–159, 169, 172, 175, 191, 193, 205, 229
Sharma, Dr Shankar Dayal, 116–117, 169
Sharma, Neki Ram, 115–116

Shastri, Bhola Paswan, 199, 242
Shastri, Lal Bahadur, 55
Shekhar, Chandra, 137, 179, 182, 186, 197, 215, 217
Shivanna, Sahur, 220
Shukla, V.C., 108, 110, 112, 152
Sikri, S.M., 63, 68
Sindh United Party, 16
Singh, Bhishma Narain, 229, 233, 238
Singh, Buta, 116, 140, 152, 157–159, 169, 210
Singh, Charan, 10, 54, 58, 118–119, 137–138, 147, 151, 177–185, 187–193, 196, 203, 208, 212–213
Singh, Chaudhary Randhir, 159
Singh, Darbara, 152, 205
Singh, Dharam, 220
Singh, Dinesh, 232
Singh, Dorendra, 214
Singh, D.P., 159
Singh, Dr Ram Subhag, 116, 121
Singh, Govind Narayan, 10, 54
Singh, Karan, 115–116
Singh, Manmohan, 230
Singh, Narendra, 232
Singh, N.K., 135
Singh, Pratibha, 122, 126, 148–150
Singh, Professor N. Tombi, 171
Singh, Ram Dulari, 172
Singh, Ram Subhag, 121
Singh, R.K. Dorendra, 171
Singh, Sardar Baldev, 20
Singh, Shankar Dayal, 109
Singh, Swaran, 41, 108, 114–115, 139, 216
Singh, Zail, 116, 152, 169, 212, 238, 245
Sinha, Atish, 124
Sinha, Dharamvir, 239

Sinha, Justice Jagmohan Lal, 70
Sinha, Mahamaya Prasad, 9-10, 54
Sinha, S.C., 153
Sinha, Tarkeshwari, 217
Smugglers and Foreign Exchange Manipulators (Forfeiture of Property Act), 87
smuggling and other economic offences, legal measures against, 85–89
Socialist Unity Centre, 7
Solanki, Madhav Singh, 169, 205
Soni, Ambika, 125
'State of Emergency,' Article 353, 44
Stephen, C.M., 79, 108, 115–117, 169–170, 188, 205, 214, 219, 238, 242
Subramaniam, C., 52–54, 94, 99, 101, 115–116, 139, 166
Suhrawardy, H.S., 17–18, 23–25, 27–28
Suhrawardy-led Muslim League government in Bengal, 1946, 18–19
Sultana, Rukhsana, 152
Swamy, Venkat, 126
Swatantra Party, 55, 58

Tagore, Rabindranath, 4
Taimur, Syeda Anwara, 171, 173
Talukdar, Harendra Nath, 171, 173
Talwar, R.K., 122
Tarkabagish, Maulana Abdur Rashid, 31
taxation proposals, 19745-76, 52
tax collection, 'survey-search-seizure' method, 89–92
'Tebhaga' movement of 1946-48, 1
Thakur, Janardan, 149, 178, 180, 208

Thakur, Karpoori, 179, 183–185
Thanhawla, Lal, 171, 214
Thatcher, Margaret, 206
Thungan, P.K., 117, 214
Thursday Club, 129, 148
Tirpude, N.K., 174, 221–222
Tripathi, Kamalapati, 109, 115–116,
    134, 140, 142, 144, 146–147,
    153, 155, 157–159, 169–170,
    175, 188–190, 193–194, 199,
    214, 219, 228, 238, 242
Tytler, Jagdish, 159

UNIDO (United Nations
    Industrial Development
    Organization)-III, 229
United Front government, West
    Bengal, 1967, 7–12, 29
United Left Front (ULF), 7
Unnikrishnan, K.P., 139, 216
Urs, Devaraj, 143–143, 147, 152–153,
    157, 159, 162, 169, 175, 183–
    184, 203–204, 215, 217–222, 231

Vajpayee, A.B., 178, 197, 209

Varadachary, T.R., 113
Vasudev, Uma, 134
Venkataraman, R., 99, 227, 229,
    238
Verma, Virendra, 116–117, 169
Voluntary Disclosure Scheme, 93–
    97, 122. see also tax collection,
    'survey-search-seizure'
    method

Wajed, Sheikh Hasina, 239
Wanchoo Committee Report, 92,
    95, 97
Wavell, Governor General Lord
    Archibald, 20

Yadav, Chandrajit, 108, 110, 115,
    116, 201
Yadav, Ramanand, 191
Yadav, Ram Naresh, 183
Yadav, Shyamlal, 10, 191
Yazdani, Dr Golam, 224
Youth Congress, 125–127

Zaheer, Syed Ali, 20

www.ingramcontent.com/pod-product-compliance
Lightning Source LLC
Chambersburg PA
CBHW020339100426
42812CB00029B/3185/J